The
SPARK

The
SPARK

Sex, Love and Spirituality in a Toxic Dating World

Rosalind Moody

1 3 5 7 9 10 8 6 4 2

First published in 2024 by September Publishing

Typeset by RefineCatch Limited, www.refinecatch.com
Printed in Poland on paper from responsibly managed, sustainable sources
by Hussar Books

ISBN 9781914613487
Ebook ISBN 9781914613494

September Publishing
www.septemberpublishing.org

To my two grandmothers, both called Betty,
and to you

Some of the people in this book have had their names changed to protect their privacy. The stories, my feelings and my journey are all very much real.

The suggested rituals and practices in this book are for entertainment purposes only and should not replace medical or professional guidance.

Contents

Spark: noun

- the first flicker of fire
- immediate chemistry between two people
- the beginning of something powerful

PART I

Welcome to the Spiritual Single World

Affirmation: I open my love life up to the Divine, surrendering it to the Universe. I step into my self-loving self with pride, and let my higher self help me speak my truth.

It was a Sunday morning and we'd had another argument.

He refused to look at me, busy packing his bag to go home.

'Look, just calm down, I'm going to take a shower then we can go out. Please don't leave. Promise?' I asked.

'Fine,' his reply came curtly.

I washed my hair at lightning speed, praying I didn't hear the front door go. I quickly wrapped myself in a towel and walked back into my bedroom to find both the bags and the boy gone.

I sat on the bed still dripping wet and called him. No answer – he must be halfway to the train station by now. The voicemail message I left him was the saddest thing I've ever spoken. I sounded as feeble as a dying mouse telling him I couldn't believe he'd left when he'd *promised me*, he'd *said* that he wouldn't go. My voice kept breaking and croaking and I sounded distant, even though I was speaking straight into the mouthpiece. Maybe you've been there too, stonewalled into physical anxiety, expected to know what you've done to deserve the silent treatment. Maybe you still hold the trauma in your body.

I felt empty and devastated, anxious and shivering from my toes to my crown. It was just like any other argument we had, where I was chasing the chaos, the anxious lows of each conflict and the dizzying relief of each make-up session. I was 23 years old, but it would take me writing this seven years later, at 30, before I would realise that what I was addicted to wasn't just people who treated me badly, it was this emotional rollercoaster.

'How was your shower?' He strode in.

'You're still … here?'

'Yeah, I was just moving my bags for later.' I was pretty sure he'd done it to make me assume that he'd left. He never mentioned my voicemail, and because I was ashamed, I never brought it up. I hope he deleted it before he indulged in the desperation and the need I felt for him. Or maybe he replayed it a few times just to remind himself how much this empath–narcissist relationship benefitted his ego so well.

Or maybe it was all in my head.

Freedom after abuse

Supernova wasn't my first emotionally abusive relationship. The same as a lot of us, I had established a pattern of going for the 'bad boy' in my teens, the one who we measured our worth by. The evident lack of self-worth meant when a relationship at university had become coercive and controlling, to the point of him threatening suicide, it never crossed my mind that I deserved better. I felt too guilty for causing suicidal thoughts, though of course I could never have been responsible. The groundwork had already been laid for Supernova to swoop in and love-bomb me into submission, a textbook way to start a toxic relationship. He wasn't the only, or the first, but he was the one who sparked a spiritual epiphany in me, awakening me to a different, more divine perspective on the world.

4

WELCOME TO THE SPIRITUAL SINGLE WORLD

The beginning of a typical toxic romantic relationship typically consists of love-bombing and grand gestures, showing all too strong feelings and all too fast promises of commitment. Then come the put-downs, gaslighting, threats and intimidation. Some relationships can descend further into abuse such as financial control, violence and isolation. You can never see how bad it's got when you're the one in it, because you're often convinced all these sanctions are totally accidental, or worse yet deserved, for your own good. It becomes a vicious cycle because you can't see outside it, and to dare to try may come across as a punishable act of arrogance.

You may never have been in a toxic romantic relationship; the abusive person in your life may have been a parent, or boss, or a best friend. A classic sign of a toxic relationship is that everything is on their terms; the plans, the concerned emotions, the allowed reactions. But despite the differences between your experience and mine, our resulting level of low self-esteem will be similar. We crave external validation, because another person's word always feels truer to us than our own. We stay submissive, because if we're being 'the good girl', we don't have to walk on eggshells that day, our environment feels safer to us, more conducive to survival. Along with seeking approval, we constantly doubt ourselves and subconsciously wait for permission, because we don't trust our next move will be the right one.

You can take back your permission and make your own choices again. You can give yourself permission to be the autonomous, free and single person you deserve to be. You already are that person, in fact. You already hold all the love you need without seeking it externally. The whole Universe is inside you. Believe in your own thoughts and feelings again. This will help you fill the void that feels so empty when *they're* not paying you attention or texting you back and to quell the anxiety you feel when they're stone-walling or giving you the silent treatment. I can guide you to follow your own intuition and show you how it's already operating, and that the answers are already within you. And it will be the best gift of self-love you ever gave to yourself.

Your intuition, higher self and your psychic senses are all already within you. These 'spidey senses' might just be dormant and need teasing out. The various practices I've included in this book are going to crank their volume right up, so loud you won't be able to ignore them any longer. But that's good; you'll no longer feel alone in your search for your soulmate, because you'll sense your spiritual tag team with you too. You'll be *awakened* to them. I believe you already have the ingredients for a life of true self-love and self-respect, and all I'm giving you are the recipes.

Above all, I want this book to act as a confidante for you, which is why I'm telling you my own story too, including the bits where I could have made more conscious choices. If only I'd had a friend like me dating and awakening at the same time, rather than me just stumbling around in the dating pool following the lead of anyone that chose me. Like a form of spiritual CBT (cognitive behavioural therapy), I could have used the resources in this book to activate healing before the damage these encounters caused settled into scars, before I set in mental concrete the false belief that I was single because *I* wasn't enough, or I was *too* much. I never gave myself the benefit of the doubt that maybe I wasn't the problem. I never let myself off the hook that our twenties are just for trying people on, and if our relationship didn't stick, it had little to do with my worth. If only I had had a book like this to make me feel like less of a black sheep and no longer The Only Single Person On The Planet.

Cosmic beginnings

A supernova is the biggest explosion that can happen in the Universe, and this boyfriend was so nicknamed because our relationship burst my heart and soul wide open, like an explosion of light in a life I didn't know was dark. Your big bang may come by giving birth to your first child, or making your first connection with spirit after losing a loved one. Supernova's knowledge of the Universe and his love for me literally was the definition of enlightening. But when a supernova explodes, it leaves a black hole behind. My narcissist Supernova may have been the big bang of my spiritual awakening, but in the end, he sucked all confidence, joy and light out of me.

I met him at a friend's birthday that summer, a glorious real-life meet-cute. I was largely oblivious to any kinds of serious spiritual thought before I met him, though I'd always been called the 'hippy' one in my friendship group. Occasionally I'd pick up the spiritual magazine the company I worked for published, *Soul & Spirit*, because in the craft editorial department we liked the oracle card packs that came with each issue, despite not having a clue how to use them. I'd always been open-minded and intrigued by less materialistic, more alternative ways of living life. (I mean, I studied philosophy at university, for goddess's sake. It was written in the stars.)

This book was never meant to be a book; it started out life as a journal that I used to make sense of my confusion and hurt after each break-up, after and including Supernova. It was a document which exponentially multiplied itself without too much conscious effort on my part. I wanted each sad page and every break-up to be my last. My notes were never meant to see the light of day until I realised they might be useful for other people. It's alchemy, I've realised, to transmute our pain into power. As my old wounds become words on the page, I hope they will trigger positive change in your own life. As we slowly move into the Age of Aquarius, represented by the powerful planets that cluster into this humanitarian sign, and what some people see as a time of humanitarian uplevelling, I have decided that now is the right time for that healing chain reaction.

A lot of people begin their own spiritual journey, as it were, not out of choice but out of trauma. It's like spirituality finds *them*, rather than the other way round. It could be the grief of a loved one's passing that makes us question what happens when we die and helps us truly begin living, a near-death experience that leaves us psychic or, like me, a trail of toxic relationships that leaves us without a sense of self. Maybe you're reading this book because you went through the same. Maybe your awakening hasn't happened yet, or you're just curious for more meaning where you can get it. Our spiritual journeys can be as varied and as personal as our love stories.

Seeking your soulmate

For me, spirituality was always going to be about love and relationships. I love love. I love being in love. I became aware of the opposite sex as well as my own body quite young, at about six years old, which I'm now told is very normal. I've always thrived off the will-they-won't-they storylines in my own life, as well as being addicted to those Hollywood and Disney 'happy ever after' stories. I'm rarely interested in a story unless there's a romantic plotline in it somewhere.

Growing up, *Beauty and the Beast* was my favourite. Didn't we baby empaths all see ourselves in Belle, who was the only one earnest enough to discover the Beast's inner beauty? As I would learn in Philosophy of Love, my favourite module in my degree, Ancient Greek philosopher Plato defined our soulmate as literally the other half of our soul, separated before incarnation. Since Supernova and my awakening, I've desperately wanted to meet the other half of my soul, no matter how far I would have to travel. I'm going to tell you what I learnt, and it was more devastating, and more divine, than I could have imagined.

I found Plato's theory less than practical. Couldn't we have various soulmates depending on which path in life we take, all equally fulfilling? I used to assume it was my responsibility to search for my soulmate, distrusting that he would find me. I've gradually come to realise that it's literally the Universe's purpose to throw the soulmate our way when it deems us to be truly ready, living on the right vibration to attract him in. Maybe you've pondered on that, too.

Similarly, I believe it is our astrology that looks after us, not the other way around. Our person will come, whatever life we choose. Call it destiny, call it fate, call it the Universe, even call it God, but I believe we really are divinely cared for. You are never alone when you truly believe whatever cosmic being you believe in has always got you covered. Whether you think of yourself as spiritual or not, labels don't matter here. Opening yourself up to the *possibility* of a higher power is all I ask of you.

Graze from the buffet of spirituality

I didn't just wake up all spiritual one morning and begin singing along with the birdsong like a lunatic, and neither did Supernova shove it down my throat. It was a process of watching him and learning in what ways I wanted to connect with the Universe and what worked for *me*. For example, perhaps from listening to him preach about mindfulness with various meditation practices, I was inspired to look for my own favourite practices, and from his trust in the powerful qualities of crystals, I was open to them, too. I found his way of looking at the Universe so positively, so trustfully, persuasive as hell. So, for me, I keep the Law of Attraction, an intuitive card-reading practice and yoga in my spiritual and emotional toolbox and leave topics like near-death experiences, astral travel and past-life regression on the spiritual buffet table. That's just how my story has gone so far, but I may lean into those things later if they seem useful on my journey to my partner and beyond – hopefully *with* my partner, too.

At 18, my choice to study an abstract subject such as philosophy thrilled the existential teenager in me but completely fazed my traditional parents. To me, even back then, the Universe seemed more secular and even more omnipresent that a male divinity can be, even if He has such a special name. If I get married, I doubt He'll be there – I mean, He's welcome, but we're not really friends.

I'd prefer to tie the knot at a civil ceremony or a handfasting, as is the tradition of pagans, not that I class myself as a pagan either. See what I mean about spiritual buffet? Take what matters to you, leave the rest available for others. As I, and maybe you, need to rebuild our own identities after suffering within toxic relationships, knowing what spiritual techniques work for us as individuals can really help.

Over the years of dating, loving and lusting, I have collected and created certain rituals, tips and tricks that have presented themselves to me, and tucked them safely away in my mental resources folder. They use a wide mix of wonderful healing modalities, all simple and beginner-friendly, and they mostly centre on boosting self-love, self-awareness and self-confidence. Neo-witchcraft would call this collection of rites a *Book of Shadows*, but I'd call mine a *Book of Light*, and I mostly use pretty floral notebooks to keep them in. Such rituals, however basic and quick they are, have saved me in some dark dating times. However, if you're not into the whole spiritual thing, just know the rituals will boost your self-esteem and make you truly happier in your own skin and soul. If you're really into the spiritual thing, I've also included some serious stuff that you can sink your teeth into.

This book is for you if you folded those paper origami fortune-tellers in the school playground, wondering what answer the cosmos was going to give you as random numbers decided the amount of times the corners were moved in and out. This book is for you if you grew up reading all you could about witches, making up your own spells with sticks, leaves and salt while muttering funny words. And finally, this book is for you if you've lost count of how many times you've quietly asked an unknown entity whether or not you're on the right path, in the right place, or doing the right thing, with the right person, even if you thought you weren't 'spiritual'.

Manifestation is central to this book, so I've got to outline how well backed it is by science. Quantum physics says that our emotions emit energy, and everything in our universe is made of energy. Then, quantum entanglement suggests particles can link up wherever they're coming from, connecting these emotions to the energy of the universe. Supernova may have been like a guru to me, but he never was that intellectual.

Say Hello to Your Chakras

Up and down our 'energy' bodies are seven energy centres called chakras, which translated from Sanskrit means 'wheels'. They go from bottom to top, root to crown, and the best way to describe their appearance is like a mini mandala or wheel emoji. To heal them all, we must start at the first chakra, the root, at the tailbone, and work our way upwards. These energy centres don't lie on our physical body but do serve as hotspots that spiritual healers use to diagnose psychosomatic problems and heal them. Each energy centre relates to a different part of the human experience, whether that's identity, relationships, communication and so on, so the system to tell where we might need help is, in theory, quite straightforward.

We all have these primary seven chakras; even kids and animals do. There are more chakra systems within our energy body, but we'll stick to just the main ones. Each time I've been to see a healer, my blocked areas were normally always around my heart chakra, as well as my sacral, which sits around our tummy button and relates to our connections with others. It was these healing sessions that paved the way to making up my own rituals that I'll share with you.

The Spiritual Single Revolution

Raise your single pride

If you're anything like me, in my lowest times I felt so alien from my cohabiting, engaged, married and pregnant friends I may as well have had green scaly skin and no hair. Though they really could empathise from their own single days, as well as cheer me up as best they could with lengthy phone chats, I still felt alone. I felt sad and pathetic to admit it, too. The shame kept me from reaching out to new single friends I could have met via Meetup or Bumble Friends Mode. I should just be able to attract a lad, just like my friends had, I told myself (I now have a vendetta against the word 'should'). Yes, we try to look on the bright side of our single status, and yes, we might get a bit touchy about it, too.

But why now?

To my delight, the 2021 UK census declared witches and shamanism as recognised, veritable trends. In times of uncertainty, like political crises or wartime, it's thought that more people turn to fortune-tellers to light their way back to certainty. As I write this, the world certainly feels like it's gripped by a case of wait it out and hope for the best. Established institutions such as the monarchy and the NHS are threatening to crumble, strikes are everywhere and climate change now feels terrifyingly close to home.

Finding a real connection online is harder than ever, even though it was projected that in 2024, according to Statista, almost 600 million people would use dating apps across the world. According to dating app Badoo, the reason first dates fail is a 'repeated dating app disconnection', something we never would have analysed before Tinder was created in 2012. With the rising cost of living, I don't think it's just me finding dating *expensive*. According to Badoo, the average bad first date costs us £47.50. If one of us has six 'failed' (not my word) romantic connections in the last year, they've spent £285. That's the cost of a weekend spiritual retreat!

There is so much change in our modern world it's like trying to catch sage smoke with your bare hands. All of these stress factors have been building up for the last few years and a lot of people I know are at crisis point. We are downbeat and done, and I wouldn't tease even the most cynical among us if they turned to psychics, astrologers, moonologers (those who map our destiny by the moon's movements rather than other planets') and other such cosmic experts for answers. Okay, I would, but only gently, because I love watching someone find sense in the spiritual where before they saw none.

Spirituality is now a way we can relate to each other, even a way to flirt, connecting over our mutual star signs, love languages and past lives parallels. For bonus points on your date, name-drop epigenetics expert Joe Dispenza or the Headspace app, both more on the neuroscience spectrum of spirituality and thus seen as more scientific and manly, and see their eyes light up.

As our external modern world becomes more stressful and intense, spirituality as a faith system can soothe the harder edges of life. We can find softness in the messages we channel through an oracle card reading, and we can feel truly seen and loved when we connect with our passed-on loved ones via a medium, for example. Spirituality is not a blanket cure for bad mental health, but there are studies that prove it helps to protect against it. Even prescribing complementary therapies (meaning in addition to medical treatment) such as mindfulness walks in nature saves the NHS over

£185 million every year, according to leading organisation Forest Research. Reiki is now a recognised complementary therapy and belief in its power of rehabilitation is so strong that clinics are now being set up within NHS mental health services. For me, being somewhere magical like a bluebell wood humbles me and quietens my ego. I know living in tune with nature really can help to relieve my melancholy, as well as explain my moods, for example when there's a full moon in a watery emotional sign of Pisces, Cancer or Scorpio. Understanding that the Universe also experiences dark phases, like the period of a dark moon preceding a crescent (new moon), can help us accept our own shadow sides and need for downtime.

Telling people you're in touch with your spiritual side doesn't arouse suspicion like it used to and the term 'black magic' is hardly bandied around anymore. Witchcraft and astrology aren't that out-there if you look at what we're brought up to believe in from an early age. Christianity celebrates the resurrection of a dead guy on the Sunday after the first full moon of the spring equinox. We call it Easter. We bring trees into our home because pagans marked winter solstice and beckoned an abundant spring with decorated evergreen branches. It's now seen as glam to be in a state of gratitude or blessedness – it's a woke revolution, and the hashtag #spiritualtok has over one billion views and counting on TikTok. 'Lucky girl syndrome' became a mainstream trend that credited an (arguably privileged) life to positive affirmations and abundant mindset. Though that all sounds pretty trite, I'm here for anything that boosts people's positive energy. The global spiritual industry was predicted to be worth £218 billion a year in 2024. Modern spirituality's force and magic continue to grow as it fights its way into the mainstream consciousness.

Not that the Universe minds it finally coming into public consciousness – I can feel it rolling its eyes that it's only *now* getting the reverence it deserves. What we mean by consciousness is a perspective on life free from ego and subjectivity, as neutral and 'awakened' as possible. But while it's all well and good that spirituality is booming, my best romantic life is between me and my spirit guides, who are like my personal cherub squad, my spiritual tag team. I visualise this gang of angels like a Greek chorus, a troupe of wonderfully camp, kind and beautifully bedazzled drag queens. They brandish diamond-studded bows and arrows and their gowns made of liquid colourless satin, but that's just what they look like in my imagination. The personal angels in your mind's eye might look punky, have piercings, wear purple leather and resemble more of a biker gang, and that's fine; as long as you know this ethereal motley crew have always got your back, that's all that matters. Learn to meet your own spirit guides on page 76 and you'll never look back.

And luckily for us all, the boom in the spirituality industry means we have a plentiful supply of crystals and other spiritual means now even compared to five years ago. Just picking an oracle card out of a deck is a way to commune directly with the Universe, and you can do it yourself. You and your spiritual tag team are more than capable. My service is to empower my fellow soul sisters to manifest their *own* self-loving happy-ever-after.

The Alchemy of The Spark

A spark is the product of elements interacting correctly at the right time, such as air and fire, but with zero water raining on its parade or damaging winds. I imagine this young flickering fire like the start of a relationship that will stick, when everything just falls into place at once, where the two lovers feel being together is totally natural.

Even when we're not in a relationship, as single spiritual women we have a fire burning inside us. That fire was sparked in the late fifteenth century when our foremothers were hung (or burnt, in Scotland) for daring to be different, wild or unpopular, citing witchcraft as their justification. But they can't deny us our innately magical intuition, our psychic truths, or our passionate knowledge of nature now. We are the proud, wild ones they never got to be, with all the eggs we'll ever carry inside us, and all the eggs our daughters, their daughters and so on will ever carry. That means we also still carry our ancestors' trauma, their hurt, their witch wound. Now that's epigenetics in action.

There are plenty of questions you might have about what a spark is or can be. I will show you what it's looked like for me, how it's redefined itself, grown with me, in the following chapters. Our soul wants the spark, just not up on the surface level where the ego is concerned.

'But,' you might ask, 'I'm in a steady long-term relationship and the spark has gone out. What does that mean?' Well, I haven't been there for a while, but I do know you deserve to live a spark-filled life, and the spark may well have gone out within you first. Actively healing the self will help you get it back in all areas of your life, similar to a domino effect. Everything comes back to you and the way you feel about yourself first, and the better you can communicate with yourself, the better it will get with your partner. Remember what spark *means*, and think what it means to *you*, because it will be different to everyone.

So as in all stories, let's start from the beginning and see what kind of sparks flew with Supernova. And know that, like me, you deserve so much better.

Sign your self-love vow to yourself

Read this vow out loud, then sign your name at the end to commit to your new approach.

I, ..., promise to put myself, my feelings and my boundaries first from this moment onwards. I vow to fiercely approve of myself, to validate myself, and trust myself. I promise to ask for help from my loved ones when I need it and stop wasting my fantastic self on people who do not appreciate me. I vow to meet my own unmet needs first and foremost and work to heal myself as only I can. I have all the love I need already inside me and I hereby welcome in my spiritual tag team and acknowledge that they are working overtime for my happiness. I know great romance is waiting for me.

And so it is.

Sign: ....

Date: ....

18

PART II

1

Root Chakra: Supernova

Affirmation: I am so worthy of love. I am worth more than how you make me feel. I am worth more than how you speak to me. I know and value myself more than you do. I am worth more than you say I am.

My story must start at the beginning. At its seed, at its root.

Our first chakra is the root chakra, called the *muladhara*. It sits invisibly behind our pelvic bone, at the bottom of our spine. It represents our home, our safe base, how secure we feel in it, and sets our foundation from which we grow. It also represents our physical desire. That all makes sense since its neighbour is the womb, our first home. Well, Supernova was the root from which my heart bloomed open like a flower. He was where I felt at home. His sandalwood-scented musk aftershave, his big smile and energy, all making me feel grounded and welcome in a world where I didn't yet understand who I was as an adult.

Supernova was different. He wasn't a normal fuckboy you can find all over dating apps. (The official term, in fact, is fuckperson, as regardless of gender and age, we are all capable of manipulation, and we are all energy beings, so the term deserves a neutral cover-all pronoun. But as I am heterosexual, I'll refer mostly to fuckboys.) Fuckboys (FB) are normally good-looking blokes who can use their looks to their advantage. This is just the new name for them; you may know them as players, playboys, Casanovas and so on. They've taken full advantage of women's sexual liberation for their own pleasure, and their idea of a romantic question is 'does your place have parking?' Their dating profile will probably be blank – they don't even know what they have to offer – and include a ripped body or a pout pic. Their hot-and-cold approach is addictive to people who rate themselves directly by how much attention they're fed. They'll probably expect of you all the perks of a relationship while telling you they're not looking for anything serious right now.

Supernova wasn't even a Spiritual Fuckboy. Spiritual Fuckboys do all the same things fuckboys do in the emotionally unavailable way they do it, just using spirituality to woo. You know the type; the kind of person to write on their dating profile something like 'I'm into the subjectivities of souls that will never be fully captured by unawakened brains' and who show off their six-pack wearing an undone shirt in front of a Balinese sunset. Sanskrit is probably listed as one of the languages they speak. They're a performative, woke mindfuck. And we spiritual single girls can be magpies.

In fact, Supernova would turn out to be the top rung of toxic, way more dangerous than just a Spiritual FB. He didn't just reel me in for sex, it was for love. Ladies, meet my spiritual narcissist.

If you're lucky enough not to know what a narcissist is, they're typically defined as someone with 'a persistent pattern of grandiosity, fantasies of unlimited power or importance, and the need for admiration or special treatment', according to a study in the *Journal of Behavioural Medicine*. If you're immediately wondering if this could be you, the same study tells us that up to three quarters of narcissists are men. If you even have the self-awareness to question if you're a narcissist, you're probably not.

Spiritual narcissists are not like a regular narc; they're a cool narc. By comparison to the classic narcissist, their snobbery is manifested in their 'guru' ego, as if they're a cult leader. They'll have a reverence for their own voice and a vanity for their own look. Watch out for god-like excess, rather than authentic modesty. Take their long hair – they're likely to think this defines them, so it's a mask to hide behind. Take these things and the signs I'm about to show you, and you'll be staring directly at a spiritual narcissist. Knowing them, they'll probably sense your attention and be making sultry eyes right back at you. And they'll probably always choose their love of the Universe over us.

Not all people who seem or look like this will be one. The crucial way to tell is how they make you feel about yourself in their company, which we'll get into in this chapter.

Though I didn't meet Supernova online, his profile might have said something similar. He would make long preachy speeches about his spiritual beliefs (I, the unknowing disciple, nodded and smiled in all the right places). He had dreadlocks he'd wrap up into a man bun, sleeves of spiritual clichéd tattoos, muscular shoulders he liked to show off, a devastatingly gorgeous face with dreamy hypnotising eyes and charismatic energy which crowned him a showman. Like any narc would be, he was completely addictive to me because I couldn't exist without his validation. In turn, he was addicted to my attention.

Zero to hero

When we lack an internal validation system, we use the people around us for external validation. This is commonly where the 'I'm not good enough' issues arise. I had not one iota of self-esteem, but plenty of outer confidence that masked it.

The weekend before I met Supernova, I'd created – or perhaps reinforced – a humdinger of an inferiority complex for myself: that I was only desirable enough to men for a one-night stand. My best friend Lotti and I had been out clubbing in Edinburgh and we discovered the following days that both guys who'd pulled me were, in fact, married or in a relationship. I felt horrid for being lied to, not just once, but twice, in totally unrelated scenarios. I thought I'd really connected with both these guys. Jesus, who can be *that* naïve? I felt like a right loser. Where I should have sent out a 'fuck you' into the ether, hoping that energy reached them both remotely, sent not just their ears burning but their souls, instead I internalised it and that message came straight back to me like a karmic boomerang. Fuck *me*, I thought, for thinking I could be chosen for more than a snog or sex. I was 22, fresh out of my uni bubble, and it was a rude awakening into seeing how some adult relationships operated, undermining their own value by opening it up to strangers.

Ah, then here comes our ego, jumping to the safety of the conclusion that we'd end up like the guys' poor betrayed partners if we allowed ourselves to fall in love. 'You can't get hurt if you're never in a relationship!' we assume, thinking we've hacked the system. But that fearful approach keeps us playing small and sours our hearts in the process. While we all need an ego of some sort to have the human experience, it can really be an emotional cockblock sometimes. We need our hearts open.

Brazened like Queen Boudicca, I felt empowered to take charge of my Saturday night the following weekend. I was off to a friend's party, and I'd work the room and refuse to waste time with losers again – there was going to be not another fucking minute of that.

And then fate rocked up, as it always does when we think we're the ones in control of our story. Supernova walked in wearing a blue linen shirt that showed off his sleeve tattoos, a shark-tooth necklace around his tanned neck and a confident smile. His green eyes pinned me happily in the corner of the party for the whole night, and I hardly felt the time go by. So much for working the room, which had faded into background noise as he gently took the piss out of me for spilling my drink everywhere. (Make a girl giggle and her walls will start to come down.) Within a few hours, I'd started to dismiss all the hard resentment I felt for men, plural, because this one man was softening me with just his smile. His alternative look was not my type back then, but his confident, commanding energy was. This was a guy who would never look at another woman if we were together, I thought. And just like that, in one night, someone had chosen me. Safe to say, we had The Spark.

The joy of attachment

You know those smug couples who claim it was by some miracle they met? 'I was off men anyway, and he was meant to be somewhere else entirely that night!' I could have said it to anyone — I probably did. Within two weeks of meeting, we *were* a couple. I had made sure of that, anxious to call him mine officially. In three dates, Supernova had fast become the centre of my universe.

John Bowlby's vastly popular attachment theory explains how healthily and securely we relate to our partner. There are four styles.

1. An anxiously attached person feels worthless without communication.
2. An avoidant person dodges communication for fear of commitment.
3. Fearfully attached people (otherwise known as disorganised attached) don't trust someone would want them anyway, so they hold back entirely.
4. Secure people are where communication is honest and free flowing, and is the goal.

How do we get there?

Well, yep, you guessed it, it generally stems from how we were shown love and emotional attention from our primary caregivers in childhood. The most seen duo is anxious-avoidant, when the former craves attention of the other and the latter craves their space and freedom. They both gravitate towards each other because that's what feels familiar, just like an empath and narcissist. In both scenarios, the avoidant or narcissist is the one who can walk away as if it doesn't bother them, so they're the ones ultimately with the power, though I hate that word. It's a dance that continues until someone starts to heal their core abandonment wound, the reason they were anxious or avoidant in the first place.

Review how you often feel in relationships

Do you feel stressed or go into survival mode if you haven't heard from your partner, or if you do hear from them, you feel as though you pull away and get easily claustrophobic? Or, might you hold back entirely out of fear or distrust (or you may be secure, and relate to neither scenario. Good for you). We may think we 'swing' one way but in fact we probably swing the other. In your journal, explore the following:

In my current relationship, I ... and they ...

In my previous relationship, I ... and they ...

Here, we can use the principle that we attract our mirrors and attract our opposites. For example, I usually attract avoidant people, relegating me to the opposite, the anxious spot. But if I tackle the avoidant reflection I'm seeing head on, as if it's a mirror, I realise that though I want to find my person, I often drift off from dating app chats, avoiding making decisions on someone either way. If I discover that I may be slightly avoidant towards communicating my honest feelings, then I work through the fear of commitment within my own self – the very fear I might be sensing in my partner. I can empower myself to end the cycle, and become the partner I want and deserve. I'll go into this idea more as we carry on.

Also make a note in your journal of how much you liked yourself in your past relationships, and how much you like yourself in your current one. You will see why this is important later.

Forget panic buying – it's panic committing

When we quickly fall head over heels in love, as I soon did with Supernova, we can lose balance. With a tough history of relationships, we crave love so much, and with an official boyfriend–girlfriend label it can be ours forever, we assume. I admit to it with Supernova, and I send my past self so much love and compassion for thinking that was the best path to happiness. She didn't know what she was getting herself into, and she was too love-starved to pause. When we wear rose-tinted glasses, red flags look pink. Here are a few of the most important red flags not to paint pink, as pretty as you want them to be.

Red flag 1: they love-bomb you to seal the deal

Our age gap was only a few years (I was older), but the clear disparity was in our self-confidence.

Looking back, I went into our early days with my head screwed on and with the right intentions – that is, to be wary. I somehow knew to 'lean back and stay warm', letting the guys come to me, which is the approach I now swear by. Especially when someone is coming on so strong and leaning into us, we have no choice but to lean back to steal ourselves a bit of space. There also needs to be space for silence to hang in between, the mystery of the will they won't they. This is the very intention of flirting, even if you are already in a relationship with the person.

We all love a compliment or a gift, and to finally feel seen in a room full of other people. But too many compliments, gifts and undying messages from someone we barely know can qualify as something you may have heard of as love-bombing. It's used to reel someone in and make them commit, and it's addictive as hell.

In the early days, I was still wary when he told me it had been love at first sight for him. These days, I believe in lust at first sight for sure, but only love at *true* sight, which can be months and multiple conflicts later, when the masks have stripped back to reveal the authentic person underneath. How could he see me as so beautiful when we'd met once? I asked him tentatively. Though I hadn't had this much attention since my university boyfriend, I put aside my nagging scepticism and lapped up his words anyway. Maybe it was my outward confidence at first that Supernova wanted to feast on for himself, and maybe he sensed it secretly housed a low self-esteem that would make me give it up to him. He made the first move a day after meeting and slid into my direct messages. It was my angel number time of 14.08, so I assumed this meant he was The One, obviously.

What's your angel number?

An angel number is a number that seems to follow you. It can be one number, two, however many you like, but ones you spot anywhere, whether that's on clocks, restaurant bills, car registration plates and so on. Most people believe in the power of 11.11 and make a wish because it's seen as auspicious (and if you truly believe it is, it is). Spotting your angel numbers 'out in the wild' are the Universe's way of showing you you're exactly where you should be.

If you don't have a specific time that follows you, set the intention now to be more open to seeing repeated numbers and patterns. Just this one clear choice will invite the Universe in to show you. Some people ask their angels out loud to show them their numbers, so don't be afraid to use your voice to command divine assistance.

Read what each number below says and piece it together as a message from the Divine. Each time the number flashes up in some way, feel the Universe giving you that message once again. For example, the soul message each time I see my particular angel number time – 1, 4, 0 and 8 – I interpret to mean trust in my manifestations, and new ones are always coming true. Once you start interpreting life's signs, you'll start seeing them everywhere.

0   New opportunity incoming
1   Invitation to manifest
2   Seek balance
3   Recognise your life purpose
4   You're on the right path – keep going
5   Transform and renew
6   Stop overgiving and restore harmony
7   Sacred spiritual number; spiritual evolution is near
8   The Universe has you covered, so relax
9   A phase is about to end
10 Work on spiritual awakening
11 Make a wish!
12 Master number: keep pushing!

Journal: every time I see the number … I believe my angel number means the Universe is telling me to …

Red flag 2: they use toxic positivity to enchant

Contrary to what we're told growing up, being a positive person still does not mean always saying 'yes'. This only leads to people-pleasing, a trait of many codependent people yet to find their self-validating power within. When we say yes when we don't really mean it, it's unsolicited emotional caretaking. People want the truth, not a blind 'yes'.

So often we want to play the part of the 'yes girl' because it pleases our spiritual narcissist. I told Supernova early on that I was happy to go with the flow and be led by him. He was so cool, I wanted to be the Cool Girl on his arm. But he was thrilled I'd so easily agreed to go to a wedding with him as a first date, an event where I knew no one. I'd be happy wherever he was, I reasoned. I thought that made me an empath, but it made me a dysregulated person with no boundaries. I didn't know we should only be so submissive to one thing, as if it's our Dom (dominant partner): our intuition.

Beware, spiritual narcissists will enchant you down to your skin and bones – no, even down to your very chakras. You will let them, because you are a 'yes girl'. He was my perfect mirror, a 'yes man' with endearing golden retriever energy. I could see no shadow side to it, no off switch. He had this zing for life, and he prioritised happiness and passion over everything else. How can you not fall in love with that? We might find it devastatingly pure, but it irritates our loved ones, ones he tried to charm, too.

We fancy that wholesome love for us, and we like living in a Hallmark movie. Maybe our inner child, eager for love, is what spurs us on. She can rest easy with his compliments, taking this to mean he'll never leave us. Your intuition, your silent spiritual tag team, on the other hand, will be trying to tell you if it is too soon. If a guy tells you he's proud of you or misses you after the first date, both things that have happened to me since Supernova, I'm pretty sure your intuition will be raising red flags too.

The Divine Energy dynamics

They go together like yin and yang or wine and cheese. These symbiotic energies may be gendered, but a transgender person or couple can assume whichever role they like. Even in a heterosexual relationship, these two can consciously swap, or as they say in kink circles, switch. Divine, to our nervous systems down here in reality, simply means they feel 'safe'.

- The Divine Feminine teases, trusts and considers all possibilities and paths to wisdom. The Divine Masculine loves to be teased, needs the support to be able to trust and logically selects one solution out of all possibilities.
- The Divine Feminine is shrouded in mystery like a wedding veil, but is the one in more control because it captivates the Divine Masculine.
- Each accepts and appreciates the other's strengths and weaknesses, coming together in partnership to fill where the partner lacks.
- Each can witness the vulnerabilities of themselves and each other with strength and without judgement and attracts in the same.
- Both can take constructive criticism and hold space for the other, avoiding passive aggressive 'I'm sorry you feel that way' remarks. Divine Feminine also knows the fine line between playful sass and passive aggression, and the Divine Masculine is conscious of it on the receiving end.
- The Divine Feminine is cosmic because she carries a portal in her belly. The Divine Masculine infinitely admires how powerful she is for it, knows how he treats the mother is how he indirectly treats his child, and believes the gender pay gap (7.7 per cent in 2023 according to the Office for National Statistics) should close.

Red flag 3: their gaze makes you giddy

With these grandiose promises of love and commitment, and endearing impressions of an open heart, comes heightened anticipation. You already have a lot to lose, even by the second date.

When Supernova suggested we plan our second, third and fourth dates before we even had our first, my response was elated confusion. We desperately assess what assets we have to seal the deal in return, so my best idea was to wear a sassy red J-Lo-style bodycon dress on our first date. We women like to control, but our Divine Feminine wants us to be secure and trust that what is meant to work out will. Easier said than done when you're in a frenzy over a guy you've only kissed but who is somehow making you rethink your vow never to get married. He's not even raised the subject of marriage – just raised everything but.

With all the fairy tale storylines in your head, when you finally see them in real life, it's such dizzying relief it can feel like an out-of-body experience. You know, when you must blink a few times to believe you're in front of him, finally. On our second date, I practically jumped into his arms. I was so over the moon already, my feelings waxing like the full moon itself. I was in a horrible mood when he wasn't around, impatient to see and inhale him. His red flags were bringing out *my* red flags, my defining my day according to him and his plans. My wariness had fast become neediness.

How to retain your sense of self

While being love-bombed, a narcissist's technique is designed to build you up so that once you're dependent on their compliments and attention, they can tear you down to make themselves feel better or appear more powerful. Other signs of an unhealthy relationship are massive highs with devastating lows, harsh criticism, belittling, condescension, and empty apologies without resulting changes in behaviour.

If you think you might be being love-bombed, talk to friends and family you trust and show them messages you are comfortable showing to people. You need your reality to be validated when the love-bomber is trying to blur it. Take some space from your partner and in a few short hours your intuition will come through and you'll gain some distance and perspective. It helps to have a journal to think out loud into and reflect. Remember that the point of narcissism is to bend the truth, which is what makes it hard to tell other people what's going on, because half the time you don't even know what it is. What are their intentions for giving you quite so many compliments or gifts – might they have an agenda to raise themselves up if they put you down? If you feel comfortable, ask them to slow down the pace of your relationship to one you feel more relaxed with, for example, 'I'm not used to hearing X, you're going to have to go slower with me', or 'I'd love it if we waited to catch up on a call at the end of the day, rather than constant texts throughout the day'. Or be on your phone less without even communicating anything, and if it's meant to continue, the pace will naturally slow down. After all, they might not know they're sweeping you off your feet, but your feet need to be on the ground. Keep your heart open, but make sure to set boundaries.

Our intuition keeps silent score

We may be blissfully happy, up on surface level, but whether we want it to or not, our inner voice manifests through our dreams and body reactions, forcing us to pay attention. Do you feel properly relaxed and yourself around them, or on edge, as if you're trying to impress? Are you looking for escape by diving into your phone, or do you engage and look them in the eye when you talk? And what are your dreams telling you? One night, I dreamt of our parents meeting each other but for some reason Dream Me didn't make a good impression. Maybe I already had underlying insecurities about our relationship. Other interpretations say that dreaming of meeting a boyfriend's parents means you could have to make a tough decision soon, and putting this off might lead to unpleasant consequences. Maybe Supernova was already awakening my spiritual intuition without meaning to, now I was communicating with my inner thoughts without realising how to interpret them.

With self-knowledge comes self-empowerment

A lot of people's dating profiles these days claim communication is the 'quickest way to their hearts', but who knows how to communicate with themselves at 23, let alone with other people?

Once we know what emotional baggage we've packed, what triggers and what traumas, we know how to deal with someone else's. Our young love was too blinded by the wonder of each other to firstly ask ourselves 'what insecurities do I have that could derail this relationship?' and secondly proceed to openly share the answers.

You may have been in a similar situation, where you're so up on cloud nine that friends' or family's murmurs of concern might seem boring, negative or inspired out of jealousy. It was probably hard for our friends to be around us, for the risk of a PDA (public display of affection). It would be years later that I learnt that if a good friend thinks something enough to communicate it, at least hear them out. I got into fights with Mum, who wanted me to focus less on this new boyfriend and more on my dreams to travel. She didn't allow him to stay over for the first month of our relationship to slow us down, but I didn't realise this was necessary and I resented her for it. Little did I know, my root chakra was soon going to be going off like an alarm bell, red lights flashing saying 'danger ahead'.

To most people, especially mothers, Spiritual Fuckboys or narcissists come across as right dicks. On slow weekends at the nearby beach when we'd have each other all to ourselves, I'd watch him do elaborate handstands on the sand as he told me about his spirituality. His beliefs were wearing off on me by verbal osmosis. He told me about meditation, how he'd do 20 minutes each day, and encouraged me to do the same. For his birthday, I crocheted him something to match one of his spiritual tattoos, in blue, his favourite colour. His love for the outdoors inspired me to see nature how he did and interact with it by hugging trees and embracing mindfulness. *He* was a force of nature, like a tornado, picking me up in his life like debris. He carried crystals in his backpacks, jade stones, quartz, amethysts rolling around with his eco bottle and bamboo sunglasses. Back then, this was considered alternative and a bit weird. But it was his effortless individuality that I became hooked on, like fire to oxygen.

This is where the mirror approach comes in again. Empaths and narcissists have the same abandonment 'I'm not good enough' wound but compensate for it differently. Empaths overgive to feel useful and worthy, and narcissists need that worship to make them feel worthy. Yes, it's all very toxic, but it's beautiful too, because empaths can learn from narcissists to stop giving to others and worship themselves instead. 'You made me feel good to be who I really am, because I can see how happy it makes you. That made me feel so good about myself,' Supernova would say to me – see what I mean by them taking worth from us, and us giving it up gladly? 'You're beautiful because you genuinely seem like you care, not many girls have your sweet energy', he'd message me another day. We empaths really do care too much – and that can be our downfall. We must protect ourselves from these 'energy vampires' and retain our own magic, before we give it all away.

Cast an energy protection shield

It's so important to psychically protect ourselves from other people who might be accidentally negative or downright energy philanderers. There's a simple way to help deflect these people's energies, and quickly.

In any scenario, whether it's work, personal or romantic, where you feel like your upbeat energy and natural confidence is being sucked out of your soul, take a deep breath. In your mind's eye, imagine a rose-gold egg around you, a few inches above your skin. This is a forcefield no one can get past without your consent; any nitpickers or spiritual naysayers cannot pass, and it will stay put once you've cast it, so you can get on with your day. If you struggle with visualisation, move your hands from your crown to your feet as if to cast an invisible sheath around you. Alternatively, you could imagine an angel halo or a gladiator shield, anything that will ricochet negativity.

This is particularly handy when your mother asks you if you've gained weight.

Red flag 4: your codependency feels chaotic

The empath–narc relationship is like a closed loop, working for and against each other and continuing for eternity unless something breaks it. For me and Supernova, it was only getting more intense, which meant I had little time to take back for me to centre and ground myself. After a few months, we were collapsing into each other like a dying star. No one had ever been in love like this before, we swore. So, when he told me he'd previously tried polyamory, albeit briefly, I was totally intimidated. How could I ever match up to two girls at once? He laughed me off, but I felt riled and unworthy. I already didn't feel worthy enough for his attention, thanking my lucky stars each day that we'd met. This added insecurity then meant I needed him even more for validation and attention. I became uncomfortable again when we went to a house party together, as he only told me on the way that he'd dated the girl hosting it. He described her as crazy, that old chestnut, but she seemed really nice to me. It was total projection of his real self onto another to shift blame.

Our closed loops go round and round until they consume us, as do our arguments that seem to start out of nowhere and continue without resolution. A Supernova is a star in constant balance between two opposing forces: gravity squeezing the star inwards, and nuclear power in the core pressing outwards. Both forces resist each other, like Supernova and I were. But we still did everything we could to aid it because we refused to let it implode. We'd come too far already to walk away. We told ourselves running away is cowardly. We made ourselves stay because we are big girls who can do hard things, we told ourselves. But the narcissist knows this conflict with us – in fact, they control this.

Following are a few reasons why we enable our narcissists when we should be starving them.

We lack boundaries

We enable our narcissist because we people-please when they don't even ask us to. Though I'd contracted a UTI on a girls' holiday through too much white wine, I soldiered on with giving him birthday sex, happily putting my needs aside to please him. Because sex is the worst thing to do with a UTI, it turned into an infection that was sent directly from the devil. I was throwing up and almost hospitalised, and I didn't get to see him for what felt like weeks. I started to regret that birthday sex I'd offered up. I also started to regret needing Mum there to hand me the toilet roll as I wept each time I weed.

'Where is it all?' she gasped.

She meant my pubic hair. I'd shaved it all off because that's what blokes like, right?

Timing never was her strong suit.

Understand the mind-body connection with sex

Since my work around letting go of shame around sex, especially casual sex, I've stopped getting UTIs. And I used to get them a lot; apparently my mum did too, as did her mum, so it seems this trauma is ancestral. We women know pain well, as do all daughters of Auntie Eve ever since the supposed First Sin. Well, I am the daughter to break the cycle, as are you. Try incorporating these rituals to shake off the shame and see if it makes a physical difference.

- Close your eyes and rest your hands on your pubic bone, on top of your root chakra. Say empowering affirmations each night, out loud, such as 'I choose only excellent sexual partners who are kind, caring and supportive', 'I deserve to make this beautiful body Mother Nature gave me feel good', 'I feel so empowered when I'm with my lover'. Or make up your own. You will get more in flow with this work as you get through the book, so don't worry if more affirmations don't come – pardon the pun.

- Journal on what intimacy you would have if shame or rejection wasn't an issue. Who would it be with, and how would you have it? How would it feel, not just in your sexual organs but in your body? Can you imagine embodying that physical feeling now?
- Try some sexy self-love; do the Gratitude Gaze (page 189), subscribe to erotic audio, and buy yourself a new vibrator. It's also self-love to check that the ingredients in the condoms or lube you're using don't contain unnatural ingredients or ones you're allergic to.
- Invite the topic of sex into conversations with your friends and your partner, romantic or sexual. The more it's talked about, the less taboo it can be.

Only sometimes can a physical problem be energetically caused like this; sometimes it only has something to do with it when it's recurring, ancestral or there's no medical explanation. While you should always seek medical advice for these conditions, research into this complementary spiritual healing therapy has certainly helped me personally. Finding what natural supplements may work for you and your body qualifies as excellent self-care.

It's comfortingly familiar to us

We enable our narcissist because it's the dynamic we were used to somewhere in childhood or adolescence. Forget the inner critic we always hear about, that negative voice inside is our inner narcissist, and even gaslights us that we deserve to feel as awful as we've been told we are. This voice is totally a coping mechanism, because if we're already being this mean to ourselves, it means no one else can do worse. Our narcissistic partner and our inner voice work together as if thick as thieves, robbing us of our natural magic. Sometimes the narc–empath relationship follows a student–teacher dynamic, because it is a power imbalance we've signed up to. One has an over-inflated view of their maturity, and one assumes the immature role. It follows, then, that you feel reduced to a child-like state when one is activated. It can be triggering if you live in or visit the place you grew up because it's easy to be reminded of the trapped person you might have been before – that's where radical self-love and loving self-encouragement need to ramp up.

Having moved home two years ago after graduating, just after Supernova and I moved past the three-month mark, I wanted out – out of my parents' home, that is. One day, my ticket out of there dropped in my lap when a friend mentioned that working holiday visas to Australia were affordable.

I had wanted to travel so badly, but my university boyfriend a few years prior had fiercely opposed even my semester abroad. I'd ended up talking myself out of it to keep the peace. Now I was in an adult, mature relationship which allowed me to be free and flexible. I thought it would be the making of us. But despite us talking about it previously, Supernova didn't want to come, and so we decided we'd do long-distance. As if I was mentally trying to escape the rut we'd fallen into while holding on for dear life. And then the rut got deeper.

We listen when they spew harsh, undeserved criticism

'You think you're so superior because you have this whole career job,' he'd accuse me out of nowhere, accusing *me* of grandiosity. This change of tack can be perplexing and emotionally winding. They had just praised us in the last breath, so where do we stand now?

'You think you're so much better than me with a driving licence,' he'd spit at me another day. The weekend before, for once I wanted to be driven somewhere, able to lean back and step into a passive Divine Feminine while he took assertive action and got us there. But he didn't have a licence and wasn't interested in getting one – he preferred to walk, he said, because it saves the planet. I sensed this was more out of fear of failing the test, so I hadn't pushed it. I see now that it was his insecurity taking the microphone, but picking at me helped him feel better. It felt vicious.

But each time these cutting comments come, we stay and appease rather than walking away. We think we should take their comments personally because we wonder if the person can see something in us that we can't. We enable our narcissist because we comfort him when he beats himself up for upsetting us. Bypassing your own feelings is the first lesson of Toxic Relationships 101. Swallowing your need for space to relevel your nervous system, in the name of 'keeping the peace', is the second.

We believe their quick-fix decisions

But if I had the driving licence, I was going to use it. I could tell we were in an unhealthy cycle, and since I was leaving for a year, I made the hard decision to drive to his and break up, forced to take the masculine control again. I didn't want to break up, but I thought it was kindest thing for him, since I was the one who wanted to leave. Out of nowhere, he had a sudden change of heart. It was so in opposition to his stance of previous weeks that it gave me whiplash. Now he wanted to come. He'd never been confident enough to travel, but with me by his side, it was perfect, he said. It would be the trip we always talked about, he said. He was persuasive. I let myself be hugged and kissed in celebration, but drove home with a niggling confusion now deeper in me. And now we had to hang on to our relationship. I was happy on the surface, but full of dread underneath. When we are at war with our inner self is when the real pain starts.

Without my spirituality as a support yet, I felt alone and empty. I clung on to the fact that soon we'd be somewhere wild and free, with no parents around. But I still felt something niggling at me. I didn't have the fallback of gratitude rituals to relieve my anxiety, or the safety net of self-care practices to catch me before stress tears set in. My anxious attachment heightened each time we fell out, and it was like I didn't exist before he texted me, so I became more and more heightened when he was at work.

He's not replying and you're panicking

He hasn't replied to your double texts, and you're pining for his attention as acknowledgement that you exist and that you are important. That root chakra of yours is blocked like mad. Then you panic – maybe you've done something to upset him, and he's punishing you. Yes, we're always doing something foolish, we think, so should we punish ourselves just in case? Whatever the reason for his lack of reply, come back to you and your emotions. Shake away the shame you feel about your perceived overreaction and self-soothe. Rest your hand on your heart chakra and read the affirmations below. Come back to you, to sanity, to self-respect, to self-love, by repeating them out loud.

Try box breathing to get into a calm but focused mental space. Inhale for four counts, hold for four, exhale for four, hold out for four – even just 30 seconds of this breathing will work. This breathwork was used by Navy Seals to keep calm and cut cortisol in highly pressurised conditions, so it'll work for us.

Speak these words out loud, breathing normally. And at each full stop, take a deep breath.

> I am love. I am worthy of love.
> I create my own reality. I am love. I am worthy of love.
> I am safe. I am love. I am worthy of love.
> I am important, I am wanted, I am desired. I am love. I am worthy of love.
> I am in control. I am love. I am worthy of love.
> I am whole and I am complete as I am. I am love. I am worthy of love.
> I am calm. I can fulfil my own needs as well as letting a partner in. I am love. I am worthy of love.
> I attract divine sacred life-changing romantic love. I am love. I am worthy of love.

Now, unclench your jaw, roll back your shoulders and outstretch your fingers. They're in a fist, I know they are. Deep breath in, and out. Keep speaking these words out loud.

I will never lose myself because I am worthy just as I am. I have clear perspective and see this situation for what it is, alongside embracing my emotions. I love me, I am beautiful inside and out. What's for me will find me. What's not for me will leave. I trust the Universe. I surrender. I breathe in love, I breathe out anxiety.

I am love. I am worthy of love.

Complete this self-check-in prompt in your journal: I now feel … and …

Journaling is for overwhelmed humans, not just writers

We talk a lot about 'holding space' in the spiritual industry, and a journal holds space for us like a good non-judgemental friend or therapist. Sometimes we just need someone or something to reflect our words so we can have a dialogue with them. When we tell a page that it feels like we've done something to upset our partners, it listens without interruption. Think of it like delegating your worries to a blank page, rather than carrying them in your mind. I also found I liked and empathised with myself more when I wrote.

'Begging didn't make me feel good at all, but maybe it makes you feel wanted? What do you expect me to do?' I journaled five months into our relationship just after Showergate. My page didn't answer me.

Journal about your relationship

Answers to these questions may help inspire epiphanies around how you feel about your relationship and clear up self-doubt.

- What does your partner do to make you feel loved, safe and appreciated?
- Does your partner do anything that makes you feel hurt, unsafe or unworthy without opportunity to resolve it?

- How does your partner describe previous partners: with respect, or with put-downs?
- If you could communicate one thing you haven't before, what would it be?
- Are your feelings heard, and if not, what stops them from being heard?
- If the relationship has started to dip, what are some possible reasons?
- If your partner puts you down, is there anyone else other than your partner who shares this opinion or is it isolated to them?
- Does this person help you grow as an individual?

We don't ask for help

We enable our narcissist when our nervous system is constantly activated in a freeze response but we don't ask for help. I'd tried the flight response, or rather the 'book the flight' response – now he was travelling to Australia with me. General symptoms of a freeze response are feelings of panic, losing sleep, inability to focus and feeling stiff and heavy, and I had a full house. I had this sense of dread, so I was never able to get fully excited about our trip. I needed to be shaken out of my hazy dissociative state, and I was too confused to ask for help. I had no idea what to do to come back into myself now dizzy happiness had been replaced with dizzy anxiety.

Hacks to help ground you instantly

When anxiety hits, we usually just want to sit and stew in it. It takes too much energy to fight it, so we freeze in it, hunch in it, grind our teeth in it. Fear of what we're traumatised by keeps us paralysed, even physically. These are some active tips to use to come back into your body and relight the tiniest spark of optimism inside you again.

- Take yourself, with a friend if you like, somewhere quiet and close your eyes, or soften your gaze. Try a simple 2-to-1 breathing technique where the only rule is the outbreath is double the beats of the in-breath, for example inhaling for two but exhaling for four. This will stimulate the parasympathetic nervous system, bringing you back into balance. Close your eyes if you wish, revisiting a happy memory where you felt safe. Repeat slowly for five minutes.
- Trace your fingers and thumb across a crystal with an interesting texture, either raw (mined as is) or tumbled (polished). Choose from lepidolite, blue howlite or amethyst. If in doubt, go for any blue stone as they're most calming.
- Give yourself a hug, squeezing each arm with the opposite hand, or ask for a hug from a loved one. This helps to redefine your outline in a world where everything feels a bit fuzzy.
- Eat something very hot or cold, salty or sweet to shock your senses.
- Know that you are in a safe space, this is only a perceived threat and not real, telling any voices inside you that no harm can come to you. Repeat, out loud, the words 'I am safe'. The danger is just imagined, and you will be okay. Revisit the calming affirmations on page 40, continue taking deep breaths and find someone you can talk to who will help to reassure you.

We're camped out in them

We enable our narcissists because we can see their points sometimes even better than they can. Many empaths are highly sensitive and even psychic; because we are so tuned into others we can almost predict their feelings before they hit them or foretell their next reaction before it occurs to them. Empathising with their takes on an argument stops us from knowing what we believe and arrests us from backing ourselves. That's where boundaries are useful, so you are both safely on your own sides.

Now, with the perspective of self-love, I know I could never have inspired Supernova to be so nasty, and we simply don't have the power to influence someone else's mental health like that. He was treating me as he was, not as I was. We're always acknowledging others, but lacking it ourselves. I imagine being a mother is this on speed, never being acknowledged for how we feel in return. Everyone's feelings are valid, of course. The art of a relationship we humans must learn is both partners feeling heard and seen, thus divinely accepted.

We oblige their desire for us to heal them

It's also a widely believed idea that spiritual women attract men who need healing, but I wasn't even a 'spiritual woman' yet. Years later, when I had my birth chart explained to me, I found that my Chiron, the 'planet' of healing, was in Leo. Leo represents bold confidence, strong personality and abundance of ego. That meant, with old Chiron there too, I struggled to heal those things, and that meant I'd mirror and attract someone like Supernova. However, my confident Leo Rising makes me come across confident, so they'd flock to me like moths to a flame, thinking I could heal their lives and personalities, which Supernova had indeed thought. In retrospect, I must admit, helping Supernova and others to do this gave me a purpose and raised my self-worth, another way I found validation in others. I should have felt enough just as me, without a job to do, a way to be useful, or a person to help fix.

You may have encountered them too: men who want to be motivated to be their best selves, to do cool things, the kind of things they'd get jealous of others for doing. People who didn't know what made them happy, whose own ambitions they didn't know, they just leant on you to define those things, to be those things for them, because that was far easier.

How to plot your birth chart

Think of your birth chart like a time stamp of the moment you came out of the womb. It's a great instant way to gain insight into your personality, as well as gauge what kind of person a potential match might be. Learning your birth chart gives you information you can work with. It's free to do online, or go to a professional astrologer who can draw up your birth chart for you, as well as tell you what transits, i.e. events, will affect you and how.

1 Go online to cafeastrology.com/free-natal-chart-report or any other birth chart calculator of choice. Type in your birthday, birth time and location. If you don't know your time, leave it at the default of 12.00 p.m.

2 Scroll down to see the zodiac signs it says next to Sun, Moon and 'Asc' or Ascendant (also known as Rising). You probably already know your Sun sign, which is also called your star sign. Your Moon sign represents how you express emotion and vulnerability. Your Rising sign simply means the zodiac that was rising on the eastern horizon the minute you were born, and reflects how you give off first impressions. I'm Sun in Gemini (hence being a writer), Moon in Aries (I like leading the pack) and Leo Rising (so I give off a very confident first impression).

3 Write your signs on the following page, and don't worry about things like Black Lilith or Midheaven, or in what house which planet sits for now. Note which zodiac element or elements pop up most. For example, if you have a lot of Scorpio or Pisces, there's a lot of water in your chart, denoting an emotionally tuned-in person. Or say you have Gemini and Aries for many of your planets, there's a mix of air and fire. How does this airiness work with the fieriness or determination of your personality?

Sign compatibility

Fire (Aries, Leo, Sagittarius) and Air (Gemini, Libra, Aquarius) are most compatible together.

Earth (Taurus, Virgo, Capricorn) and Water (Cancer, Scorpio, Pisces) are most compatible together.

We all have a range of different elements scattered through our birth charts that make us the unique person we are. I love my friends whose star signs are in Earth and Water elements too, but I truly spark with fellow Air and Fire signs.

When you next read your horoscopes, read the bit for your Rising sign too, as this is said to give an even clearer picture of your future. Look to match your Rising sign to a potential partner's Sun sign or vice versa! (This explains why I like sparky, confident Leo men.)

Scroll down the webpage and list your zodiac sign for the following:

Sun in …

Jupiter in …

Ascending in …

Saturn in …

Moon in …

Uranus in …

Mercury in …

Neptune in …

Venus in …

Pluto in …

Mars in …

Chiron in …

Referring to the element guide at the top of this page, most of my signs are in .... or .... elements.

Where's your Chiron?

This question can be translated as: 'Where do you need deep, intrinsic healing but offer it to others instead?' You don't need to totally understand astrology in order to look up where your Chiron is, but I find it a fascinating part of astrology. This is not a planet, in fact, but a cheeky comet with an erratic orbit, and the zodiac in which it sits just means where it was situated when you were born.

- In Aries: it might be hard to rate yourself and your strengths because you're always applauding others.
- In Taurus: you struggle to treat yourself, because while you encourage others that they're worth it, you don't always believe it for yourself.
- In Gemini: you might criticise yourself for what you say or how you say it, but you're quick to offer genuine help and advice to others.
- In Cancer: it could prove tricky to follow your own advice or be kind to yourself, but you're the first to worry about others and offer them guidance.
- In Leo: you might have trouble with identity and ego, feeling bad for bragging or sharing achievements, but you're a powerful cheerleader for others.
- In Virgo: you have high expectations of yourself and your organisation, but always feel like you're falling short, despite offering others clever hacks.
- In Libra: though you stand for equality, you may overgive to others. You may also feel conflict deeply despite being an excellent counsellor when others fall out.
- In Scorpio: you're highly knowledgeable about psychology, but you limit your attachments for fear of losing yourself. While you make a great guru, embrace your own feelings and jealousies too.
- In Sagittarius: you're a great leader, encouraging others to use the power of thought and manifestation, but you might feel a little lost or unsure about the power of your own potential.

- In Capricorn: you need to lower your expectations of yourself, because while you beat yourself up for not being disciplined enough, you're a strong motivator for others.
- In Aquarius: you're not sure of your place within your community, but you're the glue. Push away your insecurities, because you truly know what's best when it comes to matters of the group as a whole.
- In Pisces: as with all water signs, you hold emotions within you. Consider upping your self-care, because while you forgive others easily – too easily, sometimes – you need a dose of your own softness too.

Journal on how this resonates with you. Have you attracted friends or partners who come to you with those struggles, knowing you're just the person to help? Being aware of where your insecurities lie is fantastic intel because it allows you to work on those areas in your self-love sessions. The more you work on loving yourself, to heal what's within you, the more you'll attract people committed to doing that for themselves.

The final battle

'He didn't mean it. It was a normal argument couples have, it's one of those,' I chirruped to a friend, gesticulating it all away to save face.

Her expression fell into pained worry, and in that moment, where an expression said everything, I knew I had to stop fighting with the part of myself that loved him.

The weekend before, as he became frantic, frenetic and aggressive as an argument resurfaced, he'd grabbed my phone and thrown it violently across the room. I had been on the phone to my mum – asking her to pick me up. She could tell something was wrong immediately from my cowed voice, but then our call had been cut off by him snatching my phone off me. My tone was enough to tell her she needed to come out and save her adult daughter from her boyfriend that night.

As soon as I got home with Mum, he wanted me to come back. There was no relief. We were in purgatory.

Despite it being obvious to everyone else, it can take a long time to see how consumed we are by our relationship to even breathe deeply, let alone respectfully part ways. The demise of mine had happened slowly over the autumn, but the break-up would happen quickly. I learnt years later that I was a fast manifester, because once I know what I want for my highest good, it comes fast. Maybe you do too – when you finally decide something, the Universe is set in motion and you don't understand how it happens so fast. When your mind is finally made up, life can flip like the Wheel of Fortune.

There she is. That's the spark of self-love we needed.

Crystals to keep around toxic people

Either wear these black and white rocks as jewellery or keep them in your pockets or bra:

- Black obsidian to protect from their negative energy.
- Selenite to purify your aura, boosting your optimism.
- Black tourmaline to guard against frustration and quick temper.

It took all the willpower inside me. I didn't want to do it, and he pleaded with me that he'd get better, but I knew he'd just be threatening a break-up an hour later. Once again, I took control, crystals in hand, bra, bed, everywhere. I was numb. It was over. I could breathe. I needed all the breath I could inhale as I sobbed harder than I ever had before or since.

Assessing the aftermath

Though everyone is different, it's good to know the stages of a break-up so you know what to expect.

Relief comes first. We finally have the space and peace our spiritual narcissists never permitted us, and it feels amazing. Then, the euphoria wears off. About two weeks in is when it really starts to hurt, when reality sinks in.

Anger will come on too, but for the sake of healing – it's a good sign. It shows you that your experience was unacceptable, that you asked for too little, that you deserve better. Anger is an emotion you might have found hard to bear as an adult too; it feels too masculine, too powerful to contain inside me, it makes me nauseous and my energy restless. But within a few days, I became furious at how I was belittled into submission, made a shell of myself. I can't remember how contact came about, but we had a fierce texting stand-off. Months of built-up resentment exploded out of me when I begged him to please keep to his original plan of going first to Perth and not follow me to Sydney. He was wilful, and said he'd go where he pleased, denying it was anything to do with following me. He told me he would be just fine after me because he loved himself.

It was the first time I'd really heard of self-love, but from him it came across as arrogant, selfish, everything we know today that self-love is not. I had loved him too but I'd left none for myself. How could he be in this place that felt so high and mighty? How could he be so okay without me, I wondered, when I was still trying to piece myself back together like fragments of glass? He loved himself just as he was, he said, but looking back at the unlovable things he had said and done, I think perhaps he was in a toxic relationship with himself, and I knew I couldn't help him anymore.

The next stage after anger, and realising you're done with them, is exhaustion. Emptiness. Unrootedness. It's like you have to try to get used to life without your personal brand of crack. I felt terrified of seeing him, being found by him, even though I desperately wanted to be at the same time. I felt weak and pathetic when I should have been as empathetic to myself as I had been to him.

The last stage can be described as gumption. I carried on journaling with new steam: 'How could I have stayed with someone who claimed to love me for exactly who I was, but said "you're not worth it"? Who said: "I can't spend every day with you for a year", "I love you, but …" Who said off-hand things as in, "I'm just not feeling it today", "I don't want this relationship". Who called me negative and threatened to finish with me if I dared to want to discuss something openly and honestly. But you were the awful one, and I'm done.'

And with that last word, I felt calmer than I had in weeks, and drifted into my first deep sleep in as long.

The core lesson

Though he'd shown me what a spiritual life looked life, he hadn't taught me one important lesson: it all starts within. A basic, modest respect for oneself, for one's environment, peers, world, is easy for people to see and to sense. Crucially, it means you never need to tell people that you love yourself, which rather misses the point. His insecurities had taken the microphone for months and that critical voice had drowned out any self-love voice I could have cultivated. And now I've got one, I can see that it's growth for me to reflect that I might have been my happiest ever self with Supernova. I'm grateful I know what that euphoria feels like, even if I never want to repeat the scenario. I refuse to beat myself up for going along with the fantasy he'd concocted, because I doubt anyone would have turned down their Supernova after being so emotionally neglected by former lovers. If only he'd taught me self-love too. But then again, if I'd had an ounce of self-love, self-worth or self-respect, I would never have fallen for him.

It's also said that our root chakra links to our physical immune system. Mine was definitely busted. Just before I left for Oz, I fell ill with a chest infection, plus I had a whiplashed neck from a car accident a few months before which was still causing me significant pain. This, compounded with the constant freeze response, intensified the sensation of physical tension. I would have to get on the flight with a pack of strong antibiotics and muscle tape all over my back. I was pale, exhausted and looked like I was recovering from some kind of war zone, which I was, emotionally. I was carrying guilt from getting into it at all, and more feelings I couldn't work out. My spirituality was waiting in the wings for its big moment.

The spiritual single girl break-up guide

This is the guide I wish I had to my break-up specifically, but it applies to any kind of break-up. Follow these bullets and you'll be as set up as possible for a future of successful self-love.

- Don't fall into the trap of telling them what you think of them. It's just going to feed their power supply and waste the energy you need for healing. They'll also have proof to hold over you and tell people about, making you look like the narcissist. Resist the urge to engage and if in doubt, agree with what they say to placate them.
- Give yourself permission to not be okay if that's how you feel inside. Seek all the comforts you need, eat ice cream, cry, wallow, and feel the feelings that demand to be felt, even journal on them. Refuse to feel ashamed for feeling however you feel, because you literally can't control your feelings. We're out of the toxic positivity zone now, so welcome in the emotion, don't push it away. Our feelings are our soul communicating with us, and evolutionarily speaking, how we naturally heal ourselves. Repressing our feelings might feel easier, but this will cause problems later on.
- Read the self-love vow again from page 18, out loud, every morning and evening. Trust me, the words are going into your subconscious, which can't tell between reality and imagination. Your brain will believe whatever it's told – that's why love-bombing works so well.
- If you have no good reason to be contacting each other, start a

30-day no-contact month. This is the only way to set boundaries and start to establish your life without them. It's your choice if you communicate the boundary or not. Enforcing it allows your own inner thoughts to flood in and let your ex's presence in your head drop away. This also means blocking them on social media if you are ready to, so that you can't snoop on their profile in a moment of weakness. If you have to maintain a relationship, for instance because you have kids, let them know you will only be conversing about such matters. It may feel cold, but it doesn't mean what you had was meaningless or throwaway, just that you are now putting yourself first. You may get pushback, but think of boundaries as a membrane rather than a 10-foot-high bulletproof prison wall keeping everyone out. You control your boundaries, they don't control you.

- Know that if you are meant to be together, you will rediscover each other. If you do fantasise about getting back together, know your hard deal-breakers, so that if you do reunite, you won't ever feel like this again. And even if your head knows it's over for good, give your feelings space and time to be heard, because it takes a while for our hearts to catch up. Don't bully yourself for not getting over it quickly, or even slowly; just allow.

- Text or voice note yourself about what thoughts and feelings are coming up about the relationship. Or, voice note people you trust, then listen back to yourself. Journal on how you would counsel the person you just heard if they were your friend, trying to have as much self-compassion for yourself as possible.

- Write or list out loud a Bye Bye Bye List, paying gratitude for all the things you won't miss. Any petty or practical reasons count as valid, and can remind you why this break-up is for your highest good. This will start designing your life without them, framing it in a positive sense. A Bye Bye Bye List is about *closure*. As NSYNC said it best, 'it might sound crazy, but it ain't no lie, baby bye bye bye'. Then, when you're ready to look to the future, flip each pointer into an affirmation to magnetise it to you. For instance, write 'I love my new mother-in-law'.

- Do the cord-cutting ritual on page 62. If you find it tough, ask yourself if it's because you still want to be attached to them.
- Do one thing to transform yourself and try on a slightly new identity, such as a new hairstyle or taking up a new exercise. Do anything to start liking yourself again but do NOT cut your OWN fringe. Some say hair holds psychological trauma, but hacking at your own with scissors won't dissolve it.
- Practise one self-care or self-therapy ritual a day. Either start up the mirror affirmations on page 174, try the yoga poses on page 59 or go for the cord-cutting spell on page 63.
- Try safe anger release, such as pushing your hands against a wall with all your weight, thumping a pillow or screaming along to loud rock music in the car. This negative energy has to go somewhere, so don't let yourself subconsciously internalise it. Recruit a friend to join you and make it a group anger therapy session; they will thank you for it. Screaming along to punk emo music in a car usually works for me.
- If he or his friends or family get in touch, try the energy protection technique again, and if you need it boosted, meditate first before visualising your rose-gold egg.
- Prioritise compassion, softness and connection and find friends who are good at listening. Borrow strength from them and, if you can, schedule the next catch-up so you know you will be caught again soon. Whatever whoever did to whom in the relationship, your priority right now has to be you.

Begin the Fool's journey

We are the Fool in our own Fool's journey, our life's arc. We are the protagonist in our own spiritual awakening story. I don't mean to say all non-spiritual people are foolish. Rather that we're just at the start of an educational journey of some sort. To even start a Fool's journey requires a leap of faith, and faith is hard to keep hold of in this modern world sometimes. This is where being 23 years old can help; no one expects you to be wise to the world yet.

Tarot isn't just a trend you see on tote bags these days; its system is ancient, based on Italian *tarocchi* cards of the fifteenth century. The Milanese simply added the Major Arcana, consisting of 22 character cards, to a classic playing card deck. The characters of the Major Arcana make up the Fool's journey, and are sometimes described as 'power' cards because they help to predict bigger life events than the original deck. This deck was relegated to the Minor Arcana and the suits of this 56-card stack became cups, pentacles, swords and wands. It's still enjoyed like a game; one I've loved ever since Lotti's mum did readings for us at sleepovers.

The thing I love most about tarot is that the picture cards, in the order each deck comes in, tells a coming-of-age story of the 'The Fool's Journey'. This story depicts a tale of epic mystical medieval adventure, meeting all the other characters in the cards who are instrumental in the Fool's story, culminating in ultimate wisdom on their return depicted with the last card: The World. The High Priestess, for example, helps us to be still, to sit with our psychic ability, and the Hanged Man is said to remind ourselves to hang in the balance and let life work itself out, plus more enthrallingly helpful characters. We are all the Fool in our own journey, and it's a reminder that all of these characters come into our life at one time or other for a reason. I didn't know I was embarking on my own Fool's journey ahead of me when I got on the plane. But I was ready for novelty, for throwing myself into risk, to prove what I could do alone. I was ready to see what I was made of now I was a solo traveller and single woman.

The Fool's journey is a great place to start learning about how tarot works, and why each reading of specific cards pulled at a specific time paints a snapshot about where you are on that plotline. It's far more than a yes or no answer to the querent's question. Think back to when you were at the start of a story arc of some kind, about to meet all the people that brought you to where you are today. It could have been starting a new school, new job or a new physical adventure. If you had had a tarot reading around that time, the Fool card may well have come up.

Though tarot is one small part of spirituality, it might become your favourite way of conversing with your spirit guides. You might wish to get your hands on a tarot deck as we'll be using it in parts of this book.

Don't go anywhere without activating your root chakra first!

This is great to do around the new moon, when we traditionally make wishes and set intentions. Go straight to savasana (corpse pose), lying stretched out on your back, letting your legs drop open wide. Rest your hands where they feel comfortable and feel the floor beneath your body, supporting your weight. Light a candle or diffuser with woody, earthy smells, such as cedar or frankincense. Imagine growing roots into the floor like you're a tree. Don't worry, you don't need an artist's imagination to do this, you just need to connect with the feeling even a basic image gives you.

1 Take a few deep breaths and close your eyes. Ask yourself: could you be wasting, leaking or giving away your precious energy to anyone or anything? See what your intuition flashes up as an answer. What might be an unwise use of your energy at the moment? Set an intention to recycle your good energy back into you and your life.

2 With your intention set, imagine a red light at the base of your spine. Send that glowing red light up through your spine, breathing deeply and imagining it spreading in your body with warmth, then feel it evaporate through your crown.

3 For the rest of the moon cycle, note how much stronger and more confident you feel in your energy boundaries. You could visualise yourself with a glowing red forcefield around you to protect you from leaking energy.

4 Look out for ways to incorporate more red into your life; from wearing the colour, to using crystals like carnelian and garnet, to eating red fruits and vegetables. Feel strong and empowered.

2

Sacral Chakra: On the Rebound

Affirmation: I am free to travel the world as I like, and I fully embrace my passion for travel and connecting with others. I am divinely protected by Angel Raphael and invite myself to feel whatever I am meant to feel in each moment.

Some people change their hairstyle post break-up; I changed my hemisphere. I arrived in Sydney and into the welcoming arms of my friends from home, the ones who had mentioned the working holiday visa in the first place. They'd lined up for us a small flat down the coast from the set of *Home and Away*. It was paradise and I was determined to make the most of my new opportunities and reinvent myself.

Sounds like bypassing to me, some silent voice inside me said.

Our second chakra is our sacral. Called *svadhisthana* in Sanskrit, which means 'one's abode', it is the energy centre concerned with self-connection and pleasure. It's also where we hold subconscious emotions like guilt. Mine was ready for some cheap attention and so blocked it was a wonder I couldn't hear it practically stuttering right there behind my navel. As soon as I surfaced from my jetlag around Valentine's Day, neither of the guys I went with for cheap beers on the beach probably remembered my name. There were no follow-up texts afterwards, let alone second dates. But I was just getting warmed up, both to the Australian summer heat and the Tinder scene down under.

The more we repress any uncomfortable feelings about our exes, the more depressed we'll become. I'm not saying we should allow ourselves to wallow forever; rumination is low vibrational energy because it is full of remorse and regret. Instead, we must actively heal by allowing ourselves to feel our feelings. That's the only way to release them. We need to consciously say to ourselves, 'okay, I acknowledge I feel absolutely horrendous and miss him terribly'. I wish someone had slapped that into me; I needed to hear it badly. Instead, I spent half my free time swiping on Tinder and the other half spying on Supernova on Facebook. Each six-foot tall man-bunned hunk I spotted on the street would make my heart jump, and our local beach town, Manly, was full of them.

Sexual healing, or sexual hopping?

In the absence of active healing, we unconsciously bunny hop from one toxic boy to another in the name of 'fun'. Think less Playboy Bunny, more rabbit in the headlights, scared stiff of more rejection. I sometimes cringe when people call casual sex 'sexual healing', because I don't see how unconsciously infecting ourselves with strangers' energies can be justified as fun. (I think when done consciously, with consent and communication, it can work – more on this later.) My first proper rebound was a total cliché, with a beautifully tanned, athletic but horrifically vain surf lifesaver who I had to convince to wear a condom. I was on the pill, but you can't be too careful, and I didn't trust him ...

If you don't trust him at all, why sleep with him ...

If Supernova wasn't my most recent sexual partner, I thought I could further detach from him and it would hurt less. 'The more interest I get, the more he'll fade into memory', went my illogic. Hey, no one said healing from a toxic relationship made any sense.

After being told exactly what we were by our exes – too confident, not positive enough, too sensitive – it's easy to throw a guard up and have only anonymous, identity-less sex so they can't see the 'real us' and pass judgement. When it's that lacking in connection, hooking up with a stranger can feel like hooking up with the act of sex itself, because there's rarely much kissing, intimacy or many face-to-face opportunities for eye contact. Sex with Supernova had been the polar opposite, especially as I'd felt so secure, having both already said 'I love you' and become a couple before we consummated. I hadn't pegged myself as a traditionalist, but I loved making love to him as an individual, as opposed to this rebound experience, which felt like fulfilling a mechanical ego-fuelled act. Supernova and I had needed each other so much that we really did become one in love, simply made and exquisitely executed. Now it was just me, physically connected to a stranger by our bodies but feeling all alone. I walked home along the beach the next day with an oncoming hangover, nauseous down to my sacral chakra. It's easy to miss how loved and connected our exes made us feel, both to their body and to your own.

Use yin yoga to surrender to difficult emotions

Do this short restorative ritual every night to help soften a hard heart. You could try the following yoga poses at home, especially around the full moon, to release the trauma or tension in your body. Remember why you want to heal, and let any emotions ebb out of your hips, where we store it. Put on some soft melodic music, grab your mat, light a candle and do the following hip-opening poses. Healing rituals like this empower us to meet our own expectations and stop depending on other people to soothe us. However, if you're a beginner yogi, do only what feels good for you and your body. This is about being gentle, not about being in competition with yourself.

- Spinal twist (supta matsyendrasana): on your back, extend your arms to the sides and pull up your knees. Drop them both to one side and look over your opposite shoulder, relaxing into the pose for five minutes, heart to the sky as you gently try to get your shoulder towards or on the floor. Direct your breath there on each exhale. Switch sides gently. Roll from your side to upright, then onto all fours.

- Dragon/Lizard pose (utthan pristhasana): from this tabletop position (on all fours), step your right foot to the outside of your hands, placing the heel directly under your knee so the leg is at a right angle. Reach the straight leg back as far as it will go, pushing into the hip of the bent leg, so it looks like a plank on one leg. Stay on the hands, or for a deeper stretch, go down to your elbows. Stay for five deep breaths and feel the emotion trickling out of your hips, breathing light and oxygen to your hips if you find it intense. Stretch out in downward dog (adho mukha svanasana), then repeat on the other side.

- Melting heart into child's pose (balasana): from tabletop on all fours, melt your heart space towards the ground and rest your forehead on the floor, feeling safe with your chest to the floor. Pull your hips back and lower them to rest your body weight on your heels, moving your arms flat by your side. With each deep exhale, know how safe you are here in your body, on your mat, in your sanctuary.

Come into the reclined goddess pose, lying down with pillows longways under your spine, knees bent and out to the sides and heart open. This yin pose allows you to know what it feels like to feel vulnerable at the same time as powerful.

End with a cup of herbal tea, a bath and a book, and notice how much more peace is in your mind, body and spirit after a few evenings doing this ritual. Look out for any opportunities to stretch your hips, even if it's being on top in sex. Now that really is sexual healing.

The Magician sets intentions in motion

When we're feeling ungrounded, a spiritual faith can help us ground into ourselves and intuitively feel into the best next move to make. A conscious approach to life helps us see that our 'why' is everything; intention is where every spell, astral travel trip, even every first date occurs, because it's all about why we say 'yes'. We take this intention, add some positive energy, good technique and a bit of luck, and boom, if it's our highest good, a spectacular experience manifests. The hardest thing is knowing what our intention is, when deciding on it can overwhelm and stagnate us. Especially when we're hungover from a one-night stand.

Our intention massively matters in our healing, too. My intention could have been 'I want to move on emotionally so that I can find new love, otherwise I'll be frozen in this bereft feeling forever'. We can always change it; what matters is having a destination in mind at all. But I had no idea how to create my own post-break-up sanctuary, in my rented single room in Sydney suburbia, or in my heart. I had never even had a chance to set a bloody intention for my trip, having been so consumed by events leading up to it. I tried a yoga class but I found downward dog uncomfortable, although now after practice I really understand why it's called the 'recovery pose'. It's where we take a deep, much needed exhale from the difficult flow we've just moved through, or difficult break-up. However, I did eventually set my intention to connect with people on a friendship level, rather than on a sexual one, and booked a backpacker tour in Tasmania. This was my Magician moment – when plans start being prepared.

Connected by a cord

During a mutual break-up, it can still feel like we're outrunning someone who is chasing us. Even though he was 11,000 miles away, I could feel Supernova near, as if he was still lodging in my mind. Not surprising really, seeing as we became so enmeshed mere months before that the boundary between us still felt blurred. It seems obvious to me now, but the reason we can miss other people so much is because our energetic cord, a metaphysical umbilical cord, has not been cut. Flying even further away from the UK felt like the further escape into the unknown that I needed, to evade the difficult feelings I was running from.

Cut the cord with your ex

I didn't hear about this energy-releasing technique until years after Supernova, but it works with anyone negative or painful you want to evict from your mental, emotional and spiritual space. They won't know you've done it, but over practice and time, they may wonder how come you've been able to move on so well from them. This is their problem, not yours.

You should also do this to clear away the bad energy at the end of the relationship, even if you want it to repair it in the future. The perfect time to do this is towards or on a full moon, where we traditionally release and surrender the old.

1   Light a candle and clear your space with sage. Take some deep breaths and close your eyes to see the person you want to sever ties with. Imagine an umbilical cord going from your belly button to theirs. Ask yourself what colour it is. Is it glowing, or is there a particular texture to it?
2   Take a pair of scissors in your mind's eye (the scissors you did *not* use to cut your own fringe) and sever the cord. In your own time, imagine him or her floating away into outer space, finally untethered to you.
3   Journal how this felt: good, bad or sad? Did you start to feel your shoulders drop as their draining personality stopped affecting you, or did you start to feel more positive without their negative outlook on life? Meditate on how this change felt.
4   Do this as many times per week as you need to feel distance

between you and them. You'll start to feel less of them in your mind and more space for you.

You could also perform it as less of a meditation and more of a spell, using an actual spool of string and scissors as you imagine severing your connection. Use a lighter or a match to burn both ends to represent the finality of that relationship or phase.

Alcohol blinds, not buries

Even though you're trying to outrun your feelings, surprise surprise, they'll catch up with you. When you want to drunk-call your ex, read this again and you'll be turned off the idea for life. Or have your friends read it to you. Either way, please be cautioned and think twice.

For even further escape, a literal vacation from feeling, binge drinking is an all-too-easy coping mechanism. Scientifically speaking, it blocks your prefrontal cortex and gatekeeps emotions, perfect for staying emotionally unavailable to yourself and others. As a backpacker working in an Australian pub, alcohol was a religion in itself. I even had to complete an online qualification to legally serve it. But you don't need to set an intention for drinking, thus it isn't a conscious activity conducive to healing. These days, I drink mostly just to celebrate special occasions, or to taste something truly delicious – that means top-shelf stuff if I have been manifesting a good income that month. For me back then, it was a dopamine binge, an artificial bout of authentic happiness. But that one night, before I left for Hobart, even that couldn't stop me doing what I spent two months trying not to. Sometimes we run out of energy to repress our feelings, and finally need to surrender to them.

As I keyed in his number on a night out before I flew, I knew it was a bad idea – maybe my intuition was screaming that at me internally through all the booze fog. There was no answer each time I tried – maybe he didn't want to pick up an unknown number, even though seeing the Australian area code, he knew it would be me. I gave up eventually, still feeling his presence inside me somehow, knowing I needed to speak to him.

As the UK woke up a few hours later and I received several bewildered texts, shame and embarrassment came with rapid force. He asked if I was okay, at least. I lied and told him I was. My need was met but not really, and totally devoid of drama, leaving me unsatisfied. Expectations I had to be saved like a damsel in distress had been totally dashed. I cursed myself for having given him my new phone number in the process, knowing that I'd feel even more rejected if he didn't use it to contact me again.

Our spiritual narcissist is our god, our guru, our master, up until the point where we finally lose all respect and reverence for them. We only break up with them because the relationship is exhausting, but keep our feelings for them like a souvenir. He was still my anchor, my gravity; all I'd needed – and subconsciously expected – was the familiar sound of his voice to acknowledge me in this world where I felt so untethered. But his voice is actually really annoying. I wish I'd called a friend instead who would have told me what I needed to hear – that he was not obligated to help me, but I was, and this was all a natural part of trying to fall out of love with a narcissist.

The High Priestess sets our soul alight

Leading a spiritual single life in a couple-obsessed world can be tough. Three particular Spiritual Single Girl commandments should be helpful when you find yourself feeling lost or lonely. See these three tenets as reminders that you are exactly on the path you should be on right now. We'll dive into them in more detail on page 201, but the Third Commandment states that if we want to find our soulmate, we need to drop the ego and swipe with soul. It applies to life off the apps too. We need to find the magic in each new moment for us, rather than for the story and entertainment of others.

As soon as I got into my travelling stride in Tasmania, this felt like my High Priestess card moment on my Fool's journey, finding what set my soul on fire. It was like my inner child hooted nostalgically at the art galleries and craft stalls in Hobart. Going back to basics is the best way to heal, I realised. So think back to what your inner child loved to do, then do it. Do it to fill the BBB gap (booze, bars and boys). After hitting rock bottom on the plane going out there, my smile gradually came back. I was making a success of my new life. The tea tree oils in the Tasmanian lakes, with the natural oil softening my skin and giving my bleached blonde hair new lift, didn't hurt either.

What reignites your spark? For you, it could be learning new skills to open your understanding of life, feeling safe spending time with family, or getting in touch with nature. As your spark returns, watch how you spend the energy it generates, your own divine nuclear fuel. But watch as you channel your relit spark straight into the empty, bottomless BBB hole. As I came back to life, so did my hyper-flirty self, like a Tasmanian devil in female form. Our hyper-feminised self attracts in its mirror: hyper-sexual men.

Riskiest rebound for the highest ego reward

This powerful energy will attract anyone on the same vibration. It was like I was armed and dangerous; first off it was my tour leader, who I'd sparked off with during the week, and then it was his housemate, who I met when our tour returned to Hobart. Oops, I did it again. Having turned them both down, feeling guilty for accidentally leading them on, I went home with someone I met on a night out. He worked at the Cadbury factory (a real-life Willy Wonka, I lamely joked) and took me back to his for fumbled sex.

These days, it feels as though guys on dating apps seem to assume women are so up for sex straightaway that I worry sex-workers have gone out of business. I was practically giving out free sex in return for closeness. I felt resentful and shameful of myself, but I didn't know how else to get the intimacy I craved.

The Empress sparks our self-worth

When a male fuckboy friend I travelled onwards to Melbourne with came on to me one drunken night, I turned him down. Luckily, thanks to divine timing, I was on my period anyway. It was like the Empress character had got hold of me to say 'you know you're worth better'. Though I felt awkward after probably giving him the come on, it felt empowering to say no to someone I would have otherwise said yes to. Eckhart Tolle might have had *The Power of Now*, but we spiritual single girls have The Power of No.

Crystals for your period

We may as well do some crystal healing in this sacred rest time.

- Peach moonstone – for Divine Feminine and to stabilise emotions.
- Lapis lazuli – to make communication clear and calm.
- Rose quartz – to heal heart and sacral chakras.
- Smoky quartz – a good pain-reliever.

Microdosing gratitude in hard times

When you're in an emotional hole, as I was on my return to Sydney, it can be very lonely and easy to spiral. We've become tired of the do, do, do and chase, chase, chase, unaware that the key to life is the effortless employment of the Law of Attraction. If you're in a new city, or a new lifestyle, or new anything, one good plan or piece of news a day will keep you buoyant and be a life-saving shred of light. It could be anything from getting a manicure to a new job trial, or a coffee date with a friend planned for next week.

As I've said, keep it simple, or as inspired by Coco Chanel, don't add, just subtract. Even though she meant subtracting an accessory from your outfit, I will go into why simplicity is central to the Divine Feminine energy in general. For instance, start subtracting BBB, even just for the sake of experiment, and see how quickly you feel better. On good days, this will come naturally, and the Universe will get into lockstep with you and the positive momentum it creates. Gratitude is addictive – way more addictive than fuckboys.

The Emperor empowers us

This gratitude is like an invisible force behind you, like a gust of cosmic wind. I got offered an interview for a third job by randomly chatting to a woman in a bar. Well, the Emperor card is all about material success and leadership, and I was making myself a lot of money for a backpacker. I had to move out of my friends' place as they needed the spare room back, so I'd found an even better room in a stunning headland apartment which looked over two beaches either side. As Carrie Bradshaw would have said, it really was 'where they kept the light'.

But as self-help guru Louise Hay professed, if you manifest something and still don't believe you're worthy of it, it will slip away. We must always keep the faith and accept our manifestations gladly and gratefully, as if gratitude is the 'z' bookend to our 'a' intention.

Count your blessings, not sheep

Talking of the alphabet, if stress is keeping you up at night, play a gratitude game to get to sleep. Think of something starting with 'A' you're grateful for, however minuscule a positive change it made to your day. Then, shoot for 'B'. You can say boys if you want, but only if they've made you happy that day, not given you a chance to make them happy. You'll be asleep by the time you reach G for gratitude itself.

Life was anything but a highlight reel

As I worked 70-hour weeks at three jobs back in Sydney, I forgot to do my daily gratitude. My 24th birthday was coming up and I had FOMO (fear of missing out) on summer at home. Though I'd tried to keep my homesick sobs quiet on nightly phone calls with home, my new housemates' patience dwindled fast in our open-plan apartment. My bar job boss picked on me, and I still missed Supernova terribly, who now only lived half an hour up the road. My happiness was at an all-time low, and my weight at an all-time high, like I comfort ate for energetic armour against the world. I had manifested the amazing flat and all the jobs, but it was making me miserable. I felt like I was failing my twenties, the heyday we're meant to look back on happily. I needed some spiritual advice to apply to my practical reality.

Enter, the Hierophant

Then the Hierophant character appeared at our table at the pub one night. A traditional pope-like figure, he – in my case, she – asks us if the societal norm of working ourselves into the ground is really our spiritual calling.

'If you're unhappy, move on,' was this stranger's simple guidance.

'I can't,' I said, my excuse ready. 'I'll never get an apartment as beautiful as this one, and I have three jobs I've committed to now.'

She shrugged. 'Okay. But I've learnt not to stick at what doesn't work. Change something or leave. If something wasn't meant to be, don't push at it.'

I never saw her again, and I never got her number. She slipped through the void, and sometimes I wonder if she was an angel, heaven-sent.

It's empowering to accept we're in a rut and even more so to do something about it. I needed a change from my current stagnated path, like I was in *Inception* and needed the kick to wake up. I needed to do something equivalent to the pain I was in to energetically match it and clear it.

The Chariot resparks a stagnant situation

Sometimes it takes a freefall to wake us up. When we've spent long enough in dissociation, numbed to our pain, it's like we need overwhelming fear to shake us up. That's the exact purpose of the Chariot, to jolt us into motivation. So that June, I took another quick trip away from Australia and arrived in snowy Queenstown, New Zealand, to tick off one big bucket list item. If nothing else, it would ensure no Sunday Scaries would ever feel as bad.

That Monday morning, as my nerves ramped up as steadily as the plane's altitude, I started regretting every decision I'd ever made – to come to Australia, to want to travel in the first place, and to skydive. But that was just fear talking. As in a spiritual awakening, it was going to be uncomfortable, and there was no going back. I didn't know it was going to be the moment for the Lovers card, asking me to take a leap of faith.

Suddenly I was 12,000 feet in the air with my legs dangling out of a small plane, my life in the hands of a stranger. A big fat nothingness awaited me, the surprising depth of three dimensions of thin air taking my breath away. Petrified as my human instinct told me to be, something inside me also welcomed it, recognising a big fat nothingness inside me too. I didn't have spirituality to fill that void yet. I'd tried to fill it with oxytocin, but one-night stands hadn't stimulated that hormone. I'd have to make do with adrenaline. I let myself be tipped over into the void.

My stomach did an Olympics-worthy synchronised belly flop and every muscle in my body tensed for impact with nothing. I squeezed my eyes shut as if to dissociate further with reality. We were in freefall but it felt like being pushed up, like a feather in a flurry. For those blissful moments, I couldn't think, I couldn't panic, I could only feel the intense anti-gravity illusion, my body

69

now a mere plaything for the elements. Who'd decided this was the way our Universe works?

Open your eyes. NOW! Open your eyes!

I blinked them open at the instruction of a strange inner voice, as the tandem diver strapped to my back tapped my arms for me to open them wide. The wind was flapping my cheeks open, and I looked like a hamster shoving wind into the sides of my cheeks for winter.

Take a mental snapshot and vow to remember this moment forever.

Honestly, what was that? As I did what it said, the view of the planet from directly above was indescribable. Fierce blue sky reflecting deep blue water, the only white to be seen on the tops of the mountain ranges. Witnessing something this novel changed something in me, as it affirmed some part of me that doubted I could do something as brave. The decision to come out travelling simply couldn't be the wrong one with this outstanding view, I reasoned once the parachute caught us. The means to experience this came from totally unexpected compensation from the car accident months before, my whiplash thankfully now gone. Did the Universe want me to be able to experience something so out of my comfort zone? Was this high-altitude, no-safety-net moment what had jolted me back into consciousness?

Asking such abstract questions is the first sign we're awakening. It means we're seeing more than we did before, more than what we just accepted, and we're leaning in with curiosity. I was starting to consider that there was more to life, more to me, than my comfort zone of ego-fuelled emotions.

Look out for the Lovers

Euphoria hit as soon as we landed on our feet. I was back on Planet Earth with new information at my fingertips of how beautiful the world could be. It wasn't all hard doom and gloom and work and horrible housemates. I could now fly. I forgot all about the little voice as soon as I clapped eyes on a guy who'd been on my dive. I must have been really scared if I hadn't noticed him before. Little did I know the Lovers tarot card, which depicts an opportunity that requires a leap of faith, was going to turn out quite so literally.

Finding my spirituality in strength

'Hakey,' Fernanda recommended in her thick accent when I got back to Sydney. Again, I had been feeling ungrounded and stressed since returning.

'Say that again?'

'Haaaakey.' When I got her to write it down, it spelt Reiki.

As if she picked up on my exact needs, my kind Brazilian colleague at the shop had told me she'd just had an amazing session with a healer. Divine timing for me.

Sold on the premise that it was like a spiritual massage, I booked myself in. Reiki, I learnt that day, is a type of energy work where a trained practitioner will scan and heal your chakras. They don't touch you at all, but many people claim they do feel something, so since this first experience, I've always thought of Reiki like an invisible healing massage. We're all energy beings, and Reiki healers just move energy. It's a simple process, if you're willing to believe. It was the simple things that were best for us, I was now sure of it.

In my session, I felt like I rose above the massage bed, *Exorcist*-style, but instead of being possessed by the devil, I was floating on air, my body feeling almost tickled. I saw colours behind my eyelids, and had drifted into some meditational sleepy trance. In our consultation afterwards, my healer instructed me to go downstairs to the market and find a sodalite crystal, looking for it with my non-dominant hand, which was my left. Sodalite, she told me, a dark blue crystal with marble-looking veins running through it, was good for writers. Why wasn't I writing, she asked, when I found it so therapeutic? The crystal was also good with the thyroid, a gland that sits within the base of our throat and releases a hormone that allows us to grow and develop throughout childhood, puberty and adulthood. I had been born with hypothyroidism, so my gland didn't release a damn thing. How could she have known that? I was grateful to find a real connection in this town, finally, though I didn't bargain for it to be a psychic one. I felt unafraid, chakras clear, ready to take on Sydney.

Girls just want to set fun intentions

We're so hung up trying to meet the one, we forget about meeting *people*. I can't stress enough the importance of a wingwoman for companionship and emotional intimacy, especially on sacred times of the week: Friday and Saturday nights (or for backpackers, Tuesday or Wednesday nights). Your goal is to steal kisses from as many boys as possible. Thick as thieves, and better than boyfriends.

When Tina from Kentucky joined the bar, it was like my prayers had been answered. She was athletic and at first I thought she looked too 'cool girl' to want to be friends with me. As soon as she revealed her goofy side, calling herself a 'Scorpitattius', her birthday on the brink of Scorpio and Sag season, we clicked. Now that I was in a new house share that welcomed visitors, we had nights out and girly sleepovers that helped me feel even more at home. But my time in Sydney was coming to an end and I was suddenly sad to say goodbye. It's better to be sad to leave a place than desperate to escape it, I learnt.

Happy breakdowns can help heal us

Looking back, sometimes it's okay to cringe and laugh at ourselves. Our twenties are the years leading up to an important astrological 'coming of age' transit called our Saturn Return, when Saturn returns to the same place it was when you were born. The theory is that the planet has moved through all 12 zodiacs, testing you in all areas of life. Our twenties are for learning lessons, not excelling at them. Travelling is one of those times when you're allowed to just be reckless, careless and full of freedom. My sweet hedonistic self set the intention to live in the moment, not like dating apps now where hook-ups seem to be scheduled in like appointments (or was that just with Virgos?). I was swiping right on the future, not the past. I was making way for happy breakdowns instead of sad.

Happy breakdowns are moments of gratitude that stop us in our tracks with wonder, happy tears that temporarily yank us out of our heartbreak. I've had many in the process of writing this book. They're made up of glimmers, the opposite of triggers. They install hope and happiness back into our sad hearts or overloaded nervous systems. As soon as I took my focus off boys, bars and booze in Byron Bay, I started having them daily, just by looking out for novelty and magic.

In weed wonderland village Nimbin I found my first crystal friend, a tiger's eye ring in a ramshackle little hippy shop. My tiger's eye has helped keep me confident, abundant and focused since she became mine that day. My excess Sydney weight started dropping off me. I took myself to yoga, I ate fresh sushi and spent every day at the beach with the Chilean backpacker I'd rideshared with from Sydney and our new hostel friends. We had a shared happy breakdown a few mornings later when we drove up to the Cape Byron lighthouse for sunrise. It's one of the most easterly points in the world, on the edge of the Australian continent, so, arm in arm, our ten-person-strong hostel gang were treated to the first light of the day in the whole country. The land was sacred too, this headland having once been an important place for Aboriginal spiritual ceremony and ritual. Experiencing the quiet dawn with this group I'd known a mere few weeks, eating dinner nightly together at the hostel, after months of loneliness in Sydney, set my soul on fire. I liked myself here; no, I *fancied* myself here. My soul felt the same colour as the burning golden sun that morning.

Fuckboys are destiny deterrents

We know fuckboys get between us and our destiny – that's why we use them, because deep down, we're scared of our own success. We can't live in denial forever, we know, but we assume 'one day' it'll figure itself out. In the meantime, we are more than happy to waste our lives on their instant validation. Though I was travelling with direction, to get to Cairns to meet Lotti who was flying in, it was still mostly without intention.

Some people go to Byron Bay just to have sex on the beach. Even that would have been a more valiant intention than having none at all. Though I did have my own fun when my friendship with the Chilean unexpectedly developed one night. Some people raise an eyebrow; 'You slept with someone you met giving a lift from Sydney to?' they ask, disappointed in the comparison to meeting someone on a skydive. Yes, yes I did, and I don't regret it – my Chilean helped me see through time and space for the first time since Supernova. It was much better than my hook-up with Irish guy a few weeks later, who apologised as he cut the experience rather short. That was pure sex for the sake of it, which never goes down well.

Sightseeing with spirit

Lost loved ones are only ever a heartbeat away, say many angel experts. Death doesn't end a relationship, just a life, say others. I hadn't realised my beloved paternal grandmother Betty had been with me as part of my spiritual tag team until I left Byron and crossed the border officially into Queensland. The next day, I was going to walk in her footsteps and meet her brother-in-law. Betty had been here and stayed with him about two decades before me, and I felt closer to her spirit.

Think back to your own inner child. What age are they frozen at? If it's around six, that's the age our feeling brain turns into more of a thinking brain. It was the age I was when Stanley, my grandfather and Betty's sweetheart since she was 18, passed away. But here I was, 11,000 miles from home, in a stranger's house, in front of Stanley's brother George, who was his spitting image. His cockney accent was enough to trigger a tsunami of tears. Always a weird moment when you realise you can skydive with a stranger, have sex with strangers, but a reunion with long-lost family is the most bizarre experience you can have down under.

Your spiritual first-aid kit

The mental stamina it takes to keep travelling solo and making constant decisions alone can be exhausting. It would have been interesting to see how quickly anxiety could creep back into my mind if I let it, tiptoeing past my consciousness as a rebellious lover past their curfew, if only it wasn't so annoying. If only I'd known that I was being divinely guided, I could have relaxed and trusted my journey far more. Too much alcohol and too much giving out my strong sacral energy to others meant I had no good energy left for myself. I needed replenishing.

At any point on your travels or daily life at home, hold your spiritual first-aid kit close. I now credit mine with keeping me sane and spiritually balanced in this chaotic world. Please note, your first-aid kit cannot be another person. If there's a day you feel uneasy and need to speed dial the Universe for guidance, turn off your phone and dive into your spiritual first-aid kit to help ground you, or settle down into the meditation below to see how your spirit guide can help advise.

Your first-aid kit list won't take up too much room or weight in your bag but it's worth carrying in case you just need to take five minutes away from others to recentre. No one will know you have a whole soul survival kit in your back pocket. Mix and match as you wish, but your dependence on such a kit may grow as you become more in tune with spirituality.

- Grounding crystals to aid root chakra, page 56.
- Pendulum (if you don't have one, start to use your body as one, knowing what bodily sensation indicates a 'yes' and which might indicate a 'no'. For me, a 'yes' makes my heart lift, and 'no' is a belly drop).
- Oracle cards of any type, or make your own.
- Teabags, tissues for any healing tears and a snack.
- Essential oils; I like grounding frankincense, energising citrus or comforting lavender.

Meet your spirit guides

We all have a spirit guide, whether or not we're in touch with them. Think of them as the leader of your spirit team, that motley crew up in your mind. Some people have a spirit animal, some swear by their guardian angels, a mystical entity or goddess, and others know it's an ancestor looking over them. Psychic mediums use their spirit guides to facilitate the clairvoyant or clairaudient connection with those who have passed over. Fear not: you don't have to be a psychic medium to connect with your spirit guide. This meditation below, like most spiritual work, will help them step forward in your consciousness. It might take some practice, so just enjoy it until a recurring figure keeps coming through each time you try.

1 Excuse yourself to somewhere quiet, and start off by closing your eyes or softening your gaze ahead of you; in yoga this focused gaze is called *dristi*.

2 Put a hand on your belly, resting just above your sacral area. Do box breathing again, repeating that 4-4-4-4 pattern by taking a deep belly inhale, holding it, exhaling and pausing.

3 Visualise yourself sitting somewhere safe and warm, like your sofa at home. Inside your mind, ask your spirit guide to step forward and into the room. They might be a loved one who has passed, or they might look like a mythical being. Notice how you feel calmer with them there – your body will tell you, so pay attention to your sensations. What do they look like? If they're not a loved one, ask them their name and what they're here to help you with.

4 Once you're acquainted, ask them any questions you have in your mind's voice, and actively watch their reactions and listen to their replies. The more you practise this meditation, the faster their answers will come. Even if you weren't old enough to know what your loved ones would say, your intuition will fill in the gaps.

5 Alternatively, ask your pendulum or set of oracle or tarot cards the questions, and see what they reveal. Again, don't worry if you're new at this. The more self-care and spiritual work you do, the stronger the intuition muscle will get.

Finding your gateway to mindfulness

I know how hard it is just to sit down and meditate. Your foot itches, your mind wanders, and you start thinking about what to make for dinner or how to respond to that email. You need a gateway to mindfulness practice. Yours could be washing up, driving or walking in nature. My mindfulness method used to be sex. Running replaced that far before meditation did.

A lot of unawakened men still use sex as their mindfulness method *and* their only way to connect. The reason a lot of them don't manage it is because they only know how to connect physically – with their sexual partner or themselves. John Gray's book *Men Are from Mars, Women Are from Venus* is so true; it really is like we're from different planets sometimes. Men tend to want to problem-solve, and women tend to want to be listened to. Men are attracted by physical appearance and touch, and women by expansive conversations and acts of service. Few of us are taught to connect through vulnerability and active listening, whatever gender we are, though I'm confident men are gradually having deeper conversations or seeking emotional help in this new age.

I met the Dutchman in Hobart and he has since become one of my most trusted travel buddies. In Brisbane he offered for me to move into his home for free while he worked his night shifts. So when the Dutchman suddenly came on to me that first evening, I felt any shred of solid ground and safe friendship I'd trusted crumble. I felt suddenly unwelcome and, weirdly, unwanted and unseen. Safety is the most important quality in any kind of relationship, and the ground fell out from under me. Years later, he'd tell me he felt equally as unwanted, even though he only wanted something casual. We were both wanting connection but feeling disconnected.

Even if it's just deep breaths with a hand on any chakra that needs the love at that moment, know your go-to stress relief chore and pack it into your spiritual first-aid kit. Making a cuppa to calm myself, I then found out his roommate had just got out of prison. In that moment of acute anxiety, I didn't find spirituality – my angel chorus I hear now didn't start singing gospel in my ear – but I did feel called to go for a run. This had become my meditation, the strength of my newly supple body, my trusted safe place, my home, and what would become a place of worship in the self-love years to come. It gets you into the habit of seeking mindfulness rather than external validation in crisis. Above all, it gets you back into your body if you feel your soul become loose from your skin, like Peter Pan's shadow.

In my hermit era

You know you're a hermit healing your sacral chakra when aching loneliness from before is replaced with a desire to be alone. Even if it's being alone with others, like passing solo time in public or going to a gym class, it's a whole new way to live an empowered life. In the daytimes, when Dutchman was at work, I explored Brisbane and its festivals on its very own South Bank. I found thrift shops I loved, Himalayan vegan cafés and hipster coffee shops in studenty high streets. But it was some enlightening time I needed, to regroup after finding a whole new branch of my family tree, my ancestors, knowing one day I wanted to dedicate something I'd created to Betty. I'd regrouped just in time to meet up with my fellow skydiver from a few months before in New Zealand.

Why do I feel nervous? I asked myself the day before we had dinner. Come on, it's not like this is a date.

It's so a date. You want it to be, and it is, a silent voice answered.

Bring out The Eyes

Now, if you'll allow me to briefly revisit my leap of faith Lovers card, this is my drop-dead signature move that worked on the person that card was concerned with. I've seen this move stun people's very souls where they sit. I needed it the night when Gap Year Guy arrived – he was even more attractive than I remembered, his aura totally relaxed and authentic. Our catch-up turned into a date at some point around the end of the starter.

It's ideal if you're sitting adjacent or side by side with your date, but it can be done sat opposite them, you just need to choose which shoulder to lean into them with. Choose a time when you want them to absolutely crumble at your beauty and aura, maybe around halfway through the date. It's more of a deal sealer move than a starter move, because you need them to be leant in already.

Don't waste this move – only whip it out to when you really need to captivate. It's too powerful to fritter, and their reaction will make you feel very powerful indeed.

1   Ask them a question where you're sure they might be talking for a little while without asking you a question in return, like something about them or their favourite hobby. (Here's hoping they do have hobbies.)

2   If you're sat opposite them, lean back, choosing a shoulder to face them with. Make a point of taking a deep breath. Look down at the arm not facing them, like something caught your attention there. Keeping your chin down, slowly sweep your eyeline in their direction, bringing it to rest on the shoulder that's leaning into them. Your subject may be wondering what you're doing by now, but that's good – they're watching.

3   They've probably finished talking by now, so now's your time to strike. Within about five seconds of chin to shoulder, take a very subtle, innocent shrug on that shoulder. Then the move: slowly blink your eyes up, locking on their eyes immediately. Bam! They'll be hit with the sight of your big, beautiful eyes looking straight into their soul, and they will feel immediately seen.

4   Personalise your move with whatever expression you like, either an earnest gaze, a naughty sparkle in your eyes, or even pout your lips as if to blow them a kiss. A serious look or smoulder can work too, given the right mood. If you want to go cheesy, add a wink, but I save that gimmick for my girlfriends who get me to do it as a party trick. And for the better photographers among your friends, get them to snap a picture of you as you sweep your eyes up. Tinder won't be able to resist.

Spin the Wheel of Fortune

Remember what I said about gratitude gathering momentum for the good things to manifest? You'll know when the tide is turning from bad to good. Unfortunately, we can't spin the Wheel of Fortune until it spins itself. We must stand the Universe's tests before it rewards us, like the Dom (dominant) it is. This is the card that tells us life is about turn around for us.

Maybe starting to date someone good for you, as I did with Gap Year Guy, was what spun the wheel. Or maybe it was when you took the leap of faith that it started to tick – I'd landed a moonlit date just because, a few months earlier, I'd wanted to know what freefall felt like. Regardless of what started it, more good things, totally disconnected from him and one another, were set in motion also. One day the Universe flashed up an advert online for a promotional video shoot for a hostel chain, and I got cast in it. Gap Year Guy was in contact throughout, and we fitted in dates when the shoot schedule allowed. Then I volunteered at a horse farm in the Glasshouse Mountains, an oasis with grassy green peaks until ancient volcanic rock shot up vertically forming crystal tower-like structures. I got to start my days feeding baby goats and finish them riding horses in stunning scenery. I was living all kinds of backpacker dreams, with Gap Year Guy on the sidelines of it all. I loved both city and country, ever the alter ego Gemini.

Just like friends, Justice keeps us balanced

It's a strange transition, school or adolescent friendships into adult friendships. We change into so many different people as we grow up, and even more as we spiritually awaken (be warned, select people you think will stick around won't). If we're lucky, our paths with the right people continue running parallel, or they might cross once and never again. We can practise detaching from outcomes, releasing people with love and clearing the energetic path so that one day, when you're both ready, you stumble onto the same vibration once again.

Just like the time difference was savage between Oz and the UK, the difference between you and your pals' lives can be glaring too. When Lotti came out to visit me, she'd go home to get engaged and I'd go off to road trip Western Australia. I was so grateful my Taurean anchor came out to join me on my reckless adventure. Though travel was always on my radar, I had only met her because I'd missed my original university offer and had to go through clearing. She told me a few years later she was thankful to me, her Gemini hypewoman, for giving her, a homebird, the courage to come all that way. Just like the Justice card in a tarot reading, symbolising harmony and good advice, look out for whoever balances you out like a pair of scales.

Send your bestie gratitude

Journal on the following questions, either in your own notebook so they feel your energetic gratitude remotely or in a letter you're going to send them.

- What things wouldn't you have done without their giving you the idea or support, or lending you money or tools towards it?
- What things have you inspired them to do in return, or always encouraged them to do?
- When have they risked upsetting you to tell you some truth you needed to hear? How did it change your life for the better? How have you both repaired any conflict and how did it strengthen your relationship?
- List three of your favourite things about them.
- Express your wishes for the future of your friendship, writing your wishes into the cosmos, and watch them come true!
- To make this last exercise more of a spell, whisper 'and mote it be' as you finish writing the sentence, then print a lipstick kiss on the paper.

Be rebirthed like the Hanged Man

I've always been an indoor girl, more drawn to gossip about who fancied who rather than get outside. But if boys are deterrents from our destiny, being out in nature is the best deterrent to boys. You have no signal anyway, and the sensation of washing your naked body in the energizingly cold Indian Ocean is better than any physical feeling a fuckboy can give you – well, most. I lay down to sunbathe on my front on this private beach my road trip buddies and I had found and took a cheeky selfie over my shoulder of my white bikini-lined bum, the stark contrast in my skin tones itself a record of how long I'd been travelling, like tree rings in nature. Who was I kidding – I probably sent it to Gap Year Guy.

I could practise mindfulness now I was running and doing yoga, but my slowly burgeoning spirituality had been largely dormant for a month or two, the culture on the backpacking east coast more drinking than deities. However, the Hanged Man character on my Fool's journey was about to remind me to stop resisting my bigger thinking and gain illumination.

There, in a remote corner of the west coast desert, it was one stop in particular where I quite literally started to question everything, just as I had falling back to Earth in New Zealand. On my breaks from driving, I was reading a classic backpacker text: *Shantaram*. Gregory David Roberts' intricate story of redemption and destiny in India, which I'd picked up from a free shelf, sparked my spirituality again, and it was as alive as the organisms we went to see that day.

As we already established, a big bang defines an instant jump start of something. But if we're talking about the real big bang, where did that begin, what was the spark? Australia was the oldest continent on Earth, so I was about to see spirituality and science together in action.

The stromatolites look like perfectly unremarkable and quite ugly underwater rock blobs. They almost resemble stepping stones to the unawakened eye. Now, excuse me while I get my geek on, but they were the very first single-cell organism. They are billions of years old, and were present at the dawn of time, when the air was orange with methane. Biologically speaking, we as human beings are related to them. These rocks even let off bubbles of oxygen too; they were doing bloody *breathwork*.

My road trip mates walked straight past but I felt I wanted to spend time here, getting my head around how these could be our non-human ancestors. The Hanged Man wants us to pause and reflect too. How could I, a conscious, walking, talking, writing, sex-having dot on the record of the human race, have evolved from this pool of rocks? It was stardust in action, right in front of my eyes. This spark of humanity was a catalyst for my own secular faith. We are spiritual beings having a human experience on this wild, beautiful planet. Who decided this was the way the Universe worked? Surely some sort of higher power?

Though I now felt part of the greater nature ecosystem, believing in the oneness of the Universe, I was almost envious of mama turtles we caught one night on the beach burying their eggs in the sand. Away they worked in the full moonlight, doing what they had done for millennia, blissfully unaware of the swiping strife humans needed to do to find someone to have babies with. If match.com hadn't been invented in 1995, maybe we'd still be starting relationships the traditional way our species always had done, I thought. Though it didn't totally revolutionise dating, it did offer us hundreds more partners than even a polyamorous person can deal with, leaving us as befuddled as we are trying to set an intention for healing.

Cards are your cosmic travel agent

I recommend you travel with a tarot deck. It's a great way to let the Universe assist you with your next adventure or even add direction to your next moves at home.

Tarot cards can help you choose your next destination whereas oracle cards are softer and more open to interpretation, so they can help show you how you feel about where you've been and where you're going.

Tarot is also a great new icebreaker with hostel friends, who'll probably ask you what 'game' you're playing. Remember to take a quiet moment to regroup before a reading, and always take three deep circular breaths, which means in through your nose and out through your mouth, at the start.

Tarot card reading

Either ask the cards a direct question and interpret your answer through the guidebook that came with the cards, or mix it up a bit. Assign one of your four options of a next destination to a suit, e.g. assign cups to a waterside place, or trust in the Universe by assigning a direction, e.g. cups is north, swords is east, wands is south and pentacles is west. See which card you pull and let the Universe lead the way. Use the amount depicted on the card too; for instance, one of cups could mean you go ten miles north, two of cups means twenty miles, and so on. If you get a character card from the Major Arcana, pick a wild card place! That's a message from the Universe saying say 'yes' to the next person who invites you where they're going (safety and gut-feeling permitting).

Oracle card reading

For a more insightful look at your trip so far, pull three cards, one at a time, from wherever in the deck calls to you. Lay them down on the table in front of you in a row.

Turn over the card on the left. This represents the place you've just come from and how you found it. How does it ring true?

The middle card represents where you are now.

The card on the right describes the next place you're going. Where springs to mind when you read this last card's message?

Pendulum

Make sure your pendulum is coded to you so you know what yes and no both look like, and hold it over a map.

Ask yes/no or either/or questions to the pendulum or see where it points to.

Death means new beginnings

Not a card that predicts a heart attack, the Death card foretells new beginnings – just not totally easy ones, and an ending has to come first. Get this in a reading and expect transformation. I was about to accept a challenge I'd given myself by heading back to Sydney. Supernova and all my triggers were still there, but with my alcohol-serving licence valid only in New South Wales, I booked my flight. I was ready for my rebirth and to make the city my bitch.

The reason writing our affirmations and wishes down comes true is because when we journal, we are channelling. That triggers the Universe into action. 'I am coming full circle and directly reflected on the person I was when I first got here,' I wrote in my journal around this time. 'I have learnt to trust that things will be okay if you give them their own time to happen.' Boyfriends had called me headstrong before, and this time, they were right. I had almost done what I set out to do; make a fulfilling life for myself on the other side of the world from home, just to prove I could.

If you're struggling with something

Life is no easy journey. So when life feels tough, play.

Hold whatever it is you're struggling with in your mind, be it your job, dating, your relationship, a creative project, a course, parenting, you name it. Take a deep breath. What questions and ultimatums is your ego throwing at you right now? 'What if I can't do it?' is one that springs to mind. 'What if I miss something?' is another. I diagnose a case of perfectionism. 'What if they discover that I'm a fraud?' That'll be your imposter syndrome talking, not your soul.

We want to shy away from the thing itself, but know that we only procrastinate and play small because we're fearful of missing our full potential. Call yourself out on your own perfectionist ego, because it makes us believe each little risk is a life and death matter. But this book is all about leading with soul and enjoying the process so that we can raise our vibe and attract our soul partner. We don't want people we attract at ego level, and they don't truly want us.

Start by playing, even if you have to pretend it's a bully whose face you're going to laugh in just to intimidate it. Take a light approach when you next tackle your dilemma. If you changed the way you did A, for example, be curious at what effect it has on B. If you gave C a few different options, could it fix the problem with D? Playing could reveal the solution you'd been agonisingly looking for all along. Why do you think role play is so successful at reconnecting two partners who have lost their spark?

Playing feels low risk enough to get you to step up to the plate, desk or therapist's office, and once you're there, playing helps keep your heart light enough to tackle any obstacles without stress. Cut it down into smaller, more digestible chunks to keep your ego from screaming when it catches wind of what you're up to. And remember, everything always works out the way it was always meant to, so no sweat. You can't change it, because it's already happened and been divinely recorded (don't let me get into Akashic Records here).

Start how you mean to go on

Despite Western beliefs, life doesn't just start again on 1st January. The beginning of the zodiac year is 21st March, with the sign Aries. The Chinese calendar starts in February. Witches' new year is 31st October, otherwise known as Hallowe'en, though its pagan name is Samhain (pronounced sow-en). Each new start can remind us to set new intentions, and we can do this at any point in the year we fancy, such as at every new moon. But as I was observing the Western calendar at this point, I made my New Year count, with Sydney Harbour fireworks and a date on New Year's Day. As if the orgasms I had were micro manifestation boosters (just you wait), on my way home I got a text inviting me to work at a beautiful boho gift shop where I'd left my CV. My year had started strong and it better stay that way, I dared it. I felt magnetic.

You know you're magnetic when:

- things, people, jobs, fun opportunities and plans come to you with ease, without you having to overthink or push;
- you feel comfortable putting yourself first and don't feel the need to people-please;
- you're excited to go to bed purely because you're excited to get up tomorrow;
- you recognise happiness in other people, loved ones, acquaintances or strangers – and you reflect it, not resent it;
- you feel worthy, knowing what is destined for you is yours already;
- you slightly buzz with adrenaline when journaling, planning or talking about what you want to call in; and
- you feel light, calm and connected to your life.

Focus on what is in flow

Before being taught by manifestation experts, I had an intuitive feeling to concentrate my energy on what was fun rather than what wasn't. I let anything that wasn't immediately fruitful catch up in its own divine time, less caught up in hopes and expectations. I was only in Sydney for six weeks before my visa ran out, so I vowed to take whatever jobs that came. Magical things happen when you take pressure off situations, and I was in play mode with work. I put it down to this flow state that I managed to manifest four jobs in total, all of which worked around each other perfectly. Somehow, I remember still having quite a lot of free time. That is the idea of effortless manifestation: getting more by doing less.

I'd learn an important thing in my new day job door-knocking for charity. The more 'no' answers you get, the closer you are to a 'yes' (true for jobs, relationships, book deals etc.). The Law of Probability becomes the Law of Attraction, and you can smell success when no's keep popping up. With each sign-up it also incrementally reinstalled my faith in humanity. One day, a young

Lebanese woman who spoke very little English and seemed a little lonely invited me in for lunch, and I've still never tasted anything more delicious. Other people gave me fresh cold fruit or cans of soft drink as they happily signed up to help people they'd never meet. I got another job from a girl at a hostel in Perth going to extra lengths to recommend me to an agency. Day-to-day life at home can be lonely – in fact, charity Campaign to End Loneliness reports the loneliest people in society are likely to be between 16 and 24 years old, are female or are single. I was all three of those things, so travel was my best antidote to loneliness. A good backpacker community works like an ecosystem, knowing someone will be there to give you a tampon, hug or advice whenever you need it.

Temperance reminds us to tread carefully

Funny how priorities evolve through your twenties. Now, I value authenticity, honesty and loyalty above all else. To land most of the jobs, however, I had seen no other way than to bluff that my visa was good for six more months. Looking back, that desperation was coming from a scarcity mindset, which never works long term. It's the same for dating. It works to get us the jobs, or the guys, but eventually it's not destined for us and we have to leave 'prematurely'. So when the time came to step into my inner Fleabag and orchestrate the final white lies so I could leave the country, I was ready with my excuse that I had to rush home to my grandmother's funeral. Please forgive me, Betty.

I'd tried to get fired from the bar job because my inner good girl fancied it for my bucket list, so it worked in my favour that my train back from the suburb I'd been stationed in that day was extremely delayed. Once I finally got there, two hours late, I was pulled into a back room by my boss. 'Rosalind, we don't want to let you go. We like your spirit. We love how you are with customers. Please try not to be late again,' he said, far more nicely than I deserved.

Seriously? My personality was the thing that kept me this job

I didn't want? Damn me for being so naturally effervescent and charming.

I had dodged the Temperance card's warning, to have a strict moral code to reach my goals. In fact, I was operating more as if it had been reversed. An upside-down tarot card could be read with the opposite message, in its simplest explanation. In this case, a reversed Temperance card indicates recklessness and greedy behaviour.

After a final goodbye tour to friends in town and family in Brisbane, I was ready to leave Oz for good this time. There was just one thing left to do before I got on the plane to New Zealand.

Keep good karmic hygiene

- Donate to charity each pay cheque or bonus, even if it's a tiny consistent amount. That exchange of energy is not just monetary, but each transfer will also send healing and high-vibrational energy to its recipient. The money is just a bonus!
- Talk up your soul sisters in networking, introducing your friends if they live in the same city as each other. Know that the sisterly love and support will come back to you tenfold.
- Love people the way you want to be loved, and give people the honesty you would want in return. It's the way to show the Universe how you want to align.
- If it's safe, offer help to someone who looks like they need it, like someone who looks lost or upset. They may be scared or shy to ask, but you're not too shy to offer it. The worst they can say is 'no' and it helps keep the faith that when you need help, assistance from strangers will be there.

All good things must come to an end

'I'm downstairs, baby.'

'I'll be right there. I can't wait to see you.'

I checked into my Auckland flight early, as I had about six hours till I left Australia. Gap Year Guy had just got back from spending a long Christmas at his parents'.

I urge you to cling on, like I did with Gap Year Guy, to those you feel give you permission to be your sweet, soft self. Those you can relax with and let your guard down around. He didn't even have to try to be in his Divine Masculine; he was already modest, authentic and comfortable in himself, and I felt safe to be in my romantic Divine Feminine. What was most impressive about carefree travel me was that though sometimes I'd count the seconds till I saw him again, I never stepped out of my own life into his. Maybe what we miss most about men like Gap Year Guy is that part of us, the us that feels so desirable, special and worthy of another.

'Want some chocolate for the flight?' he asked me back at the terminal.

Um, was there ever a better question asked in an airport? We had just consummated our goodbye in an airport hotel – four star, thank you very much – and in our cuddled-up selfies, our eyes glitter with dizzy, don't-care-what-happens-next happiness.

'I love you,' I sputtered instead of saying yes. Maybe I was still high on oxytocin.

What the fuck she just say?

'Ummm.' I went red. Classic. I ran away to the other side of the shop, and we both pretended I had just thanked him.

Luckily, he still wanted to kiss me goodbye, not scared off by my post-fuck faux pas. I stole one glance back, wondering what fate would have made of us if I could have stayed. A girl like me only comes around once in a lifetime, he'd said. But then again, the man we are truly destined for will make it clear if he wants us to stay. He was The One That Got Away, but he'd let me get away from him.

A part of me is glad he stayed Gap Year Guy, rather than forcing him to become just Guy. Our real lives never came into play and responsibilities like kids and bills never dulled the spark of our connection. Maybe some sparks are meant to be temporary, but no less beautiful. But the goodbyes are never easy when they're for forever.

Look in the direction you want to go

I was surfing in wonderful Raglan, New Zealand, having booked onto a backpacker jump-on-jump-off bus trip around the North Island. This motto seemed apt for navigating both the sea and life. I wanted my own autonomy and to make my own decisions, so that no visa had to wrench me apart from someone like Gap Year Guy ever again. There was me thinking I had control.

In my post-surf, post-yoga high, I felt like I had the travel thing down now.

'I just feel so relaxed, Mum. I've got this travelling stuff down now. Like, it's so easy,' I told her from 12 hours ahead.

'Hmm, okay. Well, I'm glad. But just be careful still, please.'

When the Devil appears, expect downfall

Spiritual experts talk about opening our hearts and trusting, and not to take it personally when people can't meet us at that vibration. But like me, you know we also don't live in a world of rainbows and smiles. We're often too scared to relax in the unlikely case something bad happens to us. On our travels, it's still worth being open-hearted and trusting more people than not. But when the Devil card appears, expect strange occurrences or even disasters to come your way. It also shows where we don't listen to our intuition. Yet, like all tarot cards, it wants you to action it so you can transform. If failure or downfall does happen, it can give us invaluable perspective and euphoric gratitude for what did go right, and what it taught us.

'Leave all your things here, guys,' the tour leader had told us before he locked the bus and led us to the viewpoint. We had the car park and viewing area to ourselves.

It was a normal day on the tour, and when I was picked up that morning in Rotorua, I'd made automatic friends with the packers already on the bus. The driver on that leg was a good-looking, madly toned guy who had previously been a bouncer, he had boasted. Sounds like my type, I know, but I felt some odd aversion to him, some awkward edges I didn't want to try to unravel.

Don't trust him, my intuition said to no one, still back on mute.

After longer up on a windy viewpoint than I personally thought necessary, where he even served refreshments, as we returned to the bus I heard some weird gasps. Then my eyes clapped on the window glass lying shattered on the tarmac.

Everything I owned that had value had gone: my handbag, which had contained my purse, cash and passport. My day pack with my laptop. My dental retainers. My keyring from Gap Year Guy, notes and numbers from new travel friends. Even my bag of groceries. All gone.

You sort of dissociate in a personal disaster like that. Everything goes a little fuzzy, and your knees go weak, and not in a good way. I glanced at the two rows of seats behind me, and everything was still there, untouched on their seats. I was the last seat to have been swept. The hot seat.

All I had with me was my phone, which, thank the Universe, encased my Aussie debit card and UK driver's licence, and our suitcases were still safely locked in the trailer. A few days before, on Valentine's Day, I'd posted a few silly stories to Instagram claiming that my passport was my Valentine. It all seemed so silly now.

Was it a fluke, a wrong-place-at-the-wrong-time situation, we asked ourselves? Was the Universe teaching me a lesson about lying about my visa back in Sydney, I wondered, as if the Universe had gifted me the earnings only to snatch them back?

In truth, it was one of the local gangs who had snatched our stuff, but I was searching for a more cosmic reason.

Gratitude makes you euphoric

While everyone draws the line between fate and coincidence somewhere slightly different, my biggest takeaway was the perspective it gave to crisis situations. Sanne, a blonde, kind-faced Dutchie I'd met that morning, saw me panic and repeated comforting words over and over for many minutes as I slowly calmed down. A kind fellow bus mate whose stuff had gone untouched lent me her phone to cancel my passport once my phone died. Thank goddess we hadn't been intimidated or attacked, and possessions can be replaced, but people can't be. I was almost euphoric, buzzing with gratitude that we all were fine, no accident had happened, and there truly was no disaster.

The warning of the Devil card is to expect disaster or tension on some level, and especially on a material realm. But I would carry on travelling anyway, even though I'd now been on the receiving end of humanity's shadow. I'd put my best flip-flopped foot forward. It's very easy to take crime like that personally, but how could it have been? They didn't know us personally. In that moment, I understood money as a free-flowing energy, and I knew I could easily replace what they'd taken. It wasn't a loss, because nothing truly important could ever truly be lost.

And whether the bus driver who boasted of his links with local gangs had anything to do with it, I would never know. He would sleep with one of the girls from the tour though, so my intuition had been on the right lines.

Crystals to keep you safe abroad

No one can ward against other people's free will, but carrying these stones buzzing with the intention you place in them will always help attract more positive experiences and give you a sense of peace. They make great gifts for travellers, too.

- Shungite guards against the electrical energy burnout from airports, planes, taxis and other transport.
- Aquamarine is an excellent companion when travelling on water.
- Smoky quartz is a very protective crystal and can shield you from other people's unwanted energy.
- Malachite inspires safe travel and also invokes Archangel Raphael, the patron of safe and smooth journeys.

Having a Tower moment

You may have heard of a Tower moment, when every ideal comes crashing down in a sudden crisis. This, again, is the Universe testing us, but it's also making space for something new, chucking us off one course and onto another.

It's such a romantic idea to see where the wind blows us, and towards what man. Most people waft around Southeast Asia following the usual backpacker flow north into Laos, taking the two-day slow boat cruise down the Mekong to Luang Prabang, and then on to Cambodia. I'd also heard from a friend back at home that she'd had firsthand experience of a blind monk who did a cracking butt massage in Siem Reap, though sadly I'd have to forgo it. Now that I had an emergency passport, I was only allowed to pass through five countries on it, and one of them had to be home. Being rigid and regimental greatly disappointed the free spirit in me, but perhaps it was a blessing in disguise. I had to travel with much more focused intention, and now I had to go home rather than stay away forever.

But when a crisis comes, we cling on to cheap comforts, how to feel better the fastest we can. The Devil card was here to deliver temptation, back into old habits of using fuckboys as soul path deterrents. My sacral chakra was crying out again for comfort. Where I had come to grow in my relationship to boys, I was shrinking again when a French former firefighter with a fantastic torso took a fancy to me. After a night of flirting, I gladly went outside with him to smoke, even though I didn't smoke.

'Yeah, you could lose a pound or two,' he negged me in his thick accent, as if in answer to a question I'd posed. Was that his idea of flirting? I scoffed at him, disagreeing. How dare we let men take us down a few pegs so we'd feel desperate enough to do what they wanted?

Well, it worked. Male attention still seemed to be my familiar place, my stress-reliever, my unhappy place.

So it was sweet revenge when I chose a different dopamine fix the next day, opting for hot yoga while he nursed a hangover.

Thanks for the push, cochon.

Rebalance your sacral chakra

Firstly, the Gratitude Gaze (page 189) and cord-cutting any lovers are great for this, but here's another one you can even do on your travels to help further unblock it. As with the others, find somewhere quiet and peaceful to be alone and close your eyes.

Imagine an orange ball of light in your belly. Put your hand there and feel its warmth through your flesh. What do you visualise it doing? Is it stock still, spinning frantically, or bouncing around? With that held in your mind's eye, meditate or journal on the following three questions:

1   What are my coping mechanisms or addictions, and in what scenarios do they most often pop up, especially around sex?
2   What triggers guilt and shame in me, and in what scenarios do they most often pop up, especially around sex?
3   What are my best ways of creatively expressing myself and when do I most often feel like doing them?

If you're anything like me, you may look to coping mechanisms, such as casual sex, when you're in a time of hardship or conflict. If it's hard for you to think back on a time of conflict to investigate your triggers and subsequent coping mechanisms, take some deep breaths, do some self-care from page 189, and perhaps take some time to do the things you answered in question 3 above. You can come back to the first two another time, or you may find yourself wondering about them in the back of your head from day to day. I always find the sacral a really stubborn chakra to get good energy flowing into again, so perhaps go and see a Reiki professional who can help you to clear it and you can consult them on how to keep it invigorated in future. Holding orange crystals such as carnelian and peach moonstone is good for this, as is wearing orange and eating foods with orange colours, and spices such as cinnamon and ginger. The more you consciously think of it glowing brighter, the more it will.

3

Solar Plexus Chakra: A Spark of Intuition

Affirmation: I decide who I want to be in this life. My world is up to me and I follow my intuition wherever it goes without question. I find and serve my soul purpose with ease. Every day the fire within me burns brighter with sacred self-love.

Bali. Land of new age spirituality seekers. There's yoga everywhere, birds sing their chorus in tropical bushes, and banana pancakes are otherwise known as breakfast. The sweet cloying smells on the streets stick in my memory, the smoky incense and flower offerings to the Hindu gods every few metres.

Now, with two chakras spurred into action, you might be in a position to look at the world as it is, not just scanning for attention with old unawakened eyes. You might feel more confident in your own perspective, not asking those around you how they see the world. That's one subconscious lesson of solo travel too. My identity was completely my own now, detached from any man who had broken my heart. If anyone asked about my relationship status, it wasn't 'I'm getting over someone', it was 'I'm single'. It's a really empowering moment when your status changes like that, because it marks a shift in your healing journey. It means your relationship with yourself can truly begin.

This is where our solar plexus chakra perks up its ears. The home of self-esteem, this energy centre is an important one. It sits in our abdomen (also supervising the gut intuition) and stores our personal power. Its Sanskrit name, *manipura*, means 'city of gems', and if that's not the most fabulous piece of spiritual trivia in this book, I don't know what is. Just like the sacral was a stubborn one for dating junkies like me, a lot of people also struggle with the solar plexus because it is the centre of ego. But I love this third chakra because its element is fire, as opposed to the previous chakra's element of water. It's where we spark up our very purpose and how we'll be of service.

Experts say our chakras will never be unblocked unless we unblock both sides. They are double-sided; its front side is you, and the outer world is its back side. If you are of service to yourself and others, never to 'convert' but help them to grow on their own path, the chakra can then be fully unblocked. My Reiki master tells me that when he gives Reiki massage, he gets up to 30 per cent of the healing back for himself. In other words, when you help others win, you win too. That's not too big a spiritual epiphany, but sometimes feels long forgotten in our fast modern world. But we can do it on a small scale such as a Tinder chat; even if we don't end up going out with the guy, we can share a nice evening exchange or brighten up both our days with a flirt or a cheeky compliment.

Caring for the other's welfare is the basic groundwork for any relationship, so it's a good feeling to start with yourself. The rest of my trip would be about raising my spiritual and emotional intelligence by collecting self-knowledge. We can't master a craft before we understand how it works, and we are our own craft. The better we know ourselves, the better we can recover from difficulties, becoming the very definition of resilient. Being consciously out of your comfort zone on a new trip, job, city or even a new relationship is where the groundwork can really get going.

You never forget your first ritual

Though it's heavily Westernised now, it's easy to still be culture shocked in Bali. But the best way to get past that uncomfortable feeling is through it, seeing it not as a negative but as a tool of self-discovery. The best way to embrace it is try a traditional Hindu purification ritual at the Tirta Empul, a holy temple near Ubud. As the locals showed me, you dip your head under spouts of holy water, chest-deep in cold water with fish swimming around you, working your way from the leftmost to the rightmost. As with rituals we've made since we learnt to blow out candles on our birthday cakes, we make a wish. You could have spotted me in a line-up, looking less *The Craft*, more Boho Barbie in a tie-dye pink sarong to respectfully cover my red bikini. Well, to each her own shade of spirituality. While I'd always recommend a 'you do you' approach, I wouldn't recommend dipping your head under the kitchen tap at home like a thirsty cat. A mindful bath with salts, meditation and intention setting will also do the trick.

Unlike these ancient longstanding traditions of Bali, the Western spiritual industry can sometimes feel full of spiritual novelties. The same as any industry, it goes on trends, so that service providers can offer what everyone is talking about. Astral travel one moment, cacao the next, and devotional womb ceremonies tomorrow. Oh wait, don't forget the blue lotus tea ceremonies, because if you don't offer them, you're way behind the game. It can be exhausting. They are all great healing modalities, but without a true intention, partaking in them is like playing lucky dip at spirituality. Letting it permeate you at surface level, you can't transform on a deeper level. Just as when a break-up fringe won't magically relieve your sadness, and a tattoo can't automatically cover it up either. I'd had a tattoo done of a fiery arrow on my inner bicep in Sydney to signify self-love, but it hadn't made my self-talk suddenly positive overnight. We have to consciously do those things. Newsflash: real self-love happens in the tough, ugly bits of life, in the things you don't broadcast on Instagram.

So a few days after the purification ritual, an unsettled feeling stopped me in my tracks, like some peculiar feeling was trapped under my skin. The fad I tried to solve it was a turmeric shot at the yoga centre *kafe*, as if by doing that once, I would suddenly qualify as enlightened. Suffice to say, the turmeric didn't do a thing apart from speed up my bowel movements. The itchy inner feeling carried on. I needed a deep, inner healing, and I didn't know why. I was restless for it.

An itchy soul ... Who you gonna call?

A healer, I decided. And I'd find one the very next day from a girl next to me at yoga.

'He's a little out in the sticks, though. Can you drive a scooter?' she asked. I nodded, glad to have learnt as soon as I got to Bali in the hope of riding around with a man-bunned hunk.

She wrote his name down. 'Tell him Em sent you.'

My Dutch hostel mate was curious to join me, but neither of us had any idea what to expect. I just knew I had to go. We arrived early that next morning, got wrapped in long colourful sarongs by his wife and then waited in the central yard. The healer, in traditional Balinese smock, wrap skirt and turban, emerged from his little hut to beckon me in.

Buckle in, sweetheart, my inner voice carried on silently.

Who knows what to do in that scenario any more than they know what to do on a one-night stand? Stand there and look awkward until you get down to the task in hand? In my healer's hut, I was instructed to sit down cross legged in front of him, lower my eyes and be still. He meditated in front of me for what felt like a long time. I felt self-conscious. Was he reading my thoughts? Did I need to keep my mind clear so he wouldn't see the filth in there?

His old, wise and sincere eyes slowly opened and centred on me. Always a tad unnerving.

'When you get home, you will be offered a job. Just take it, it will be good for communication.'

I thought it was going to be more energy work than talking. Had I booked the wrong kind of 'healer'? I'd been told by a palm reader years before in Hong Kong various things that hadn't come true, yet at least. I was open to this healer's reading, but felt guarded over my privacy and sense of free will.

'You will meet your partner in years to come and they will be from abroad. I can't tell you where they will be from, but they will not be from either South Africa or the Netherlands. You will go into business together also. You will die and be buried abroad.'

'So ... it's not going to be someone I've already met?' bypassing the profound prediction and instead gutted for Gap Year Guy. The same as a child who was promised a whole candy shop but just wanted one thing from the bakery.

'No. And drink black coffee with sugar. No milk.'

Ah, medicinal advice. This feels more *Eat Pray Love* now.

If I can advise you at all, it's to audio record your psychic sessions like my clever bird of a Dutch travel buddy did. I can't remember much else than the end, when he sat me up against the wall and pressed down hard on my sternum with his thumb. Making whooooosh sounds with his breath, he then told me to join in. I felt like a human wind instrument being played, but I experienced the same powerful whistle-like exhales in another healing session back in the UK years later – it's how they channel the stagnant energy out of you. If they cough, it's even more powerful energy moving through them and out of them, but so many of us need this hands-on support to get rid of old pain stored in our body. If it was easy to do alone, we'd all be much more healed than we are.

We did this heavy breathwork for about ten minutes, and I emerged from his hut slightly lightheaded. Years later, I'd know I was more into my healers than my hook-ups when my moans were releasing repressed emotions rather than orgasmic screams.

I sat down to process my first healing session. Did I believe it all? What job could he mean, was it going to be in London as I wanted it to be? Who was the guy going to be? And, to live up to being the strong-minded person I had been told I was, did I have any say in my own future? I thought I was going to get answers, not more questions.

But I did feel better – I had a suggestion of a direction now, even if I didn't believe it was set in stone. Say he was right, and I wasn't going to meet The One for a while. That meant I could afford to have both my eyes on myself. I had permission to be just me, single. Because that felt like the empowering win-win option, I took it. And sometimes the best thing we can get from a reading is validation for feeling a certain way, and to finally release our own critical self-judgement. We can rest easy knowing our path is set up for success.

How to have a psychic reading

It can be easy to get scammed in any industry, but unfortunately, psychics, card readers, mediums and other spiritual professionals are automatically painted with the same cynical brush. So to make sure you spend your buck on the best reading possible, here are a few tips, as well as how to be ready for one, too.

- Does the marketing look professional? Are the advertising words spelt correctly? If there's only a few five-star reviews, without much context or good use of the English language, it might not be good to go.
- Read the reviews and see what your intuition tells you as you read. If it's telling you not to trust this person, believe it, and choose someone that does make you feel calm and confident.
- If it's a company phoneline, always read the small print to see what you'll be charged upfront and then per minute. Opt for Zoom calls or in-person readings so you feel as present as possible.
- Look in the classified sections of spiritual magazines, ask your friends for recommendations or post in community groups in your area to gather names.
- Some fantastic psychics and mediums do live reading sessions broadcast on social media, so it's a great way to get a free taster of their style and energy. Alternatively, see when they are next

appearing at a mind-body-spirit event and let your intuition see if you gel. ·

- In the reading, treat it like a house party – you never know whose spirit is going to show up. Be open to receiving messages, otherwise your loved ones may not step forward. Messages won't always be clear so be ready to receive anything that happens – once, my watch stopped the morning of a reading, only to resume after it. Be ready to connect with spirits over anything; spirits don't like to be interrogated, and may give you messages you don't want to hear. Note them down, and carry on living your life as you were. Come back a few months later and reassess how it aligns with reality.

Look upwards for the Star's spiritual insight

It doesn't matter if you're in Birmingham or Bali – start to seek cosmic interaction however you like, whether that's seeing comforting shapes in clouds or your angel number on a bus timetable. Knowing that the Universe has your back will help you heal your heart. And we can't see these cosmic comforts until we stop navel-gazing in our phones.

I had arrived in coastal Canggu for Balinese New Year, a sacred festival called Nyepi. I'd watched the locals build massive effigies made out of bamboo poles and papier mâché for weeks, and witnessed some dances in rehearsal for the big New Year's Eve. Think you've seen a country go hard on the New Year celebrations? You've seen nothing compared to the Balinese. The tradition goes that everyone gathers to watch the villagers burn gigantic ghoulish monsters called Ogoh-Ogoh, who represent the evil demons. Some had eight arms or legs and all had gruesome expressions, towering over us at 12 feet tall. For the whole of the next day, the Day of Silence, we were all to stay indoors silently hiding as if these monsters were checking we'd fled. Everything was on lockdown;

flights, WiFi, even noise and light after the sun went down. And then the show started.

Stars lit up the sky like fireworks I'd watched on Sydney Harbour. With no light pollution, it was a blanket cover saturated with lights, some faintly glowing, some strongly twinkling. These stars didn't need permission to shine bright, I thought. And yet, we women are always trying to dim our own sparkle. We don't believe people when they compliment us, and we wait for permission to join in approving of ourselves. Most anxious attachers and recovering people-pleasers might also feel the same way. I mean, are we meant to tell ourselves we've been good girls?

Yes. That's the whole point of affirmations.

No one, other than the healer in Ubud, had ever given me true permission to be single, just to be me, alone, because they practically followed up the advice 'play the field, enjoy yourself' with 'but have you met anyone yet?' I was inspired by the bright sky above me: these stars weren't competing to outshine the others, they just were sparkling on their own terms, individually, independently, unbothered by their neighbours. As soon as we try to stop dwelling on our break-up with our old guru, our Spiritual Fuckboy, we can look up to our new one, the Universe. And we realise we can twinkle just as bright as the other girls in the bar, or office, or red carpet, and no one takes away from each other's light. We're just mirrors reflecting each other's shine back to her.

Conscious boundary pushing

The Gili islands each have their own different personalities. Gili Trawangan (nicknamed Gili T) is the party island everyone flocks to. Gili Air is the chilled backpackers' island. I would try new things on both. The first new thing might have led to more, um, fraternising with the opposite sex, shall we say. But the second new thing, done with Tina and which encouraged me to be still, would be far more meaningful. As we push our boundaries of what defines us and what doesn't, we strengthen our solar plexus.

In most tourist hotspots in Southeast Asia, you don't need to have booked lodging before turning up in a new place, unless it's late at night. All you really need to know is two things: how the local currency works, and how to say 'thank you' in the language. Part of the fun of travelling was being shown around accommodations, then haggling for your nightly rate.

On the first island, Gili T, we opted for Dodo's thatched bungalows, which probably were designed to be couples' getaway shacks, given that the towels rolled up on the beds as swans looked more like erect penises. It was perfect for two bachelorettes like us. Dodo was a man in his sixties from Java, and given I was the blonde one, he promptly fell in love with me. I loved him right back; he looked like the Indonesian Barry Chuckle, height, face shape, moustache and all. He didn't quite understand my name – the 'r' sound in Indonesian phonetics is more an 'er' sound. I improvised.

'Rosalind, but call me Rosie.' Confused looks. He shook his head.

'Rosie,' I tried again. 'Like the rose ... um, you know, like the flower.'

'Ah! Flower!'

And so my pseudonym in Indonesia became Flower, like the hippy flower child I now looked like with frangipani blossom in my hair. Before my Saturn Return showed me who I really was, I'd be a chameleon.

I urge you, however many trips round the sun you've had, try on other identities. Stretch yourself out like pizza dough – it's your prerogative as a human. Try on nicknames. Show different sides to yourself with new hobbies, such as burlesque – anything to have playful, intentional fun. With this same conscious logic, if I had tried skydiving, it followed that I also needed to try scuba-diving. I was in the right place for it, after all. This choice felt good. I knew that on the other side of our fear lies expansion.

The act it would lead to, almost as a 'well done' gift to myself, was the opposite, and would only shrink me.

You know the scene; you're on a night out with the crew and a guy is making eyes your way. You can spot a real fuckboy now, because sure, he'd mentioned a girl, his ex-girlfriend, coming to see him next week, but he has his eyes on you at that point. You don't even have to be particularly intuitive to know that he will, at some point, make a move. My guy was good-looking in a punky way, but universes apart from my beloved Gap Year Guy. Beggars can't be choosers, I thought.

They bloody well can.

Besides, I deserved to celebrate my not dying on my dive with someone, right? The citrine pendant I'd bought myself wasn't treat enough; sexual validation was the ultimate reward.

I'm a supporter of casual sex if it's conscious, with everyone being very honest with their intentions with each other and, even more importantly, themselves. We can only have casual sex if we want the orgasm, not the oxytocin (though research shows oxytocin increases during sexual arousal, so we could be screwed both ways). The very definition of unconscious sexual experimentation is to allow what we don't like without even questioning what we like in its place. Schrödinger never theorised how we learn what we like in bed without checking what we don't. When we don't know our boundaries, we can't communicate them, so we go into a one-night stand blind. And when booze lowers our inhibitions, we're on 'yes' autopilot.

The Moon sheds light on our insecurities

The way to check if the guy is interested in us is by leaving. This is a recent conclusion of mine, but it checks out across a cross-section of men in my experience, including this one. He knows his time is up to swoop in or say goodbye, so he's forced to approach. He knows it's now or never.

'You can go get food if you like, or you can come back with me and let me fuck you,' my guy said, his head bowed down to me, his nose almost touching mine.

'What – what did you just say to me?' I half laughed, half choked in his face. I would have been disappointed if he hadn't asked me to go home with him, but in this way? Who said romance was dead?

'You heard,' he replied, cocking his chin, a serious look on his face. The glint in his eye was not sparkly and inviting but matte and cold, like hard metal. I was intimidated, but that was a turn-on for drunk unconscious me. Intimidating me made me want to keep them close. I hadn't yet understood that what I feared, I craved.

Pay careful attention to how you feel in this moment. Intrigue? If it's safe, follow it. Butterflies? Take them with a pinch of salt. Intimidated? That's probably your nervous system stuttering. I started shrinking into my submissive with an anxiously fast heartbeat while walking back to his. We want to live up to his sexual expectations, where he doesn't care to question ours.

Don't we always assume the next sex we have might be the best we ever have? The one where we meet God, shake his hand, then come back down to Earth integrally different? Was this my Moon moment? Its card shows us there are secrets and illusions at play, and things are not what they seem. Maybe this ex was still his girlfriend, but I didn't need to know. I needed to see what I could be missing. Forget FOMO. For single girls, it can be Fear of Missing Out On Great Sex, but FOMOOGS doesn't quite have the same ring.

I know how much you want to be sexually liberated. Witnessed for who you are. But this is not the way.

We feel comfortable in the submissive, because all decision-making responsibilities are taken out of our hands. If to surrender is your kink, have at it, but this sex was rough, and though I had fully consented, I hadn't consented to the kink. I went with it, ever the sheep. But so often we are being too nice and don't say anything, and so often they know this and our silence is their enabler. We are scared to say no in case they laugh us off. Though we can rarely stop and just walk out the door because we're often nowhere near our familiar surroundings externally, it's almost safer to stay in the semi-safety of where we already are. It's why I choose to bring people back to mine these days, because now I'd rather ask them to leave than do the walk of no shame.

The kink conundrum

Sex, like many newbies to yoga, can be all about performance rather than feeling safe in authentic connection. I put on my best porn routine, though I was probably subconsciously moaning more out of discomfort rather than pleasure. My inner narcissist was telling me I deserved this, or at least didn't deserve it to be loving. Just take it, the negative old voice said. But life is not porn. We don't see the actors being asked their boundaries before the camera starts rolling. The difference between conscious and unconscious kink is the consent.

No darling, no. You don't need to feel any shame. Your body. Your say.

But if I'd stopped it, how could I have people-pleased and ensured he'd had a good time? How could I say no once I'd said yes?

You can always say no, whenever you want to, even if you've just said yes the second before.

And then it was over, and I was sober, and he was satisfied. The novelty of the night had quickly worn off, and any compliment I took from his attention with it.

Tina stirred as I got back into our room. And as I began to feel safe in the comforting company of my friend, I felt a tiny trauma break a chip off me. Sex had been my dopamine dose. So why did I feel like this? It was easy to hide away from my emotional abyss in sex, to be able to keep vulnerability at bay by taking all my clothes off instead of the layers of myself. I'd never felt like this before. Was it the culture shock raising my senses?

We can't see our patterns at the time because we're so in it, and we'd probably get defensive if anyone reflected to us without our permission. The only thing that had caused me concern was that passersby on the way back had seen his red eyes and stumbling feet. Through their worried faces, I'd realised I'd placed my safety, my body, even my measure of worth in the hands of someone off his face. Must choose better bunk mates next time, was all I thought. My senses were sharpening, but not sharp enough yet to stop me.

What would be a conscious reward?

Journal your unhealthy coping mechanisms, minor addictions – anything from dating apps to sugary snacks to sex, from shopping to social media, from gambling to booze. We all have them, and they are nothing to guilt yourself with. We use these things to keep ourselves playing small, to discharge our lives rather than supercharge them. Once we admit them to ourselves, we can master them.

Now, what else would be dopamine-inducing? Look at what you put above; if you put group activities of some kind, what would connect your true self with others? If you put solitary tasks above, what would connect you more with yourself? Try a few days of the second list and avoid the first list, and journal on what differences you're feeling.

Note what you feel on Day 1, Day 3 and Day 5.

When the Sun starts shining, expect joy

It was the Sun card's time to shine on our next destination. This tarot card predicts all the good stuff, fun in the sun, confidence, love, success, pleasure, pure fucking happiness, a rebirth after the Death card. And though Dodo walked us to the ferry stop, insisting on carrying my broken pack and asking me very sweetly to marry him, I was off men. It would be the Day Everything Shifted.

Writer and guru Vex King published a book called *Healing is the New High*, and I'd be inclined to agree, but I had to get high first just to check. Psilocybin is the ingredient in many psychedelic drugs such as magic mushrooms. It has been said to help heal depression, PTSD and anxiety. Though I didn't have any spiritual perspective on it yet, it seemed like a fun new novelty to try. Again, you don't have to go to such extremes at home. Plant medicine such as cacao (see page 148) and herbal teas such as mugwort can help aid spiritual transformation just as powerfully. We were told by the bartender of the space bar that one large cone of magic mushrooms could be blended up with Coca-Cola and pineapple juice and split between two people. It was not as disgusting as it sounds, but it is as illegal as it sounds – it's a class A drug in the UK too. Right then, a Western man strode right up to us and asked us rather urgently if we knew what we were doing.

Fuck, he's undercover for the government, we telepathically assumed. I'm on an emergency passport; what will the authorities think of me without even a proper sodding passport? We could be imprisoned, or worse.

Deep breath, stay cool.

'Umm ...' we stuttered, then nodded.

Relief – he only wanted to tell us what to expect. Then he left us to it, as if he'd cautioned Cinderella that her awakening spell would last only until midnight.

And cosmic princesses we would feel like, watching the deepest pink, orange, watercolour-like magical sunset one could ever hope to experience, despite the almost total cloud cover and the fact that it was actually just an average sunset. But as the Sun card wishes us to feel safe and loved, we did. I felt as if held in a glass snow globe so universally beautiful, so safe, that I was suspended in love, like it filled every atom in the air. The mellowness I felt, the way it could make me smile and exhale, how I just knew the Universe had my back – it was a total sensory and spiritual awakening. It would be an inner knowing, a quiet peace, that was just between me, Tina and the Universe. I could feel the Universe almost hugging me, a more intimate affection than the person who'd been inside me mere days before had given me.

We would likely have seemed quite obnoxious to others on the beach as we tried to capture an Instagram-worthy shot of each other leisurely walking along the sunset shore. The sound of the water lapping up on the coral shore felt deliciously tickly to our ears, like a wind chime, as though we had suddenly transcended into shamans. This was a better orgasmic feeling than sex, I remember thinking. My imagination was on fire, and I scribbled down stories in my journal as if I was six years old again. My inner child was nudged awake, happy once again like she had been in arty hotspots of Raglan, Byron Bay and Hobart.

The best tool we can pack

In much the same way as a knife, the sharper our sixth sense gets, the better it works. Ignoring it will blunt it. The more you listen to its messages of growth through conscious experimentation, the less you will fall into irritating patterns of the past. Let my next adventures be a lesson to you that if in doubt, you should feel it out.

Sharpen your skills as you travel

You've heard of brain-training. Now try intuition training, perfect when you're travelling at home or abroad.

- Set yourself daily guessing games. If a flight is waiting for its gate, what gate will it be? If your phone buzzes, who is it likely to be? This will also tell you who you *want* it to be. What song is likely to be on the radio when you turn on your car ignition? Keep the faith that your guess will start to overlap with reality and the Universe will show you. There are games all over social media and YouTube too.
- Likewise, when an old friend or odd memory to do with a certain thing or place pops into your head, note it down. Don't ignore it just because you don't understand it. Note down anything that played out to validate your premonitions. Once you start seeing synchronicities, you'll be more open to them.
- Meditate with amethyst and quartz to let the intuitive energy of the stones transfer to you and carry them in your bag. You can even get drinking bottles that infuse water with their energy.

- Take a tarot or oracle deck with you and practise with card readings for yourself and friends, or even use it to break the ice with strangers. Keep them free of charge while you practise so that the financial energy exchange is fair.
- Avoid alcohol to let your mind clear. Drop dating – in fact, drop anything that sparks your ego, because it loves to get in the way of your intuition.

If in doubt, slow it down

It was mid-April when I arrived in Thailand for Songkran, Thai New Year. This would be my third New Year celebration that year already, but I took it as an opportunity to set a whole new intention after my mushroom-fuelled awakening. No single girl could welcome in another New Year without a New Year's kiss, after all.

I met a tall, gorgeous guy from California at an outside DJ set. It started raining, not that it mattered, because we were all soaked anyway (Songkran was celebrated with one holy, serious ritual: a national multi-day water fight on the streets). We started kissing, dancing, writhing together under this warm falling water, feeling so alive. Looking him up and down to double-check I wanted this (my belly didn't sink and my heart didn't lift, so I had no answer as a pendulum yet), he looked like a Spiritual Fuckboy. He was wearing many quirky things, leather bracelets, hairbands on wrists and a marvellous man-bun, and he had a distracting set of hunky shoulders. As with many travellers, he was just travelling functionally. We were messing around kissing and chatting and he was keen to come back with me. My suspicions were raised for some reason. Usually I'd wave them off, but something told me to slow him down. Slow. My first experimentation with the word.

When we slow things down, we catch on quicker. Whether that's being able to lean back and ask more insightful questions to gauge what someone's real intentions are, or just being able to enjoy the ride more, we never lose by slowing down. The right man will never hold it against us for going too slowly. So on the walk back to my hostel, rather than running to jump into bed together, I stalled. Besides, I had lovely Canadian roommates I didn't want to embarrass. When I insisted on saying goodbye to him at the gate, my WiFi kicked in and he insisted on connecting on Facebook. He added himself, and suddenly he had vanished. I looked down at my phone and scrolled his profile, stopping when it got to relationship status. Houdini was married. To a woman whose profile was full of happy pictures of them together.

As our patterns reinforce themselves over and over again, we cement them even more into our subconscious belief systems and continuously manifest them. A little-told fact is that we manifest our fears, not the man we put on our manifestation boards. I could have kissed any backpacker guy in Chiang Mai that night, and I found the married one. I was still a magnet for unavailable people, narcissists who wanted to have their cake and eat it too. My fear had stood right there kissing me, using me as an ego-inflator. Looking at it with sober eyes now, maybe I had used him to validate me and my ego in return.

Their marriage and relationships are their problem, and none of them knew the real you. How could you take it personally when they didn't even know you personally?

The same as the gang robbing us in New Zealand, people can be enabled by pure opportunity. It's nothing we single girls do other than go along with it. We can say 'no', or at least ask to take a pause so we can stand back and assess our situation; easier said than done when alcohol has disabled our judgement. I came across Anaïs Nin's quote 'we don't see things as they are, we see things as we are' years later, but I could have done with hearing it back then. Instead, I just felt guilty. I felt like crawling under the bunk bed and hiding. And that's when a reply dropped into my inbox.

In my drunken fury the night before, I'd found the wife's email address on her Facebook page and sent her a rushed though somehow totally grammatical memo telling her what her lying, cheating, travelling husband had done. I could get some good out of this by helping his wife find justice, and I could honour girl code. Maybe she'd already thrown his stuff out of the house, left him furious voicemails, filed for custody for any kids. This was girl karma.

She emailed back grateful, of all things. 'But I appreciate you getting in touch!' she'd written. 'You are welcome to see him again. Did you guys meet on Tinder? Didn't he tell you about our open marriage?'

What the fuck, please, Universe? Open marriages, like they actually existed?

This woman deserved a reply. 'Hi, sorry, weird day,' I typed back once I'd plucked up the courage. 'Things make a bit more sense now.' I explained how I'd met him. 'Is there anything else you need me to clear up for you?'

'No worries, we're used to questions, honestly,' she responded. 'You seemed pretty set on telling me, so I'm grateful you thought I deserved to know. You also seemed pretty upset.' Yep, more than he would have ever known. And his wife was the one apologising.

'The green silicone band is his wedding ring – they are very common with alternative guys like him,' she went on. That was the small hairband thing he'd placed on his right hand. Had I missed it when he'd moved it across?

Why are you blaming yourself for missing a trick?

She continued. 'He told you about my boyfriend, yes? Why did you think he was joking when he told you he was married?'

I replied describing his insincere story. It all came racing back to me then – he actually had told me he was married, and in an open relationship, but it seemed so outlandish, and he'd coupled it with so many shrugs, I laughed at him instead of believing him. 'It was such an intense night – I was on a hostel pub crawl,' I admitted. 'He was nice but I think he could have been more transparent to make sure I understood, he would have got a lot more from me if he had. Sorry again for contacting you and good luck with the open marriage!'

'That checks out. Sounds like one of those drunken nights we all have! Have a great rest of your trip!'

And that's how I made friends with the wife of an almost one-night stand. Not quite the type of friend I'd hoped to find in Thailand, Universe, but thanks all the same, I guess.

When they disappear or don't reply

A common trait of unavailable and avoidant people is to ghost. Otherwise, they'd have to admit they had been crossing a boundary of some sort. Only a Divine Masculine could own up to this.

So don't follow up. Their absence is your answer. The shortcut is learning to sense unavailable energy before they even open their mouth. Flirting with them anyway when you want something more might seem helpless, but it sends out the wrong message to the Universe.

If in doubt, look for role models

If you were liberated, both spiritually and sexually (by that I mean not letting fear hold you back, acting on your innermost intuition to strike forward), what would you do? Where would you go, and how would you expand yourself? Where do your favourite people or influencers go to expand themselves and how do they stay authentic and intuitive? With a rare day to myself in backpacker mecca Pai, a town outside of Chiang Mai, the Universe showed me what a powerful woman who didn't need the validation of men looked like.

She was a girl in the group next to me at an acro yoga workshop, and she had this powerful energy around her, this self-acceptance, this confidence I'd never seen anyone exude before. She had blonde dreadlocks pulled back into a supersized messy bun and had this tribal aura to her and her wildly kind eyes. Roughly cut black denim shorts and a black crop top showed her tanned abs, and she had the strongest core I'd ever seen on someone as she stretched out like Superwoman, balancing her hips on a base person's feet.

The blonde hair falling all over her body seemed to follow the patterns of her muscles, as if she'd groomed herself when she was wet and her hair had dried just so. She caught the eye and had the respect of everyone there, and it had nothing to do with plastic fillers, photographic filters or fake boobs. She was just cool, and she believed she was worthy of being no one other than herself, as if she had been a warrior in a past life. I had a total girl crush – no, a girl crush on her energy.

Now as I remember her, I realise the world could do with more of these women, so we can learn how to be more ourselves by seeing how others manage it. Take that inspiration anywhere you can get it so that the next time someone offers you a ticket out of your comfort zone – maybe a more liberated lover, or an adrenaline-rushing activity, or a vulnerability-inducing photoshoot – you can consciously grab it with both hands as an opportunity for self-expansion.

This is also why doing gratitude gazing nude is so powerful, when you say no to being self-conscious and hold space for yourself. I have a picture of myself nude in a Thai hot spring I can gaze at from that time. In the picture, I'm a part of nature once again, and my beauty wasn't for the male gaze, it was for me, all for me.

If in doubt, go on retreat

When your mind is opened in meditation, the quiet drowns out your Western judgement and your ego drops away. It's why kids are more psychic than adults, because they don't allow cynical beliefs of the 'real world' to deny the information their senses are giving them. It's why spiritual naysayers will never evolve out of their established world mindset.

My travel buddy Julia from America and I had just returned from a forest monastery. As if the Universe was intersecting my plans, I had tried to book a yoga retreat minutes before being told about the monastery, but the WiFi in the hostel kept timing out. I didn't know then that meditation would raise my senses so high that I felt I could have given the vampires of *Twilight* a run for their money.

Culture shock had greeted Julia and I when our first impression was a slow-moving single file of people all in white walking silently around the grounds. But on learning it was not a cult practice but a walking meditation, it was actually lovely. It was slow enough to be able to soften your gaze and focus on your breathing, and you could trust the person in front of you to guide you like an unspoken trust exercise.

If you're ever in need of quick grounding, planting your bare feet on the ground will immediately root you down, and I was doing it all day every day. Though I felt calmer from each day's meditation, imposter syndrome gently crept up again. Here I was meditating, purposefully doing what looked like nothing all day, while my friends worked away in the 'real world'. In the coming days, I'd realise that I was actually doing everything. I was beginning 'the work', it was all just inside me, invisible, humble.

These days, back in the 'real world', when I get frustrated, I ask myself: am I horny, or hangry (angry from hunger)? Well, at the monastery, I had to make peace with both. Little did I know it would help my mind clear far faster. We were fasting from each 11.00 a.m. lunch until the following breakfast, and the rules stated men and women had to refrain from communication after 8.30 p.m. No distractions from the outside world existed, no WiFi and no fuckpeople to flirt with, so each day felt like it lasted a week.

I was at a sort of spiritual crossroads; one way signposted boys and the other way signposted me. It felt like something, some kind of tense energy, was bubbling up and rising up in me. I just knew that with more meditation, I'd simply evaporate it away. That trust in the process was new for me. The space I was finding inside my mind was expansive, and I felt I was able to push it outwards, clearing out room in my inner world, despite my increasing tiredness from sleeping on ceramic tiles, heightening my senses and humbling my ego.

Practise *vipassana* meditation at home

I'm not suggesting you sit under a tree like Buddha until enlightenment finds you, but there are some quick tricks to know yourself better each day.

- Practise deep breathing each time you make a cup of tea, going back to box breathing for as long as the kettle takes to boil.
- If you are medically able, practise intermittent fasting safely by not consuming anything but water for a 16-hour period each 24 hours. The intention of this is to clear the mind, *not* to lose weight.
- Microdose gratitude after each meal or drink to manifest more abundance into your life.
- Get bored on purpose and allow yourself to daydream so your subconscious mind can percolate any important life dilemmas.

If in doubt, focus on your senses

You might think solo travel is too scary for you to do because you believe you'd go wrong somewhere. You'll realise why you must be alone to have breakthroughs, because you need to be totally immersed in what is around you.

As I wandered the narrow streets of Hanoi a few weeks later, without a travel buddy or working phone, I was able to watch life playing out before me. The sights, sounds, smells of this closed-in, tall French colonial street was something to behold. I wasn't lost in conversation with someone for once; I was lost in my senses. My eyes were peeled, ears pricked up, body ready for someone to put their hand into my pocket, and my ears primed for words I might recognise in English. And in this close charming street in Hanoi's Old Quarter, with wires creating an almost opaque ceiling above me, shop signs fighting for vertical space as much as people on the ground, my senses were being hit from all angles. As I wandered through, gulping down the information being sent to my brain from my senses, I realised all my ears could recognise was one familiar sound: laughter.

Laughter, like maths, is the same in every language. My surprised brain found it could make sense of this noise coming out of a grandma's mouth as she gossiped with a neighbour, grandchild bouncing on her lap. As a feeling of 'I know this sound' registered, I felt immediately comforted. Where before I thought I was an alien, I now felt as if I belonged.

In that moment, I received a download from some unknown source: though our language and physical features may disguise it, we are all the same. We all sound the same when we laugh, and we all want the same things for ourselves, our families and our children, to live autonomously and to die with dignity. Between those two events, we have the same basic needs. And our human bodies are all hard-wired to love and connect – thank all of our gods then that there is way more that unites us than separates us.

Judgement is our cosmic wake-up call

Once you unlock the joy of being alone, knowing you inherently trust yourself now you *know yourself*, it's just a matter of time until your sixth sense really kicks in. With my short remaining time abroad, my own intuition didn't have much longer to put on a show. Similar to a boy watching me grab my coat, it had to step in.

I'm ready.

As I set off to the bus station for my flight down the coast, the cobbled streets quite quickly made it clear they hated my suitcase, breaking it more with each bounce. I resented the idea of continuing to do this across the country, but pushed on anyway. I was mid-lug when something inside me stopped me dead in that same overhung street from days before.

Go back! Something inside me bellowed.

What the hell was that? I heard something. Wait, was it coming from me? I shot around to see if someone on the street had yelled at me. It had been so firm and so decisive, totally unlike my go-with-the-flow attitude.

Repack your bags and leave this godforsaken case in the hostel lock-up. You're coming back here anyway.

But if I go back and repack I'll miss my flight, I answered.

Do not get the bus. Get a taxi directly there instead.

But I want to save the money.

GO BACK! NOW!

I probably looked like I was lost or, worse yet, crazy. But I was far from it. I was frozen, and I had no choice but to listen.

Where time had slowed down, it sped back up again. Within 15 minutes I was in a taxi with a fellow hostel mate who was going the same way, having managed to squeeze two weeks' worth of my backpacker life into my day bag. Traffic on the highway slowed down – it looked as though there'd been an accident up ahead, so cars had to filter from two lanes into one.

As we passed the scene, something looked familiar. There was the bus I had been meaning to catch, though it was a miracle I could read the number on the front at all. It had skimmed into the grassy knoll on its right (in Vietnam, you drive on the right) and passengers who looked shocked and stressed, but thankfully not hurt, were being escorted out of the wreckage.

Did that internal alarm voice stop me from getting anywhere near it? Had my wish back at the Tirta Empul in Bali come true, to be safe on my onward journey? Had the Balinese gods or Thai goddesses made it happen, or had I?

Now that I think about it, I know it was my first claircognisant download, and the strongest I've had to this day. Our spirit team really likes to put on a show, the utter queens.

The World: completed it, mate

After the Judgement character wants us to finally evaluate ourselves, the World card tells us we've done so correctly. When Judgement asks us our place in the game of life, the World card predicts fulfilment there. It is very fitting to the solar plexus chakra and its continuous search for purpose. It also can foretell homesickness, so it was apt that I was finally on my way home. I woke up from my plane nap to the pilot saying 'Welcome to Heathrow' and my travel brain kicked in once more – how do we pay and say 'thank you' here? Wait, I already know this one.

As I lifted my case off the baggage carousel, the handle snapped off. It was like a sign that said 'you're ready to throw that thing away'. I was ready to walk through Nothing to Declare, other than the fact I had a lot to declare; I had become a totally new person walking back into my old life.

My journey was complete now. I had triumphantly returned from the World, the final card. I was a Fool no more … right?

Be a safe spiritual single girl abroad

Though I'd always encourage you doing a trip your way and no one else's, these do's and don'ts will help you have the safest trip possible. It also means that, crucially, you're the one in control when it matters.

- If you are feeling the urge to go on your own *Eat Pray Love* trip, you must go. If you don't, you'll always wonder 'what if'. Trust that the time you do go will always be when you are meant to. Use the money manifestation rituals on page 171 to save up, and book the ticket as soon as you can to hold yourself accountable to actually going. Tell friends who can help you set decision deadlines.
- Do some 'Tinder tourism' by all means, but always tell someone around you where you're going and with who, as well as maybe telling someone back home too. Use Travel Mode on dating apps so you can meet locals who can show you around. Suggest a double date and bring a hostel mate with you so you can both see a new city together. Either way, keep your location turned on. Get a local SIM card or eSIM or connect to the WiFi in the bar, restaurant or venue you're spending the date in.

- Download the MAPS.ME app so you can save maps for the place you're in without needing data.
- Check out Tourina, an app that allows you to meet fellow female travel companions. Travello also helps you find other travellers around your current location, match plans for trips, share pics and join groups.
- If you're ready to meet locals or on a tight budget, stay with locals for free via Couchsurfers, who might have a spare room instead of just a sofa. Check their reviews first and have a backup plan in case you start to feel unsafe. Always trust your gut and don't worry about feeling rude for leaving.
- Be cautious about over-the-counter medicines; instead ask your hostel or phone your travel insurance company to get them to locate a doctor.
- If you're not gelling with people, move on. You may be travelling solo, but it's hard to actually get time alone to rest when you're always checking into dormitories. Be of an abundance mindset and trust a good crew will come along.
- Walking tours of cities are fantastic places to learn history and break the ice with fellow tourists. You might even get invited to meet up another day or go and see them in their home city.
- Do strike up conversations with people you get a good vibe from. They're probably wondering where you're from so just a 'hello' in your accent is enough or make a beeline for something you have in common. I've done this plenty of times, and often people are grateful for your approachability. Of course, listen to your intuition and don't be afraid to white-lie your way out of a situation. You owe strangers nothing.
- Do go out of your comfort zone in terms of activities, and you might meet someone on a skydive or a scuba-dive. This is the time where you have few inhibitions, so use it for good, for stories you'd tell your grandchildren. Be conscious not to go far out of your comfort zone in sexual situations. If you'd worry about a friend doing it, don't do it yourself.
- If you're planning on going anywhere out of mobile or WiFi service

areas, tell your people back home they won't be able to reach you for however many days.

- Before you go, carry a mini padlock and take your passport everywhere with you, unless it's in a safe. Mini padlocks are also great for fixing backpack or bumbag zips together to deter pickpockets.
- If you can't read a foreign label, Google Translate has a Photo Lens option to translate written text when you point a camera at it.

Find your personal power with three solar plexus rituals

Some chakras are worked on with gentle rituals. Not this one. These ideas will get you fired up, so grab your citrines, tiger's eyes and sunstones and spice up your life!

1 Put on some loud music at home (even better in a sunlit room) or go out to a rave or dance event. Be conscious of your movement as you dance, undulating from your waist and feeling yourself, touching or holding your abdominals, imagining the muscles beginning to stretch, move and vibrate within you. Imagine fire moving in your blood as you get it pumping. You will feel more empowered after, and any stuck energy will have left your body!

2 On a quieter night, use a safely lit candle to burn any old journal notes or letters, notes or photos from exes that you are ready to let go of. This is specifically powerful to do on a full moon, especially in a fire sign of Aries, Leo or Sagittarius. Collect the ashes and scatter them in the earth on your next nature walk.

3 During your next meditation, especially around the new moon, place citrine on your stomach, visualising heat coming out of it and penetrating through your skin. Imagine this chakra glowing with heat, spinning hotter and faster. What old opinions of yourself will you give it to burn?

What parts of yourself, memories or triggers no longer serve you? If you feel called to, journal on what you can replace them with. What kind of woman do you want to be, and crucially, what will her dating profile look like? What won't she allow on it, and who will her new fire warrior self attract? Feel emotionally resilient and completely unstoppable as you sign off your journaling with a 'so mote it be', then watch as this chakra's masculine energy rises out of you and creates real change.

4

Heart Chakra: Chaos Dating

Affirmation: I am single and a queen of my own kingdom, and I enjoy tasting the fruit of my fellow singles on offer as I wish. Tinder is full of people who want to connect with me. If it doesn't work out with someone, all is well. I return to the safety of my own heart and know my love is coming.

No one ever said what happened to the Fool when they got to the end of the Fool's journey. Coming-of-age films always end with the protagonist getting their happy ever after. There I was, broke, unemployed, being picked up alone rather than with my Prince Charming. The real world was at my feet now, but I didn't know how to navigate it. I was an opportunistic backpacker back in the real world, like someone had put a black-and-white filter on a colour photo.

No one ever tells you the truth; that coming home is way harder than leaving. After a week or two, however lovely the reunions are, people get on with their lives and expect you to do the same. It's somehow surprising to you that other people have changed, too. In my friendship group, one friend had bred, one had bought a house and one had moved in with her partner a generation older than us. We had all just turned 25, but I suddenly felt very young compared to them.

Though I couldn't wait to be that fun hippy auntie to my friend's new baby, the kind who writes magazine columns, wears ten colours at once, travels often and can teach swear words in a dozen different languages, I felt rootless once again. I was also unemployed and living at home. No wonder some people prefer instead to stay abroad, going on constant visa runs just for the privilege. But how can we see our true reflection in water that never is still? How can we fulfil our life's purpose when we're always distracted by a pub crawl, flight admin or the hostel hottie?

Putting down your roots

In manifestation, our mindset determines how quickly something will happen. It took me a long time to realise just the heavy word 'relationship' triggered subconscious fear of commitment, because commitment had previously meant control. No wonder we run away to the other side of the world, not ready to properly commit. We barely reply to most of our Tinder messages.

That's where the heart chakra comes in, the energy centre most concerned with sharing our joy, love and empathy with ourselves, and then others. Called the *anahata*, which means 'unhurt', experts say it develops between 21 and 28 years old. So you could say it's better to stay single in these formative years just to get the most of this self-development stage.

Now, because I know the importance of stepping into a more positive mindset, as I approach 30 years old, I see a relationship more as a symbiotic scenario, an emotional safety net to catch us rather than ensnare us. Back as a 25-year-old, I still found it hard to commit to anything, even to the UK. I'd flirted with other countries, half promising I'd move back to each. But on the plus side, I had started hearing voices in my head, and had enough stories to regale any house party crowd for years. It was time for me to come home and commit to building a life.

Ah, that word 'settling', or its full name, 'settling down'. Because what if we blink and 20 years later we're still where we were when we got home, our post-travel brains cry? Making real-life decisions seemed scary to me, the free spirit I was (I prefer that term over 'commitment-phobe').

But you have to start somewhere. Funny how we're proactive with our financial and social needs just so that we can get faster onto our romantic needs.

As a single person, good friends are everything. They add the colour to your working day, the glitter to your weekend. A single life is incomplete only in the absence of good friends. For a lot of women, our jobs are also our source of worth. Most of us are in a toxic relationship first and foremost with our jobs, so no wonder we fall into it in our love lives.

So though it was lovely to be working with my friends again back in my old job as holiday cover, it didn't feel totally aligned with my new self. It felt like backsliding into my old self. My new self was clear to see: people remarked how much more confident I was, no longer the permission-seeking person who doubted herself. Maybe I'd manifested it daydreaming of my old office as if it was my current workplace, I wasn't sure. But in one fell swoop, I had met my first two needs.

Career is one of the first things we ask a match about, or at least, it's the first thing we tell our friends about them. After that, it's what kind of car do you drive, or when was your last relationship? We need to know exactly how good to feel about ourselves by how wanted and important *they* are. We look for any way to validate ourselves by association. Yes, a couple must align on values and mutual interests. But if we filter potential partners by their work, we might miss some great personalities.

Let me interrupt that inference for you; our worth is not related to theirs at all. Besides, I feel as soon as the question 'What do you do for a living?' is brought out, I usually find it a one-way street to small talk. I want to spark off with a new match talking about anything other than our real lives; I want banter and engagement. I want to know if a guy I'm dating feels he is making a difference to people, and not just if he's an Aquarius. So maybe the question we

should be asking our matches instead is *who* are you for a living'
or 'if you hate it, do you feel empowered to change it?'

Insightful questions to ask a new match

Use these questions to lean into the real person behind the profile. 'The talking stage', i.e. the time spent messaging before meeting up, may as well help you discover new things about you, too. You never know – when the fuckboys fall away because you refuse to send them a pic or your Instagram handle, these chatty cheerful guys might be the person to win your number.

- What's one foolproof thing that always makes you smile?
- What are you hoping to gain in life from this app?
- How do you make a positive difference to other people?
- What's your love language?
- What feels like meaningful support to you?
- Do you feel like your star sign represents you? (If they say they don't know, you can explain how their star sign might be characterised. Think of it as woman-splaining.)
- What kind of connection are you ready for right now?
- What makes you insecure?
- What is the one thing you can't live without?
- What's your view on spirituality or the afterlife?
- What's the happiest you've ever been?
- And lastly, what are you not telling me? (Kidding on that last one. Maybe.)

You could also even go the whole hog and create a Google form to vet someone. That really lets you know who's serious about getting into your life, and the results open up your conversation immediately. Just keep it light and fun!

Confident in life, lacking in love

A lot of successful, popular women might feel love has let them down. We can do life just fine when it's just us, thank you very much. Introduce a partner to do life with, and that's where we get caught up and lose flow.

Our Spice Girl generation was brought up with self-empowering 'we can do anything we set our mind to' energy, so I guess I misunderstood that we shouldn't actively seek out the boys we set out hearts on. There I was, a 25-year-old control freak believing it was my responsibility to plonk *myself* in the right place at the right time, else I'd miss my Person. So to help fate along, and to tackle my boredom, I sought out dates. Well, I thought, at least I knew they'd also be single and in the same boat as me. That was already something we had in common.

I knew my slowly blossoming self-love and spiritual skills would filter through the big life things to help with the little life things too, e.g. more honest communication with others or picking a winning scratch card. My higher vibration found a role that aligned far more with me too, a role that felt destined to be mine. After three weeks back in the craft department, the editor role of *Soul & Spirit* magazine next door opened, and I slid right into it. It came with the same exact salary I'd asked for on another job interview. The Universe is nothing but pedantically exact, after all. You know the phrase 'money talks'? I had spoken the salary expectation out loud during my phone interview, rather than just sending in an email. When we do that, we hear ourselves asserting our worth, and like the genie in the lamp, the Universe listens. But I had no idea spirituality could have anything to do with dating.

Ah, it has everything to do with it, ma cherie.

Dating blind

The first two guys I dated that summer were a stab in the dark, having not used Tinder at home for a long time. The first turned out to be a work friend's stalker ex-boyfriend, which explained why she was lurking in my mind for the whole date, even mid-kiss. Thanks a lot, intuition. Bit of a mood-killer.

You're welcome, hun.

The second Tinder boy matched me on an intellectual level, discussing our career ambitions and how we desperately wanted out of our parents' houses. We went on cinema and crazy golf dates, and it all felt very senior school. He didn't take it well when I called us both out on our mutual friend-zoning energy and suggested just being friends instead. What? I was just calling the energy how I felt it.

Even though being asked out feels flattering at first, dates we don't actually want can leave us feeling even more alone than before. We wonder *why*, because we've just been on a date, and should be feeling excitement and butterflies, so why do we just feel confused? I didn't yet know that dating without conscious intention means choosing whoever chooses you without examining if your individual needs are being met.

So the one central question I introduce to you first and foremost is 'does he meet at least 80 per cent of them?' Ah, maybe that begs the next question.

What are my needs?

It can be anything from someone to make you a cup of tea, to a personal driver, to someone with specific looks. Go as shallow or as deep as you want, and see what the Universe serves up. What do you need in a partner? As soon as your needs are immortalised in ink, it's outside of you and you can have a dialogue with it. The best thing is we can always change our needs as we see fit.

Journal the phrase 'I need someone who …'

Without doing this, we can tend to romanticise dating, living in hope that our bad matches were just the bad frog-kissing stage like we're in our own Tinderella story. We don't see that we can take conscious action to get better just by asking ourselves our needs. We think we might stumble upon a prince, as if he was just hiding among the profiles waiting. Though this does happen to a lucky few, I like to think we meet the Universe halfway.

Some are born shameful, some achieve shame

And some have shame thrust upon them. As sexually liberated singletons in the new age of app dating, we don't know how to feel about casual sex. Fuckboys want it – even expect it – but our mothers shame it. Our loins lean one way and our values another. We're caught between a rock and a hard place.

Our generation has more milk and relationship alternatives than the generations before us, so I understand why there's a gap in understanding. They had slightly more important things like war to deal with, after all. When someone asks for a 'friends with benefits' set-up, this usually isn't healthy or conscious. It comes from a toxic mix of avoidance, fear of rejection and closed-heartedness, all masked by a 'come on, don't be frigid' attitude. These are all things active self-love can help to stamp out. On the flip side, when we consciously know our needs and learn to meet a lot of them ourselves, only then can we consider conscious casual situations like open relationships and ethical non-monogamy (ENM).

Having come from a Great British stiff-upper-lipped family, I'm not surprised to learn that under 10 per cent of people in the UK are interested in ENM. Interestingly, 20 per cent of people in the US have tried one. But wherever we live, shame can be thrust upon us by those of the older generation who are, shall we say, less compassionate, and their judgement can sting.

The weekend before featured someone we'll call Wedding Boy, an usher at a family friend's wedding. I hadn't quite shaken off my 'free-loving' backpacker mindset yet and was used to doing what I liked without fearing the consequences. The guy had been into me for years, so why fight something that was always going to happen eventually, I had reasoned. The sex was good, and that was something to even feel relieved about.

Wedding Boy's compliments, even if they were ultimately designed to get me into bed, were something my ego desperately wanted to hear, considering I'd been told by Mum that morning that I looked fat in my dress. What we should do is take ourselves away to breathe deeply, observe our hurt feelings and console ourselves with some sympathy and positive affirmations. Instead, I had ridden the validation train upstairs to my hotel room. The hotel room my parents, in the room next door, had paid for.

Wedding Boy seemed a very emotionally available man, but unfortunately for men like him, I wanted the chase. We confuse mystery and danger when it comes to boys. We think we want bad boys, but we need good boys with boundaries.

By the time Mum had wind of it a few days later, I was too triggered to entertain anyone, and turned him down when he asked me out properly.

Sex, I found, was a way to both connect with someone and keep them at a safe distance at the same time. I was just so scared to lose myself in another, or even to put myself out there on the line. Little did I know that being vulnerable is where the growth happens. But you couldn't have told me that then. I was a damsel in disdain, but I wouldn't let anyone near me to save me.

What to call it instead of a walk of shame

The term one-night stand originally comes from travelling bands who would only be in town for a night. Now, it describes a one-off sexual encounter, usually to the accolade of the man and the shame of the woman. To shake off this slick of outdated judgement, I like to call it a 'one-night special' or 'one-night show'. Thoughts become things, so don't let fear of judgement fester with these high vibers:

- Walk of no shame
- Stride of pride
- Post-passion promenade
- The funtime runtime
- Post hokey-kokey hike
- Single girl strut

How your moon sign represents your mum

Or at least, our perception of how our mum loved us. For example, with my moon in fiery Aries, a cardinal fire sign, it was no wonder I experienced a fiery mother. My brother's moon sign is an earth sign, so he may have experienced a more grounded, straight-laced perception of the same mother. What element is your moon sign in and how does it relate to your perception of your mum? How does your sibling's moon sign differ?

For contrast, our sun and disciplinarian Saturn represent our father. For those that only have same-sex parents, the more dominant parent may be represented by the sun and the more nurturing parent by the moon. Sometimes, it's just reaching our Saturn Return and going into our thirties when we realise the conditioning unknowingly put upon us by our mothers. How we repeat the relationships with our mother in other areas of our life to seek acknowledgement; in our friends, bosses or even therapists.

Don't shit on the house share doorstep

House hunting on one income probably means two things: the budget is small, and the place is probably going to come with free housemates.

For a sparky people person with a history of codependency, that would work just fine for me. Housemates meant readymade friends, and their friends meant readymade friends. Preferring to meet a man through mutual friends, my dating fishing net could expand overnight with the right crowd. I needed people around me to bounce off, single people, not couples. I already felt unworthy enough of love without being reminded every day that other people were worthy of it.

So when I moved in somewhere and caught the sparkling eye of a guy who lived upstairs, a tall, dark and handsome guy we'll call Housemate, a spark that said 'danger ahead' to most people but whispered 'come hang out in my room tonight, if you like', I felt I was in exactly the right place. And to think, the room I picked I almost skipped viewing completely, but again, that little intuitive voice had piped up to tell me to have a look anyway. Now I was half an hour away from my parents' musty intergenerational judgement, I was ready to follow any spark I could find down any rabbit hole it wanted me to.

She's going to have a rude awakening, my angels muttered to each other. *Maybe your mum just wants the best growth for our girl.*

Life hacks to feel loved

Sometimes, you don't even want sex, you just want a foot rub and a cuppa made for you. When you just want to feel looked after by someone who is not your parents, these hacks are great for keeping loneliness at bay, and you never know, you might even meet someone through them. Crucially, it means you don't go looking for a care-giver on Tinder or in your house share.

- Freeze healthy stews, curries, puddings and smoothies so you can dedicate time to self-care. Even if you feel you're dating a past version of you, you still have someone to appreciate, and that's important. You can pay yourself extra gratitude.
- Make male friends and try being yourself. Half the time, missing being in a relationship is just missing male company. Join social media groups in your location and interests where you might meet lovely people, such as gym classes or band nights.
- Team up with a girlfriend with whom you have a safe, compassionate friendship, and make a pact that you'll share teamwork, such as

taking kids to school on a certain day, or going on a fortnightly mate date or yearly holiday. Someone you can feel is your companion. They don't have to be single, they're just meeting your need for connection.

- Write messages to yourself and leave them on mirrors or in a jar so you don't need to look at your messages with your ex or go on Tinder just to read a compliment.
- Subscribe to BoyfriendAudio or ASMR if you like it. It's great for manifesting a boyfriend because even though it's an actor, they're talking to *you*, you're already hearing the words you want to hear, and feeling the loved, intimate feelings you want to attract.
- Don't over-glorify relationships, as being in one won't solve everything. Know that people in relationships can also feel lonely, unhappy and unloved. As a single person, you are fully empowered to go out and find a relationship that will serve you. If you were already in one, that would make things a little more complicated.

Come on down, the first fuckboy!

The easiest way to spot a fuckboy is to register how you feel when you meet him. Is your nervous system activated, puzzling why he hasn't texted back? Are you telling yourself *I must make him want me?* This energy is all you need to know to do an about turn and walk away. Does he have spiritually clichéd tattoos, grow his hair long and quote Eckhart Tolle? Oh god, he's a Spiritual Fuckboy, run!

One Friday night soon after I moved in, I met my first fuckboy since fleeing the nest. We'll call him Brandon. He was good-looking and totally my then-type, his hair a curly mop on top tapered to short on the back and sides, piercing eyes, nose piercing, height six foot and above. I couldn't stop myself making some sort of beeline to get talking to him, probably asking him and his mates what shots they were drinking. He was obviously happy about it, as his chat-up line soon came: 'I'm moving to South America next week, do you want to come with me?'

Oh, he was serious.

This guy believes his trip is what makes him interesting. Does he have no depth?

But I couldn't hear my intuition and dove in there before it could even say 'guy'. It was rare to meet this kind of ambitious man in *this* town. He was everything I would have manifested in a man. He seemed emotionally available when he told me he'd lost his dad the year before, hence the carpe diem approach to travel. And he wanted to talk to *me*? What was I doing later, he wanted to know.

A bit early to be asking that, sir.

'Sorry, friends are staying at mine tonight. But I'm free tomorrow?' I replied far too eagerly, as if his imminent leaving and absolute fuckboy language weren't red flags at all.

Get-to-know-you sex with strangers is rarely good, which is why people usually opt to be drunk for it. A hungover fumble between strangers in daylight is even worse. He couldn't stay long afterwards, he said, but I was busy that afternoon anyway, which let him off the hook. There were no red flags flying in my mind, despite them being glaringly obvious to the friends I'd been out with – the same friends who nodded along with my plans to go long-distance with Supernova, who maybe could have helpfully hinted that I was being an absolute fool. *This* time my naivety was rooted in thinking boys could fall in love with me once I'd slept with them, without a hint of a boundary, conscious need or expectation. I was the definition of 'easy'. Maybe I even hoped this guy wouldn't move after all, as if my vagina had the power to change minds and plans.

Only you have the power to change your mind.

I filled in my friend and my journal on my gossip. But reading it back years later, it was like I had thrown the growth gear I'd been in since travel into reverse and was now in shrink mode.

If you also get told by your best friends that you 'wear your heart on your sleeve' or 'fall in love too fast', then you're in the right place here, sister. Sex really screws with our brains. Our rush of oxytocin bonds us to them. When that happens, we can have good intentions to take the guy at his word, or his actions, but our expectations will likely still hit the ceiling. We grab onto anything we can as a sign that 'feels are catching'. If we invite him round and he accepts, that means he definitely likes us back. If he watches our social media stories and he likes them (it means nothing). He just can't tell us he likes us because he's busy, or he's bad at communication, or some other lame excuse. It was just like Houdini in Thailand – they don't communicate because they can rarely be honest with themselves.

I had been so concerned I'd get lost in another person, without realising that I didn't need to worry about that yet. We were so far off even a situationship (a relationship without the strings of commitment, but one which masquerades very well as a relationship to the outside world).

Journal prompts to make sure you're dating with self-love

These questions are great to journal post-first date, if there was a date. Having an insight into your feelings *before* you get emotionally attached saves you time and energy, two things that were way more precious than I realised. Take some deep breaths and still your mind. Remember, there are no wrong answers here.

- Ask yourself – do you really like this person as a person, or are you just curious about creating some dramatic fateful love story? (I'm afraid to say you need to value them as a human before casting them as your partner.)
- Do you really want to give this person your precious divine body? Is he earning you, wooing you, valuing you, or at least properly engaging you? Are you giving him a chance to earn it, or are you doing all the work for him?
- How will you feel if you sleep with him and he doesn't call? Be honest with yourself – what expectations do you have for your shared future?

- Is this person good enough for you, rather than you feeling good enough for them? Can they truly see the real you, or are you pretending to be the Cool Girl Without Needs just to impress them? What are you scared to show them?
- Does this person show vulnerability and openness? How does your nervous system feel when you're around them – are you calm, bored, hyped up, stressed or euphoric, for example? Does your stomach do flips, does your heart chakra feel fuzzy, or do you feel nervous for 24 hours before seeing them and fixate on every little thing?
- Where might you be adding potential for him where it lacks? What factual basis do you have for how lovely they are? What proof do you have of how he feels about himself?
- Are you dating him to find out more about him, or are you using your chats like writing exercises when you should be journaling? Note, if you spill personal details on your chats early, it should be in journal entries.
- Are you dating him to kill time?

Divine guidance makes us defensive

A few weeks later, I was in London to review a crystal healing session for the magazine. The night before, Brandon's mum was away, so he had asked me to go over – a rare occurrence I normally would have jumped at, despite it being a booty call. Invitations of that kind normally are any time after 10.00 p.m. (11.00 p.m. on Friday nights and weekends). Though I desperately wanted his company, something wouldn't let me go to him, and instead kept me rooted, in my bed, like a Derren Brown subject in his mentalist act. It wasn't a power move – I literally *couldn't* move, but I didn't know why. Was it a smidgen of self-respect trying to unleash itself?

Seeing a healer is half soul diagnostics, half epic girl talk. The treatment had been wonderful, her hypnotic voice guiding me into a trance as grounding crystals tinkled in her hands. She placed them around me and on me, tourmalines, obsidians, and rose quartz too, all weighing me down further into my meditation like an energetic weighted blanket. It wasn't the same as Reiki – I didn't see colours as I had before, I just felt I was in a deep dream-like sleep state. As she spoke, she stayed connected with her spirit guides, who were feeding her the information I was about to hear. Her own spiritual tag team was at work.

Yay, now it's a party!

'That boy you're seeing. He's a player.'

Woah, how did she know I was seeing someone? My back was up – don't talk about poor Brandon like that.

'The guides are telling me you are not to get involved with him. He's unreliable. He's also hurting ... did he lose someone?'

I could see his grief had enveloped him, so she was on the right lines. I think that's why I excused his bad communication, his need to run away to South America. I had run away myself, to Australia. But I had only lost a boyfriend, however trauma-bonded I was to him. I couldn't imagine losing my dad. I felt sorry for him. But ah, shit. We don't need to have sex with people we feel sorry for.

'There's someone better for you who can give you what you need.' I think I scoffed in disbelief. Well, where he is then, huh?

Chill, woman. We didn't like this guy anyway.

'You need to do some healing work of your own. And you shouldn't see him again. He's the landing pad to your last hurt,' she continued.

'How do you mean?' I asked.

She paused. 'Well, people can't land somewhere if there's not a landing strip. People who have hurt you in the past have enabled him to land on you too, like they've set up the runway for him.'

She could see me taking in the information, nodding but clearly disappointed. 'I'm getting a ringing sound, like a bell ... does that sound right?'

'His last name's Bellman.'

'Ah. Yes, well, he's not your guy. When you're ready to do some healing work, imagine a white light in your heart. Let it purify and heal you there, clearing out the hurt. I feel motherly towards you right now. Protective. But you should know that you can disregard what I'm telling you. You don't have to follow the advice. I was in a relationship for five years though I knew not to be. And I didn't go to an event last month the spirit guides wanted me to. We all have free will.' She gave me a knowing look. My defences came down, feeling safe in her empathy.

My crystal healer was right. The same as saying 'no' to spirit, you can say 'no' to anyone's advice. You have free will to choose to follow it or not, depending on what your gut is telling you. Despite taking the Bali healer's word as gospel, I feel uncomfortable following that course unless I know I agree with them, too. If you follow blindly, you become a sheep, and that's not empowering at all. In fact, it can make you dependent on your healer, or psychic, or medium and make you especially vulnerable to spiritual narcissists to guide your way for you.

'Poor guy, losing his dad. You do like the broken biscuit boys, don't you,' a friend said. Dating stories were always the dish I brought to a dinner party. 'You're like a moth to a flame if you think you can fix them up.' And so he became Brandon the Broken, inspired by the *Game of Thrones* character. And I became a little bit more suspicious of my own dating tendencies. I was starting to become ashamed of how much I needed men, or at least, validation from them.

I wasn't yet aware that entertaining the fuckboy meant I was a fuck*girl*.

How to know you're a mirror

It's a hard truth to swallow, when you realise you might attract the fuckboy because your energy is on similar vibrations. However, if we entertain the connection for whatever reason, it might mean we're a fuckgirl, the perfect yin to their yang. See if the following sounds like you, because energetically speaking, once you call it, you can clear it.

- We accept his breadcrumbs if he comes over late at night or in the morning for sex. That's the only time we're free too.
- We post lots of provocative selfies or dates with other people online for attention, in case he'll see. He will, and he will text us, for sex. It will work, until his attention wears off again.
- We are emotionally unavailable ourselves. We can't name the emotions we feel, let alone lean into them. We're then surprised when they burst out of us when we're drinking or triggered.

Meet the fuckboys of the tarot: the Knights

You learnt the messages of the 22 Major Arcana cards through my travels, and so we're on to the 56 cards of the Minor Arcana. As we've established, there are four suits in this section: pentacles, wands, swords and cups. There are ten number cards then four court cards in each suit: a Page, Knight, Queen and King. The next thing I want you to know is which element each suit portends to. I think of this as follows:

- Pentacles, in the classic Rider Waite deck, has a five-pointed pentagram on the artwork. This makes me think of a pentagram drawn in the mud as if for a witchy ritual, so this suit relates to earth. This goes with slow-moving stubborn things, such as wealth, health and groundedness. Think of someone you know who's a Capricorn, Taurus or Virgo and they'll probably be a reliable, stable type who's good with money.
- Wands look like long-neck lighters, so this suit relates to the fire element. It looks at ambition, drive and passion, and what Aries, Leo or Sagittarius do you know without a desire to do well in life?
- Swords can cut through air, or someone might say 'you could cut the tension in here with a dagger'. Use this to help you remember that swords represent the air element, and though its characters are ambitious, passionate and idealists, it can point to lower vibrational

states such as anxiety or rumination too. Think Aquarius, Gemini and Libra.
- Cups hold liquid, so this is the water suit. These cards question our (or whoever the question is about) emotions or emotional intentions, as well as psychic or creative matters. If you know a Pisces, a Cancer or a Scorpio, they'll probably have one or more of those sensitive qualities.

With that under our belt, let us talk about one court card in particular: the Knight. The Knight is like any prince; crucially, he is not the King, so he is not the master of his suit. Like many Tinder boys, he is here for a good time, not a long time, so enjoy his six-pack for a night and move on. He's pretty much just an action man who is in your reading to represent some sort of change or movement (well, when we meet a fuckboy, life does get pretty dramatic). What suit the Knight is in may shed light on his intention, because luckily, they're not all Casanovas.

- Knight of Pentacles: the man who is dragging his heels about something, such as proposing, if the question asked to the cards is about a relationship. He needs to hurry up and act more quickly.
- Knight of Wands: the fuckboy of tarot. Classic. Run from this card. He is fast moving and does not want to settle down.
- Knight of Swords: be careful and look at the cards around him, because he can be a negative Knight, sometimes even aggressive or intimidating. Give this guy space.
- Knight of Cups: because this is the emotion suit, this boy is the real charmer, the romancer. He is the positive knight, because he shows up to shake up feelings. Whether or not he'll stick around depends on further 'clarification' cards, cards we ask to give context to ones drawn before.

And when you've got multiple Knights in one reading, you may be going through quite a vast period of change. Up your self-care, make sure to stay grounded and be open to what pops up next.

Boundaries, schmoundaries

If you reached adulthood with even one personal boundary in place, I applaud you. I was 25 and didn't know the meaning of them. What was this thing you call a boundary? What do you mean I couldn't kiss my male colleague at the Christmas party – he's single! It baffled me. A hedonistic, pleasure-seeking creative like me – I didn't need boundaries to come in and curb the fun. If anything, they felt like rejection of fun instead of a tool of protection. I was a people-pleaser, satisfying everyone but myself, so how was I meant to please others if there were blocks that I couldn't get past?

Maybe you've always felt like an in-betweener too, so you relate to people who also don't quite fit in, those people who have a strange mysterious energy you can't put your finger on. I had the sense Housemate had been misunderstood in his life, and it's natural for us empaths to lean in and want to help carry some of the load. He'd just been dumped and had fled his home country as a refugee – his family was still in danger, and I admired his Divine Masculine taking it upon himself to be the remote breadwinner. Maybe he'd provide for me too, said my inner cavewoman.

Things progressed nicely with Housemate, giving me lovely false hope to comfort myself with. We had crossed the friendship line into cuddling, foreplay and sex, always in my room, never his. My guard was wrenched down enough now to let the oxytocin flow freely. It was a symbiotic situationship, and one of true unfortunate convenience.

But despite my day-to-day sense of fulfilment, avoiding asking friends for advice when judgemental expressions crossed their faces, it did frustrate me that it didn't seem to be moving in the relationship direction, despite my epic fake girlfriend act. I was pouring out so much of myself into him, a tsunami of me, but he'd turn me on and off as he wanted, like a tap. We'd watch action movies I secretly hated curled up with my head rested in his lap, and me the literal putty in his hands. I couldn't talk about us in detail with anyone other than Beth, the deputy editor I had just hired, who believed in us all the way. She was as sure as I was that, in time, I'd upgrade my status in his life.

Hmm ... Maybe I needed just a little boundary.

How to set strong boundaries

These are even more important if you're an empath, a Highly Sensitive Person or have experienced trauma. The first thing to know is that once you set them, even though it might not feel like it now, the people who care about you will generally, eventually, acknowledge them. Once that happens the first time, see where else in your life you could strengthen your overgiving tendencies. I started with dating apps, and then conversation topics with my mum, then tried it out with my relationship with work and then friends. Trust me, when you know how much easier it makes your life, it gets addictive.

Try journaling on the following.

- Most importantly, be honest with yourself. How much time do you need to yourself per day or week? What areas of your life would you rather not discuss with your mum? How slow do you need to take a new intimate relationship? These things come with being able to observe your feelings when boundaries are not in place, giving you a sign you need to investigate setting some there in future. For example, if you feel resentment or anger when you say 'yes' to something, it's time to set some limits. What could be the best compromise for you?
- You can retrospectively install boundaries; even if you said 'yes' to something a thousand times before, you can still say 'no' next time. You are not held by any law to people-please.
- Know that if we carry on without boundaries, we'll live our lives according to other people's needs. And most people wouldn't want you to be unhappy. If someone who previously benefitted from your lack of boundaries gets upset with this new act of self-respect, that's just the Universe showing you who is worthy of you and who is not.
- Practise some one-liners first, either alone in the mirror or with

friends. Phrases like 'I need some time to decompress for now', 'I'm sorry, that just doesn't work for me', or 'I'd love it if we could connect more like this or that' are good starts. You'll be able to find more that are good for you. Keep it to 'I' phrases, not accusative 'you' comments. We don't want our loved one to get hurt or defensive here, because these are *our* needs, not theirs. So say it with a smile but be kind and firm. This isn't a formal thing, and it works better the more casually and positively it's presented. If it's said over text, a smiling emoji always helps to show that this first request, at least, comes in peace.

- Give people their own space to process the new boundary you've set. You're growing, and that's great, but you don't want to push people away. Boundaries are a compromise, after all. Go gently and expect a little discomfort as you find the sweet spots. Vulnerability shows us we are growing.

Putting spirituality into practice

When we're so attached to a need for something or someone, it's the perfect time to remove ourselves to gain some perspective and question why. I needed my first retreat, and so when a residential weekend that claimed to expand one's 'inner guidance' popped up, I jumped at the invitation to review it for work. I craved both a staycation away from the house share and to practise some spirituality of my own. I needed a hard reset, a realignment, feeling myself all out of sorts from my romantic experiences of late; a cocktail of chaos. That's the thing about spirituality – you can't just read about it, it demands to be practised.

The farmhouse retreat centre was haunted, they said, but with friendly, protective presences. Well, that certainly makes it more marketable, I thought. It was classic old house stuff: ghosts in the garden, faces at the window, footsteps thudding in the corners. I never saw anything – I'm not a clairvoyant – but I could still feel some sort of presence in my room. In both houses, the retreat and my sharehouse, I had the odd energy of another hanging around me.

'The heart *is* inner wisdom. It knows best,' the retreat leader Denise told us the first night. She was a down-to-earth person with a wild past, a recovered drug addict and former alcoholic, and she and her partner ran the retreat with no alcohol, sugar or caffeine. With nothing to be addicted to, she was in 'freedom', as she called it. I wondered what that would feel like, the freedom from addiction of boys, love and sex. How weirdly empty my life might feel, but how novel. To release hope they'd even text me back would feel amazing. But that scared me even more. How the hell would I relate to men without sex?

Then came the real reason I must have been called to that retreat: to have my first legal plant medicine trip. To crack open my heart chakra and shake me with so much love it was going to feel like I had been genetically re-engineered from the inside.

Farmed in the jungle, she, as shamans refer to cacao, has aided our healing for centuries. She's packed so full of natural goodness that she needs little marketing. She's said to ease pre-menstrual syndrome and even relieve depression because she contains anandamide, the 'bliss' molecule we tend to make after exercising. I was most interested in how she could shift our emotional states, help us find self-forgiveness and release old habits. I had no idea how she was going to do that for me – I'm not sure I even understood the degree to which I needed it – so I channelled the intention I set at the start of the retreat to *trust*. A big ask for anyone with a history of narcissistic abuse.

Taking a deep swig of the rich and slightly bitter liquid, we were led into meditation. I could feel it almost expanding the capillaries in my heart, like champagne goes straight to your head. As many newbie meditators do, I found myself unable to switch off, diving head deep into self-question mode. Our egos are under attack, and they know it.

Am I lost right now in life? What the hell am I doing with boys?

146

I've been looking for an emotionally strong man who's not afraid of committing to me, but really am I just looking for a strong, focused energy source in general? It was so loud I was surprised no one else in the room could hear it. So I was grateful that as soon as we had finished our cup, we were invited to let the cacao do its work in private. We might walk, stay still, cry, laugh or sob, but whatever happened, we'd be sure to feel our feelings deeply, feel the sensations in our body, something I wasn't used to.

As I got outside into the cold air, just as the mushrooms back in Indonesia had, all at once the cacao hit its destination: my heart chakra. I remember the exact moment she seeped into me, became me. I was out walking in the misty grounds, and it spoke to me as clearly as my intuition had that day of the almost bus crash in Hanoi, so loud and solemn it almost bowled me over.

All the love you are craving is already within you.

Boom, it landed, stopping me mid-step.

You are here for a reason. Others are here for their reasons.

Bang, I came to a complete stop.

Stop looking to fix them. You can only heal yourself. They can only heal themselves.

Then the tears came.

We think we're worthless without a person by our side to validate us. But the cacao was telling me, with every molecule inside me, that I already had intrinsic value just as I was. In the eyes of friends and family, I was way more able than I thought I was. I was way more loved than I had cared to see, because I had been so focused on the lack rather than the abundance I already possessed. I choked out small, grateful tears as I processed my epiphany, as if the cacao had said to my cells 'take this message, pass it on'.

'No more lack, only love', I chanted to myself as I walked the labyrinth mowed into the short grass, a type of circular active walking meditation. With my heart chakra still buzzing with pure love vibrations, I felt my post-travel self who felt unstoppable alone flood back to me, and I knew what I had to do. I needed to tell both Housemate and my ego to kindly go away.

Do a cacao ceremony

You can do this ritual alone, with your girlfriends, your partner, or any size group. Just double up the ingredients as needed. I do this when I need a hit of self-love, but some people choose to make it a weekly ritual or on new or full moons to boost their intentions, for example.

Makes enough for 2.

Gather up:

- Large thumb-sized rock of cacao (approx 60g total)
- 220ml oat or almond milk
- 220ml water
- Squeeze of honey or coconut agave
- Pinch of paprika, chilli powder, cinnamon and/or cloves, to taste

To make:

1   Grate the cacao on a cheese grater so it becomes flakes or rubble and melt down the cacao in a saucepan. Once it looks like a paste, add the milk alternative, and add water to get to a hot chocolate consistency. Add honey or agave nectar. Simmer for at least 10 minutes, but don't let it boil. It should almost be glittering. Serve in your favourite mug with a pinch of your spice of choice on top.

2   Sit down on the floor with your back straight, opposite each other or in a circle. Have candles flickering, soft music on, low lighting and be somewhere you won't be disturbed. Close your eyes and take a deep inhale of the cacao in your mug to begin with. Let the steam inhale through your nostrils and see what first flickers in your imagination.

3   As you let it cool, still inhaling its rich smell, set an intention or question. What difficult emotion would you like this sacred plant medicine to help you unpack today? Where do you need to soften, slow down and open up?

4   Once it's cool enough to drink, close your eyes, concentrate your

senses on your tastebuds and take a deep gulp. Simply meditate as you drink, or there are many shamanic healing guided meditations to listen to as you drink on Insight Timer, YouTube, Spotify or other such platforms.

5   See what feelings come up for you as you let the cacao digest. Journal on what messages come to mind as you sit with your question or problem. What conversation is your intuition having with the cacao? What questions is it throwing up to your consciousness, and how is the cacao responding? For example, you might be feeling anxiously attached, feeling like your partner is pulling away. Listen to what words your intuition is flashing across your mind's eye right now in response. For me, it's responded in the past with 'then self-care as he works himself out, he'll come back to you when he's ready to hang out', and 'it's okay, child, take your attention back to you'. It always responds with self-love, always. That's why your ego hates it; it wants to criticise, where cacao wants to sympathise.

Keep the self-love cup topped up

After a retreat, it's prudent – no, necessary – not to let petty day-to-day life dramas drain your nicely full cup. So back at home, I clung to my new-found positivity like it was an elusive fuckperson I wanted a reply from. My default was to seduce Housemate again, and I did, but I stopped sex halfway through when I realised that this love-making felt anything but loving. I was suddenly conscious of how wrong it was. Limp, in every sense of the word.

When girlfriends go through similar experiences, I wait for their anger to come. It always does. It's a healthy emotion if channelled in the right way (see page 54). In the next few days, my need for space turned into quiet hostility. It exponentially increased by the hour, manifesting in total passive aggression. I was so angry at him for using me as rebound and myself for taking so long to see it. It was exhausting not to be able to be as upset as I needed to be in my own home, so it was a relief to be going back to Mum and Dad's for Christmas. I was finally running in the direction of the people who loved me.

What's your resolution word?

Because of my cacao-fuelled epiphany, my New Year word was 'whole', because I realised I already was, even without a partner (stick that in your pipe and smoke it, Plato). One-word resolutions replace a statement or promise that often doesn't fit our year in practice. A word like 'spark' can fit into many definitions.

Some empowering words to choose from: happy, boundaries, self-love, awe, light, fun, expansion, authenticity, surrender, family, creativity, growth, consciousness … you get the picture.

Journal your word for the year and add ideas on the intentional changes it will manifest. Then, if you wish, you can do the same for the next couple of years too.

Come on down, the second fuckboy!

If you're still dating unconsciously, you'll attract unconscious people. And the Universe will keep introducing you until you heal the part of you attracted to the chase.

Similar to retreats we come home from and immediately forget, month-long fad challenges like Dry January can be largely pointless. According to the widely regarded 21/90 rule, it takes 21 days to make a habit but 90 further days to embrace it as part of our lifestyle. It's the same as a drink on day 31 being our reward, undermining the whole point. Even if I was doing it as a novelty experiment, it would lay surprising groundwork for the future.

I took it very seriously, mostly just to prove to myself that I didn't have a drinking problem. Because I learnt hard love growing up, I continued to treat myself with it, so I also challenged myself to Veganuary, where you go vegan for January, at the same time. It was like an extended retreat in my own life, with the surprising by-product that it quietened my ego and, by extension, my interest in dating.

In February of the same year, I went back on the dating apps tentatively, but with the advantage of fresh eyes. Do it over, and do it better, I thought, as if my love life was a clay pot I could squash back down to try again.

A few weeks in, taking my time, I opened a chat with Nate. Well, I needed to cuff (hook up with) someone in time for summer drinks in pub gardens. And after my cacao epiphany, I would do this fuckboy differently.

Dating? In Spring? Groundbreaking ...

Nate was a delightfully hipster-looking interior designer. It was lumberjack lust at first sight, and I could picture myself stealing an oversized flannel shirt on a cuddly Sunday afternoon, surrounded by our adorable little lumberjack babies, watching the sunset ... Anyway, it wasn't just lust I fell into, it was trust, and far too soon.

We trust he means it when he tells us 'you might be exactly who I'm looking for'. In retrospect, he was probably as hopeful for it to be true as I was. After our first date, I trusted him enough to invite him to mine (for a tea and cuddle only – because of boundaries) and I trusted him enough to tell him what had gone down in the house (more drama had elapsed in the house, this time between Housemate and a new girl who'd moved in). I trusted in his support. He opened up about his recent depression in return, which I felt immensely special about.

That's the thing about boundaries. We may think we've got them in check, only to blindly overshare ourselves in other ways. You may not tear each other's clothes off on the first date but you can fast-track the emotional intimacy side of things before building a foundation. I clearly needed to be talking to someone I either knew better or a therapist, and so did he. We thought we were just dating but we were mirrors, both as intense and as confused about life as each other. I guess when a walking red flag sees another one, they like to join together like bunting.

Butterflies mean sparks, right?

There are two schools of thought over jitters. One says this butterfly-in-the-stomach feeling is a sure sign of the spark, and the other says it's a nervous tendency that doesn't lend itself to long-term relationship health. I've gone from idealising the former to firmly siding with the latter. When I see someone I *should* be with, I want to be totally calm and comfortable around them. You'll know you have the spark by other means.

When waiting for Nate to pick me up, I felt so nervy I needed to visit the toilet a few times too many. The jitters were trying to tell me something: 'run away before he does'. The only way to take it forward was to make it more intense. Because we had already bared our souls, the next thing to do was bare our bodies. We don't realise we want to wait and get to know each other better first, let alone say it. I must have been wearing rose-tinted glasses when I mistook his frowned sex face as suddenly strong feelings for me, and his deep eye contact as passion.

'You're like a radiator,' he mumbled as he rolled over afterwards. My stomach sank. Previous experience told me this comment meant 'I'd like you to leave right now'. He had even kindly put on the new horror film *Get Out*, my hopeful self not getting the hint. I started to feel lonely and invisible, beating myself up for staying in the hope of more intimacy. Eventually he stirred and mumbled for me to scratch his back. Relieved to finally be acknowledged, I obliged like a good little submissive.

Well, you can wave goodbye to that one. You won't see him again. Buh-bye, Natey Boy, my higher self said as I got out of his car the next morning.

Kindly fuck off, voice, you're wrong, I responded. I would see him again. I swear I would. He was just tired, and we didn't know each other very well yet.

Daddy doom

Our avoidant attachment–anxious attachment dance was about to begin. A few days later, when I checked in with him, I got the Doom Text.

You know the one: a short but lame excuse message as a precursor for the break-up text, or no more texts at all. Where they say something like they're still tired from Friday night and would drop you a text later. Coupled with the confirmation from your gut feeling, it usually foretells their losing interest, they just don't know how to cut you off. I must preface this by saying it doesn't always mean a break-up is imminent, but it does mean an honest chat is needed.

The more days went on without a reply, the more I was certain he'd freaked himself out and wanted to backtrack. It hadn't yet crossed my mind that I could spend my time relieving my own anxiety over *his* internal battle with self-care rituals, or lightening my outlook with manifesting spellwork. Or at least smudging my house share room with sage to remove both the bad Housemate and disappointing fuckboy energy I'd picked up (though I reckon if I had, I might have set the smoke alarms off). I *still* didn't realise spirituality could fill the void.

When the student is ready, the master appears. She was an old friend who had found her fiancé on Tinder, so I knew she was Wise with a capital W. She brought forth the tool that is the vibe-checker text.

It went like this: 'Hey, I feel like the vibe has changed, is everything okay?' She'd started using it after having enough of not knowing where she stood with someone. I liked it – it was short, sweet and non-incriminatory. Surprisingly, I felt like more of a 'cool girl' for putting myself out there like this, even if it meant double-texting (texting them again before a reply).

It worked, and I got my answer.

'Hi Rosie. Ah, this happens a lot to me. I get to the same point with someone and I just don't feel it anymore. I just don't know what to say other than I'm sorry.'

The word sorry doesn't cut it. We're only accepting sorry energy.

And as we do when we put so many expectations in one man's basket, when we're told not to take something personally, we do. We question what's wrong with *us* if he's not 'feeling it', whatever that means, and what we did wrong or could do better. I'd tried my best to be the perfect mix of sexy, sassy and supportive. But I was so disgusted I'd been cast in his pathetic fuck-and-chuck cliché that I didn't respond, my pride and ego avoiding dignifying that lame message with a response.

In truth, I didn't know *how* to respond. I'd invited in honesty and communication with my vibe-checker – one that arguably saved us both dragging out something that wasn't meant to be – and he'd responded with honest communication too, even though it wasn't what I wanted to hear. What I wish I'd said now is: 'Thanks for your text (shows civility). I wish you had communicated that before we slept together. I hoped we'd cultivated a safe space to share (assign responsibility). At least now I know to give someone who deserves it my amazing self (joking). At least now I know this was your experience and nothing I did (reflecting his words). A shame things didn't work out (showing regret, because it *is a shame* – you *did* like him) but all the best.' I mean, you can take whatever you want from that, and crucially, you need to mean it, unless it's redundant. I'll show you how to get so comfy in the next chapter that you will. You'll send them healing and move on.

But the me back then used my hurt as my excuse to cower out of the conversation just when I could have taken the opportunity to show the Universe how I wanted to close a connection. But I didn't, because it already stung too much. My heart still feels love and compassion for that version of me, knowing I was meant to be her to become this version of me, just like you are meant to become the more empowered version of you.

We can change, but they might never

But the Universe loves to stir the pot, doesn't it? I bumped into him at a gig that night – he saw me and ignored me – and four years later, as I write this, he's back on my Bumble carousel. The time in the bar, I ignored him out of fear of confrontation, the second, because I'd outgrown him. His profile still called him 'the UK's no. 1 nice guy', which made me scoff. I vowed to take anyone's profile that claimed something so complimentary with a massive pinch of salt in future. In fact, a whole bucket of it, stolen from my spell ingredients cabinet.

Always the bridesmaid

Now, a bit of astrology trivia to help me explain how dire my love life had become in comparison to my peers'.

When the full moon occurs, it is always in a zodiac sign, i.e. Gemini, Cancer, Leo, etc., any of the 12 zodiacs. At that exact point in time, the sun is always in the opposing zodiac, which means six months counted on. So in June, when it's Gemini season according to the sun, the full moon that occurs will always be in Sagittarius, which is the zodiac for December. In July, Cancer season, the full moon will always be in Capricorn, the January zodiac. They are always directly opposed, and so it follows that the *new* moon will always be in the same sign as the sun. That's how directly opposite my love life felt to Lotti's, at whose wedding in Sardinia I was a bridesmaid.

As is the case with avoidant people, once they see you move on, they tend to crawl back out of the woodwork because they get their thrill from the chase too. By contrast, a narcissist will never lose face by trying to get you back. As if I'd mentally summoned him by finding his French doppelganger on my solo trip to Paris, Brandon was back in town.

What was my new house share address, he asked? It wouldn't take much time, he said.

It wouldn't take *you* much time, I replied.

Tell him to clear off, or we'll do it ourselves.

I cracked and told him where I lived. I wanted company, but not like that.

Angels, assemble!

To test if you're genuinely happy with your decision to invite a guy round, see how your body feels. If you're sitting on the edge of your bed frozen, instead of excitedly dancing or immediately turned on, you don't actually want them to come.

As if it was divine intervention, the traffic suddenly got so bad that he couldn't make it in time to honour his other more important plans. Rather than shooting love arrows, cupids were clashing our schedules.

Then, on the day before Lotti's wedding, Brandon tried to book in another casual sex appointment. This time, I didn't need my angels to intervene. I told him exactly where to go. Reeling, I spent the whole day silent with anxiety, my Edinburgh complex – my mistaken theory that I was only 'good' enough to be someone's bit on the side for a night pre-Supernova – was well and truly live and kicking again.

Come on down, Ghost!

'Where attention goes, energy flows' is all you need to remind yourself when you catch yourself in a negative thought spiral. And my attention was still on boys, or the lack of them in my life. I was still so fearful of what a real commitment would require of me, I was energetically pushing it away. And so when Ghost's profile popped up, he was destined not to stick around long either.

When you picture a fuckperson, or any kind of person who would mess a fellow human around for the sake of their ego, who do you see? For me, it's a dashing, muscly guy with a fantastic face and a brooding expression. Ghost was a fuckboy in an average-looking person's body (I was shallow and judged my own worth by the same shallow criteria, too).

When Ghost slid into my Tinder messages that June, it sparked expectations in me. *This* was *definitely* a guy I'd be able to bag easily, my ego thought. He was creative like me, athletic and into running like me, funny, smiley and handsome, like me. He didn't look the same as a Spiritual Fuckboy with a flowing mane, so he'd be reliable, but he was open-minded enough to have a great chat with. This guy *does* seem just your perfect match, friends agreed. He'd even gone to the same school as one of my closest friends, so I instantly trusted him by association. Tick, tick, tick went my boxes, and down, down, down went my guard.

This was who we went through all the shit for, we believe. This is it.

But as it ticked over to July, I got tired of his excuses. If only my intuition was tuned into boys and could have told me he was probably just keeping me warm while he surveyed his options. Well, we attract our mirrors, and while he messed about with multiple weekends away with family, which was a funny name for other girls, I was keeping my options open too.

Spiritual ways to get over being ghosted

- Admit how much this stings you and acknowledge how low-vibration this behaviour is. Don't gaslight yourself; embrace the emotions this rejection brings. Name your emotions. Is there resentment in there? Disappointment? Maybe even relief, if you were really honest with yourself? Feel these and journal on them to release them.

- Know that the person ghosting you probably doesn't even have sufficient vocabulary or emotional availability to compassionately explain why they no longer want to see you. This is the Universe taking someone out of your life that doesn't deserve to be there. Is this something to be sad about?

- Ask yourself, is this about being chosen by anyone, or being chosen by the right person? The right person would not treat you like a throwaway. Affirm 'I choose myself' over and over again, as many times as it takes to forget about anyone who doesn't choose you.

- If you still need closure, you might choose to draw a line under it yourself by either sending yourself a message as if it's from them, or sending them a note to close out your thread. 'Hi there, I'm sensing you're no longer interested so I'm just going to put a full stop on this chat. Thanks and take care.' It doesn't need to be any nicer than that.

Healing from a non-relationship

A break-up can diagnose helpful things about the relationship itself. Firstly, if it felt like a relationship, the break-up is going to feel like a real one too. Don't bypass your real feelings, and refer to the break-up guide on page 52. Notice where the hurt lies too; if you're more offended than upset, as I was over Ghost, chances are it was an ego choice, not a soul choice. You might find you stay in the relief stage and stop there without ever getting into the deep pain.

The final fuckboy

One helpful thing about still being connected to someone you thought you were in love with on social media, like I was with Housemate, is you can watch how little time it takes them to move on, then use it as a gauge to feel even shittier about yourself. So as not to lose face and even the scores, I doubled down on the dating apps. I was, as Gabby Bernstein, an American manifestation guru, would call it, a 'manic manifester'. One evening when Beth was playing Tinder for me, as my many cohabiting and married friends helpfully called swiping as if they were me, she caught a good one.

Be still my beating sex chakra. He was an indie punk Jack Dawson from *Titanic*. The Model – who wasn't a model but looked like one to me – was a landscape designer, painfully good-looking and just my type. He had tattoos down his arms, a nose piercing and a floppy 1990s-style hairdo. He had full lips and vivid green eyes. Well, if Ghost was perfect but couldn't fit me in, and if

Housemate was a great match but didn't want me, I may as well just go for the fucking fuckboy who *definitely* wouldn't want me then.

Um, maybe they weren't as perfect as you thought they were? We have been trying to show you but you just keep taking it personally ...

Teaching myself the Divine Feminine

After all the dating practice I'd had, I knew the power I had at first swipe now, having the 'cool girl' act well practised. My pictures included a full-body bikini shot in Thailand, sucking my belly in of course, a shot of me looking at a pink lake to show off my bum, and a few other smiley shots. All were sure to provide the guy with an easy icebreaker: 99 per cent of the first messages I got were 'So do you like to travel?' I had learnt to give just enough information that I couldn't be confused with a catfish (someone who uses a fake identity with the intent to deceive), give mysterious and thus sexy replies to messages, and not come across too interested by replying anytime outside of Tindering Hour.

Tindering Hour is the same time as Witching Hour: 11.00 p.m. The hour witches were said to creep out and cast spells, and when my soon-to-be-acquired cat would start zooming around, and when my phone would start lighting up with dating app notifications. One message in particular was from the Model, who I 'intrigued' enough to be asked out on a first date, though he'd cancel the first try at short notice.

The problem with dating further than a five-mile radius from home is that travel becomes an issue. It's a red flag when driving and drinking happen together on a first date, because someone will then need to stay at the other's. It's a cunning trick for them to have 'one too many' and claim they'll get a hotel. If you've had a good night, and you probably fancy them, you're too nice to let them shell out. You'll invite them back to yours.

Sex with the Model on our eventual first date was consensual but fumbled, the alcohol I'd drunk on the date keeping me in a haze. As I sat on the loo afterwards to keep away the UTI demons, I needed to vomit, so I sat down on the cold tile floor of the house share bathroom.

Existential meltdowns; they're always on the fucking bathroom floor.

I felt nothing. I was emotionally numb. That feeling had been with me a while, I realised. It had been hiding out somewhere, feeding off my energy, like a negative entity of my own making. It was willing to hide no longer, despite the haze of the alcoholic content of all my mixed drinks. It was the same niggly voice as the time it told me I wouldn't see Nate again.

You can't keep doing this.

Not you again.

You feel nothing, you know you do.

Actually, I feel like shit.

You're empty.

But I just had sex. It was good, I think?

Stop this, go cold turkey.

But I'm not a sex addict. I don't need to go cold turkey on anything.

You'll thank yourself.

NO, you're WRONG this time, I said back internally. I won't ever freak out at him or make him uncomfortable or run away. This one will be different; he was definitely single, and didn't seem to have an ex he still loved – or any ex – so that was progress. He was only a fuckboy, not a boy in need. See? I've chosen better this time. I have, I have, I have. I crossed my arms indignantly.

Of course, I had only attracted the same guy in a different guise. I'd attracted my mirror self, over and over. I was only after sex, cuddles and company, to keep my life firmly untethered to someone else's in the safety zone. This guy made me feel desired, and hot, and sassy, but it still wasn't enough. I didn't feel like myself.

Wave him goodbye, sister.

I don't want to. He's too pretty.

Be on your own for a bit. Stop waiting for a text, or for someone to choose you. You *need to choose you.*

We deny and cling. We become obsessive trying to work out what he's thinking or doing. We steal his tee shirts as a bond, not to comfort us with its smell, rather as a deposit that he'd only get back by seeing us again.

We push on little things to see how they'll react to the big things. A friend had reflected to me that I 'played with my food', but experts say it's a learnt evolutionary behaviour. If you reply to this text fast, I trust you're more likely to be there for me if I die giving birth to your child, our inner cavewoman believes. We test, we nag, we play games with him, the unaware Player 2.

'There just doesn't seem to be much room in your life for me, or for any girl really,' I pointed out over text one weekend. We hadn't scheduled a next time to see each other, and we were not phone callers. Most of all, I didn't want to accuse him of anything intently malicious, or project anything on him. I was over blaming the fuckboy for being a fuckboy. I had to take responsibility for who I chose now. We wait in the tower of our house shares, calling out for a hero, not realising we have the tools to get down ourselves.

He texted back later that night agreeing. He failed my test. He submitted to my push. I felt so disappointed he didn't try to change my mind and woo me back, even though I had put the words in his mouth. Maybe that showed he was securely attached. Maybe he was sad but hid it to save face. I never knew how he felt about it.

Now I look at it, *I* was the one that called it off. I passed *him* up. I had been looking out for myself all along. As though I had fallen asleep while driving and my intuition had secretly taken over the wheel.

I came home to my parents' again that night. I also had a strange desire to be in the house I grew up in, but I had no appetite and I craved time alone.

For one moment, I stopped thinking of sex and intimacy and let my mind clear.

Hey, you! YOU!

Oh god, I come off dating for one day and these inner voices are already thinking I'm all theirs.

With my duvet pulled way over my head, nestled down deep in the soft, dark sheets, I answered the call of my intuition for the first time.

But this time, the voice wasn't my intuition, or my higher self, my chorus of sassy angels or even the omnipotent Universe in its Morgan Freeman voice. Who was waiting for me was a sad little girl, with wide eyes and a round face. She was pretty 'in a plain way' and wearing a mismatching patterned outfit of leggings and a tee shirt. She was petite, shy but angry. She also had a massive overbite – she'd need braces in a few years. She had a fringe and long soft blonde hair turning to mousey brown at the roots. She had a sparkle in both eyes. She was me, my inner child.

Suddenly, in my mind's eye, I was pulled outside to my Wendy house, a little wooden slatted playhouse my dad had built me when I was little. I had spent hours in there in the summers, sitting up on the shoulder-height mezzanine level listening to mix tapes I'd made myself. I knocked on the door as if to ask her if I could come in. There was no answer, so I popped my head in to find a sulky little girl sitting by the window.

'Hi there,' I offered.

Just a glare back.

'Can I come up?' I asked, nodding to the little ladder.

'Hm.'

I climbed up and shuffled closer to her, aware of the creaky wooden boards underneath us, wondering if any adult had ever made it up here before.

'I'm sorry.' I felt like apologising, without knowing why. I realised this little girl didn't know the word, having been on the tail end of very few apologies in her life.

'Are you?'

'Yes.'

Silence.

'Want to tell me what's going on?'

After what felt like forever, her little voice piped up. 'When we lost Grandad, all I wanted was time with *you*. You forced me to like the boys you liked, to be grateful for any little thing they did for us, but I didn't want to. You neglected me. You *ignored* me. I didn't want them in our lives, and I don't know why you did. Wasn't I enough for you?' She started crying big, fat tears.

I wrapped her up in my arms, rocking this sweet inner child of mine. She struggled against me, lashing out, angry tears now pouring down her red face. She was furious, and I suddenly could see why. I *couldn't* spend any time alone. I needed constant distraction, and had given away so much of my energy to apps, people that I probably would never meet or know or remember.

I blinked open my eyes under my duvet to realise it was me who had been crying.

I had heard the calling. My man break would start here; that January break had kickstarted some healing, but it wasn't enough, I needed more. I'd started dating at home again a year before, so I'd take one year off to energetically cancel that out.

C.S. Lewis said to love was to be vulnerable. In this modern world, to date consciously is to be vulnerable. I would finally have to let my guard down with myself and get comfortable with discomfort.

Heal your heart chakra by activating your inner child

Healing any emotional wounds from childhood is interconnected with our heart chakra as we carry those wounds into intimate relationships. Any time you feel triggered here, take a pause, go for a walk, coach yourself with some positive self-love affirmations or distract yourself with some self-care. As your inner child begins to heal, you'll feel less need of your previous survival mechanisms; you'll feel safer, because you've finally got you.

Picture your inner child. How old are they? What do they look like, how are they dressed? Do they look happy, or was there a traumatic moment or a loss of a loved one that happened that locked them at this specific age? Imagine them standing in front of you or, if you find that hard, draw them in your journal so you have something to focus on. Ask yourself:

- How do you feel towards them? How do they feel towards you? Do you even want to spend time with them?
- What's good about your inner child's life? If you were going to spend a bonding afternoon with them, what fun or creative activity would they ask to do? (Then go and take yourself to that activity.)
- How did your inner child express their emotion, or struggle to? Who do they go to with their emotion, or how does it manifest itself? Who do they learn it from? Journal on how you do the same things. How do they align?
- Can you reconnect with people who they were friends with, even though you're all grown up? What other things might make you feel nostalgic and help you to reconnect with them?
- Check in with your inner child each night before you fall asleep, checking in on their mood and what they say to you. It could be anything. Listen to them and wish them goodnight. Watch how you start making decisions with them in mind and make more self-loving choices. Realise how you owe it to yourself and them to see what self-love could do for you. What do you have to lose?

PART III

5

Throat Chakra: The Man Break

Affirmation: I commune with the Universe because I know it always wants to help. I am worthy and fulfilled without a partner. I practise my affirmations out loud with confidence, self-love and respect and when I speak my intentions, miracles unfold.

I was just a few days into my man ban, hiatus, holiday, whatever you want to call it, but I was down on my knees once more.

No, not like that.

Despite the withdrawal symptoms, I was no longer at the mercy of a man. I was at the mercy of me.

Down there on the floor, I was swimming under my bed to retrieve clothes I was selling. I was making space in my physical life as much I was in my mind, now no particular man was taking up room in it without paying rent. I was detaching from the old man-chaser version of me however I could, even from the clothes she wore to woo guys. May as well make a penny on past me, I thought, while I try to unearth my natural spark with myself.

When we break up with someone or something, it's rarely just for the reason we blame at first. I may have been breaking up with dating, but I was in fact also breaking up with my relationship with high expectations of others, with constant conversations with friends about dating, with the compulsion to check my phone twice a second. Maybe I'd uncover even more reasons as the break-up went on. Now I was prioritising the relationship with *myself*. It was late October, and though it was cuffing season, when singles tend to shackle themselves to one another so they have a definite date for Christmas and Valentine's Day, I was taking off my handcuffs and throwing away the key. Would I tell the guy I met after it that I hadn't had sex in a year? What would they think of it? I didn't know who I was going to *be* then anyway.

Connecting the flow

Just as the man break is the bridge from one part of our dating history to the next, so is the throat chakra the bridge from the lower four chakras, root, sacral, solar plexus and heart, to the two higher ones, third eye and crown. The former represent physical earthly matters whereas the latter are more in tune with our cosmic and spiritual lives. This is literally the plot twist of all your healing, the Tower moment, the middle act, if you will. This is where the magic really begins.

Concerned with speaking your inner truth, the throat chakra couldn't be linked to a more apt chapter in this book if I'd tried. The throat chakra is known as *vishuddha* in Sanskrit, which means pure, and you might be feeling pure with the lower four chakras unlocked. Just wait until you see how your throat chakra unblocks with affirmations I'll share. With this more balanced fifth chakra, you'll inspire others to share by creating a ripple effect of gentle honesty and authenticity.

Your altar can be anywhere or anything

Whether we are single or coupled up, especially when we're healing or in a life transition, I can't stress enough the importance of having our own happy place. Even if it's only a corner of a bedroom, a space next to the bath, or car dashboard, or designated journal or a place outside our home like a yoga studio or loved one's graveside, we all need a quiet sanctuary. A place with no judgement or triggers to meditate in, to actively feel our feelings in. Even a place we can metaphorically store those emotions, so we don't have to carry them all around with us, weighing us down. Instead, we can detach, view and release them. Even your desk, littered with rings, candles and crystals, can be a happy, safe and beautiful space if you approach it with that mindset.

We don't have to be spiritual to know when we've outgrown someone or somewhere, but when we do realise we need to move on, an attuned intuition sure comes in handy to help us make the right moves forward. A house share like mine had so many lives, stories and stale energies packed into its walls, I could feel the mortar almost exploding. It would need an industrial amount of sage to clear. Our landlady became more and more overbearing, turning up every day without notice, threatening mess with fines – that was my sign I'd saved up enough and had to skedaddle. She'd also moved in new couples who were all much younger than me, so the new student-house vibe, the triggering couple co-living situation and my memories of sex with the Model now I was abstaining all showed me it was also the right time to take my man break.

How you know you should take a man break

You know you need to give dating time out when:

- You get the good jitters not over men, but over moves that have nothing to do with a partner, like a new job, city, course or pet. Soon, those things fill the gap that dating left.
- You need your own love more. A break from dating is not just the absence of dates, it's the presence of self-love.
- You realise we're possibly only alive for 4,000 weeks and you know you've wasted approximately a quarter of them chasing men who don't chase you back. You realise you've got to spend the best love on yourself, like every day is your birthday.

- You realise a hyper-obsession with dating means you don't even have time for yourself, let alone friends.
- You want a relationship to escape loneliness, not to share love and life.
- You desperately want to meet someone, but it's just not happening for some unknown reason despite your being on all the apps most days.

Manifest like a spiritual single queen

Just watch; weird things start happening once you set a strong intention for your highest good and follow through. Dribs and drabs of extra money just to tide me over started trickling in. I got £100 by asking my bank for compensation for an error they'd made. I saved money by going vegetarian. I got a modest but rare pay rise from work for the successful magazine redesign I had led earlier that year. With this positive abundant energy mounting, I took to surfing property sites instead of dating apps, because I was certain what my deal-breakers were. Men are like property – you've got to know your needs. (And they are better in certain postcodes.)

When we sort our lives out, the upside is we become too busy to manhunt. I could barely even afford to take myself out for a drink either, let alone someone else. When I found the right place, the only man I'd be chasing would be my solicitor. Though I had the deposit from an inheritance and my own savings, I would still be mortgaged up to my eyeballs, and tried not to be jealous of all my couple friends buying much bigger first homes together with what looked like far more ease.

Let the deal-breaker lead

By letting the deal-breaker lead, you have an automatic filtering process. My biggest clincher was having somewhere outdoors

THROAT CHAKRA: THE MAN BREAK

where I could do my sun salutations. And by that, I mean have a glass of wine. Manifesting a man, I lead with a few most important deal-breakers: emotional availability, single, no kids. Everything else is just a bonus.

I found only one available flat with a balcony. But as with all things, partners, jobs, next moves, all you need is one special one to say 'yes'. One can change everything.

But life is not a fairy tale, and factors like price and affordability come into play. This perfect flat was out of my price range by a few grand. Well, if you look at those factors as technicalities, like the place is already yours, the man is already in love with you, you keep calm and let things work themselves out if they are meant to. I knew this flat had my name on it, and I believed the earth would move to make it mine. The legal bit just needed to catch up.

And it did. When price negotiations began, some cosmic estate agent in the sky must have donned a fantastic power suit, as I discovered the previous owner had gone to school with a close uni friend of mine. Thanks to the association, and a few thoughtful gifts I'd sent, the owner kindly made it possible for me to buy by coming down in asking price for me. And just like that, I had found my perfect first home, just because my landlady's annoying behaviour was forcing me out and my laptop had been stolen 18 months before in New Zealand, leaving my savings untouched with mounting interest. Everything had happened imperfectly perfectly. Maybe what we think isn't working out for us really does work out for us.

Manifest money

Money is a big topic that can trigger us, so if you're not ready to work with it yet, come back to it after working through the main abundance affirmations of this chapter. Money is just energy in a tangible form, and paying is just an energetic transaction. No wonder that as the cost of living crisis ensues, our collective energy seizes up in stress. We tighten our belts and, subconsciously, our jaws. It follows that to get into the energy of having an overflowing abundant bank account, we need to *believe* that we are worth all of that big, beautiful money energy. Here are some ways to be more financially abundant, so the Universe won't be able to help but rain on us with cash.

- Each new moon, especially the new moon in grounded, materialist earth signs Taurus, Virgo and Capricorn, add coins to your altar to signify abundance and set some savings goals for the next three months (these can be chocolate coins). On the full moons in those signs, if needed, burn notes that have your old money stories written on them, of tales where you lost money, where parents were careless with it or you constantly felt it slipping through your hands.
- Affirm each night 'I attract money to me every day, money loves me, I am naturally abundant', and every time you think of money, keep your thoughts positive and light. Be open to signs that it's working. If you catch adverts for high-interest savings accounts on TV, that is a sign. If you find a fiver in a pocket, that is also a sign. Be open and don't let anyone drag down your vibe – that is their fear talking.
- Pin a cheque or sketch of your banking app with a million pounds in it on your visualisation board. Imagine how it feels to be in possession of that much abundance, that much possibility. How would you invest it and keep that energy going and paying itself forward? Journal on how you'd treat yourself, your family, friends and community, what investments you'd make, how you'd grow your business, because that energy will come back to you tenfold. (If you just frittered it, that would be losing energy, and it would only speed itself up.)
- Take a practical perspective to aid the Universe's work: get a friend to look at what you are charging for work services. Are they too low, or in line with inflation? Do you need to ask for a promotion from your employer for all the great, consistent work you're doing, or are you ready for a step up elsewhere? Cut off energy-sucking subscriptions you don't use and open high-interest savings accounts to put in a pound a day or week.

Believe fully you are worthy of fantastic wealth, and it will come to you.

Hesitate or make excuses and your thoughts will likely be the block even the Universe's power can't get past.

Get your life back

On dating apps, it's possible to invest hours of your life with absolutely no guarantee of return. Maybe you'd get some matches and could look forward to a few lame messages of 'hi, how are you?' in the morning – whoopee. The one that most annoys me is when they superlike you but never reply – was it a slip of a thumb? It's hard not to overthink it, but speculation is such a waste of energy. Here's some spiritual single girl math: the chances of them even replying to your reply, then leading to a date, let alone a relationship, are exactly as low as your subconscious opinion of yourself.

As I moved into the relief stage of my break-up with all men, I regained approximately 40 per cent of my spare time and brain space. Were the apps the energy vampire all along? At 26, I had already spent ten years of my life waiting for a guy to notice me, not that those years weren't fun or fruitful in their own ways. We learn about ourselves through dating, but now we need to learn about ourselves solo. When life seems to speed up the second half of your twenties, that makes you want to make wiser, more conscious decisions with your precious energy. Tinder chats are temporary, just boosting the ego; self-love is in the soul, forever.

So if your problem is that you are love-starved, starve your natural tendencies. Switch your bedtime routine from never-ending swiping to chanting affirmations. As I flinched from the coldness of the rose quartz roller I was pressing into my faint crow's feet, I tried to trust the words would sink into my subconscious. Self-love had to be a better use of my time than 11.00 p.m. Tinder sessions, surely. I really needed some in-depth theory to trust it all the way and I knew exactly whose book to go to first.

Just as I hope this book will be a guide for your own dating break, Louise Hay's first book was a guide for me. She was, and still is in my eyes, the most influential self-love teacher that ever lived. She helped thousands of clients realise their afflictions, both emotional and, more controversially, physical, were energetically linked to a lack of self-love and self-acceptance. Then, as the inspiration she was, she wrote and published her book *You Can Heal Your Life* under her own company, Hay House, one I worked with on *Soul & Spirit* many times. Though she passed away two years before I became editor, I feel I owe Louise so much. I'll be sharing a few of my favourite techniques from her book in this chapter.

Remember, Louise Hay wrote: 'Affirmations are statements going beyond the reality of the present into the creation of the future through the words you use in the now.' So let's get started with a classic one.

I love and approve of myself exactly how I am

Start off slowly with this affirmation, out loud. Now say it again: I love and approve of myself exactly how I am.

How does that feel for you? Give it a beat. Say it a third time. Do you feel resistance or acceptance? Go to a mirror; can you look yourself dead in the eye in the mirror and say it? If not, what are you scared you might see? Relax – a lot of people struggle to really see themselves. Louise Hay reported there were days when her self-denial was so prevalent, she would occasionally slap her own face. And that was the original self-help queen talking. We all have those cringe moments when we feel self-conscious, but we've been conditioned to find anything for ourselves cringey. Please don't beat yourself up. It took me a few days to get used to it too.

If it's still too much, look at a photo of yourself that you like and go from there. If you can, repeat the affirmation above in the mirror 44 times a night for 28 days and feel the difference. If you get tongue-tied, it's a good sign – you're channelling now! Log how you feel in your journal. If you're ever in doubt, any time of day, night or type of situation, come back to this one affirmation. In fact, always come back to love, full stop.

Now personalise your affirmation

The classic affirmations will raise your general vibe, but a bespoke one will make more powerful change. Work through the following points to put together your own personal affirmation, then write it out in your journal and watch your life transform.

- Your first name starts with:
    - A–I – I naturally attract
    - J–R – I'm a magnet for
    - S–Z – I gladly welcome in

- Your star sign:
    - Aries – the confidence to achieve my dreams
    - Taurus – the means to make a wonderful life
    - Gemini – all the good things life has to offer
    - Cancer – the love of all those around me
    - Leo – beautiful experiences every day
    - Virgo – the abundance of the Universe
    - Libra – meaning in all that I do
    - Scorpio – the ability to see divine truth
    - Sagittarius – both freedom and grounding in life
    - Capricorn – the fun that the Universe provides
    - Aquarius – the sacred good innate in all humans
    - Pisces – the ability to communicate my needs and emotions

- Then your birth day number:
    - 1–10 – and let go of the need to compare myself to others
    - 11–20 – and release all my guilt and hurt from the past
    - 21–31 – and surrender the anxiety that holds me back

Write your personal affirmation in your journal and recite it 12 times a night, either just to yourself or looking in the mirror for full effect, then feel the difference in your natural confidence.

Cling on to your intention

As hard as modern dating can be, cutting it out can somehow seem even harder. As Louise Hay said, 'sometimes when we try to release a pattern, the whole situation seems to get worse for a while'. Maybe it's a cosmic test, maybe it's not, but I believe it just shows us what move we really want to play next. When I fell off the proverbial man break wagon and redownloaded Tinder, craving comforting words from a stranger, stressed from work and from the flat-buying process, Tinder totally flopped. And thank goddess it did. I got very few matches, and in 24 hours received two messages I did not feel at all inspired to respond to.

'This is not a bad thing,' Louise's words told me, quelling my inner fear of failure. 'It is a sign that the situation is beginning to move. Our affirmations are working, and we need to keep going.' I hear you, Louise. I clung on to my 'why', which was to start choosing myself and trusting the Universe was my cupid. I deleted the app again. 'We know deep down when we're ready', Louise wrote, 'to step out of the bondage of our past.' I loved that line; I couldn't help but summon a mental image of a troop of Spiritual Fuckboys in leather studded belts and reins.

Focus, please.

The time is always right

Leading a life with a solid self-love practice is like turning up the colour saturation on every day. However, a life dictated by a fearful, closed heart drones on with a rainy and dull pallor. That's why we have rose-tinted glasses on when dating, because we need to inject a bit of fake colour. Fear and ego are never going to ask more courage of you. That's why giving up something as addictive as dating is such a big life improvement. It takes bravery to become who we're meant to be.

It called to mind the time a friend in the spiritual industry said something that stuck with me. 'It took me to my forties to start the work, to become spiritual. You're so lucky to be doing it in your twenties,' she'd told me. If that was true, I'd take the opportunity now while I had most of my life ahead of me and hadn't procreated with any fuckboys, spiritual or not. They say the definition of insanity is trying the same thing over and over, without ever changing methods. Well, who has the time to be insane any longer?

Of course, if it hadn't come along at this point, it would have eventually, just like it came for my friend exactly when it did. Maybe this book is the sign you've been looking for. When our souls decide it's time to step up, we can't turn back even if we try. Our spirit squad can't be squashed.

Oh no, we can't, they repeated in camp pantomime fashion.

Alone but not lonely

Feeling alone, even though it's the thing we're most scared of, can be the thing that sets us free. The first time I was alone in my own flat was more electrifying than any one-night stand. Sorry, one-night show. I felt so much space to grow into, like a fish moved into a bigger tank that could now grow to its full potential. I ran around from wall to wall; I owned my own walls! I had a flat with shiny wooden flooring! I had my own kitchen! And the best bit, there were no locks on the outsides of the bedrooms, or noticeboards with rules in the hallway. I didn't have to compromise with any landlord or partner if I wanted to paint my walls pink, which made my inner child very happy.

With our solar plexus unlocked, and heart chakra in the process, we could activate our own healing even more when we become of service to others, too. Now that I had a lot of spare time, I needed to fill it with new friends.

That's right, girl, there's more out there in the sea for you than just fish! they said, mid-shimmy.

No longer on the lookout for men

It can be intimidating to go along to a new group alone. Especially one where you run multiple kilometres to volunteer in the January darkness. I usually leapt at the chance to meet new people, so I knew I was in a new stage of growth when I felt nervous to go along to a new running group. All those first dates and we're intimidated by more than one person's eyes on us at once.

'I am excited to make new friends, new experiences and new memories,' I chanted over and over on my way there. 'I will make *so many* friends, this will be good, it will be worth it, I will make my new best friends,' I continued, as if I was encouraging my shy inner child. I may have felt weird talking to myself on the street, but it was working. On days I find it hard to get to the desk to write, it helps too. The trick is to identify the fear that's stopping you and flip it into an active to drive that fear away. 'I am outstanding at my job' might make your inner narcissist scoff, but your brain can't tell the difference between lies and truth.

Now as the cheerleader chant goes, be aggressive, be, be aggressive! 'I am so fucking outstanding at my job I'm worthy of a promotion.' Don't tell me you don't get passionate when you're giving a friend a pep talk. That's the reckless, rebellious energy we want here. Heart open!

And that positive intention came through for me. I went back to volunteer again the next week, and the next, and the next, and cemented the best of friendships.

Try this bedtime manifestation ritual

This is where you go off-script. You're going to ad-lib your affirmations and spend time deciding what kind of partner you eventually want to bring into being. The more personal and specific to you, the better they'll work when you're ready to get back out there.

1   Stand in front of a mirror at the end of each day (or morning, if you're a morning person). Smile at yourself and give yourself permission to feel silly. Now start talking, knowing the Universe and your subconscious are listening, but no one else is.

2   As if you are channelling something, start telling yourself things about your perfect partner, or whatever it is you're calling in. Go back to your needs list on page 130 and start describing the person who can fulfil all of them. 'I love my boyfriend, he's so funny and buys me flowers every day. He makes an amazing cup of tea. He's so much fun and smart, my partner is so grounded, so self-aware, so calm and oh my god, so damn funny.' Talk them up like a mother talks up her single son. Smile at how good they sound – they're yours, after all!

3   Keep chatting about your partner as you go about your normal routine, brushing teeth, or making the bed. Talk about how they look at you, how they move, what their quirks are, and simply describe what you see. Alternatively, sketch them and pin them up in your bedroom or bathroom. For example, I want a companion, someone who makes me laugh first and foremost, and I'd probably be pulling silly faces at thin air and talking in stupid accents to this imaginary person (which is why you need to be alone to do this). Do this every night and the Universe will start to concoct the version of this *you are ready for at that moment.*

Know what growth looks like for you. You want to know that your little affirmation ritual is paying off so that when they arrive, you can grab the opportunity quickly. What would signify your growth? List three things that would show your work was worth it – a sense of inner peace? The ability to go three days without swiping and not caring? Telling someone you're dating your truth rather than lying to avoid shame? Matching with someone you fancied but actually just becoming good friends because that aligns better?

Boost manifesting with masturbation

Now for the fun bit. It's very simple – do your thing, and as you get there, picture the exact person you'd described in your affirmations. Picture the actor who'd play them in a movie, at least (hello, Henry Cavill), or if you're not a visual person, hold the words in your head. Ride the wave all the way through a movie montage of them, their appearance, their quirks, a scenario you'd imagined, romantic or otherwise. Use all that orgasmic energy to superboost your intention out there, especially powerful on a new moon in a Fire sign. The Universe won't miss this concoction.

Don't feel lame, because let's be honest – we all picture someone, so it may as well be someone we've designed to our exact needs. When we say we are horny, we're just identifying lack, so let's charge up our sexual imagination with abundance. It's the same as with affirmations; if our brain believes what we tell it, then surely we'll be as satisfied as if it had really happened. And horny someones can't date from a place of lack – it's like going food shopping hungry.

Just be careful not to picture your ex, because on the next Mercury Retrograde that's exactly who might appear.

And if you accidentally picture the wrong person, because our minds like to play that cruel trick on us, don't worry. The Universe knows you don't want to date your old maths teacher.

Saturn Return incoming

Ah, you never forget the moment someone tells you how Saturn is going to hit your birth chart and turn your life upside down in the most cosmic, chaotic way possible. It happens at around 29 years old and transforms you through challenge. Think back to when you were 29 – did you go through a big transition of some sort? Women seem to dread their 30th birthday, feeling the body clock ticking far too fast (it's worth noting that men's sperm start to deteriorate at 35, but no one talks about that). I believe we should celebrate our 30ths even bigger and brighter for surviving the challenges our Saturn Return brings!

As well as joining my running group, and manifesting my man into existence, I was also having another first that month. Now you know how to read your natal (birth) chart, see if you can read which house your Saturn sits in. At my first astrology workshop in February, I learnt that mine would hit in my 'house of relationships', my seventh house, making my love life transform in some way. If this transit meant I was going to become betrothed to my soulmate, I had three years of single time left. Plenty of time to learn to love myself so well that I could welcome him in.

It all fell into place – one year of celibacy, maybe two years practising conscious dating and sharpening my relationship skills, then bam, he'd appear. Yes, that was definitely the Universe's plan. The same as any writer, I thrived on now having a deadline. I was feeling epic, unstoppable, unrockable – my man break was totally working, and I was all mine. Then Valentine's Day came around.

As with anger, envy is healthy

No day divides a society like Valentine's Day. Luckily, spiritual single girls aren't the only ones to scoff at the consumerist chaos it brings. Married mum friends of mine could take it or leave it, that's if they even know it's Valentine's at all when they're covered in baby sick. On Valentine's Day 2020, feeling like The Most Single Person in the World even though I'd consciously chosen not to date, I got to a point where I would have swapped it for the baby sick.

I believe, if anything, envy can energise our manifestations. Two of my girlfriends had had baby girls that morning, and though I was so happy for them, I found myself with an icky case of the green-eyed monster. Our lives already seemed to have taken different paths. Why them, not me? Well, my life had not been conducive to family life, and we must meet our manifestations in the middle. As I write now, I see envy as a good thing – it showed me that I wanted my own partner and little girl one day. By acknowledging

181

what we want, on all levels of our being, we call it into our life. I'd end up having exactly the type of little girl that could fit into my life by adopting Tabitha, a Leo, later that year (I'm not saying your pet should have the same Sun sign as your Rising, but it helps). As for the partner, I had more belief blocks to burst before they could show up. We'll go into this shadow work soon.

But envy is a cunning emotion, and if you don't roadblock it immediately with a plethora of quick self-love affirmations, it can spiral fast into feelings of unworthiness. If self-love was a ladder, envy was a snake. As soon as I let myself into my friends' empty London flat where I was crashing, I rode the snake all the way down into triggers and tears. Coping mechanisms such as sex or alcohol, even just attention to validate our ego, can cover over our sore wound. In the past, I would have got straight on Tinder to fill this painful, gaping gash, and I know I would have found what I needed.

But I had a man pact with myself to keep. If I broke it, how could I ever trust myself again? It called for me to do three things instead: eat some chocolate, plug into a self-love guided meditation and pray to the Universe to help me feel easier. As I softened with each word I repeated after the host, phrases like 'I am worth everything I desire', my voice broke. Not like Showergate with self-pity but from self-compassion. I felt the release with each teardrop on my open hands at my sacral; my parasympathetic state coming back to balance.

You are still here, still loved, still important, without a romantic interest telling you that on some specified day. It's not meant to be my life right now, but it will be at some point, I mumbled out loud to myself. *This* is the work I must do first. Saving myself, rather than looking for a friend to save me, was huge progress. I simply needed to be with myself and let the Universe wipe my tears away, stroke my hair and rub my shoulders, telling me it was going to be okay. So it was, and so it is.

Ask yourself why

Imagine your inner child constantly asks 'but why?' to all of your decisions. Conscious living is questioning our habits and deciding if we want to carry them forward or not. Enjoying the experiment of the man break, I was willing to rebel, to push my known limits anywhere, try anything to feel more at home in myself, get down to deeper layers of myself. So, when it was time to shave, I chucked the razor away instead. Boycotting Valentine's Day by going to a rave with my guy mates instead led to boycotting stereotypical beauty standards too.

I'd been an adult for almost ten years, but I still had never seen my body as nature intended. It suddenly struck me: why did we shave away pubic hair like we're trying to infantilise ourselves? Habit just wasn't a good enough reason anymore. In fact, consciously ask yourself: what else is habit not a good enough reason for anymore? Wanting kids? Wearing make-up every day? People-pleasing?

I didn't want to be a perfectly groomed woman anymore. I didn't even want to try. That girl in the acro yoga class didn't. For the sake of experimenting, I would become living nature. After a few weeks, I felt primal and powerful. As a friend once said to me, and she has more recently proven to be true, it is absolutely the last thing a man in his Divine Masculine is bothered by when you're getting down to business.

Keep grounded with the moon

Another way to keep yourself mindfully in the magic of your life (and no one else's), as I was discovering, is by lunar living. It's more practical than it may seem, and we won't find these answers in our Tinder conversations.

Each time there is a new or full moon, take note of the zodiac it is in. Its zodiac sign can guide us on what to manifest under that new moon and what to release under that full moon. In theory you'll be doing a moon ritual of some kind every two weeks, in probably exactly the same time it would have taken me to shave my underarms, legs, bikini line and upper lip (but don't tell anyone). Here's some more spiritual single girl math for you: after 12 months of these rituals, once all the zodiacs have had their new and full moons, each part of life will have been examined, so if you're on the right vibration, everything you want will come to you. That's why a birth chart has 12 houses – each represents a different part of life.

Your senses are your survival

Your senses are telling your soul you're still alive. By living in tune with the moon, and growing acceptance of what you see in the shower each day and the mirror each night, start to realise how much more sensitive you're becoming. This is good – don't let anyone tell you otherwise. Our senses are where our power lies.

While raising your consciousness, be prepared to become as porous as a sponge to your surrounding energies. Make sure to use your rose-gold energy shield on page 34 daily. The energy in the world did not feel good in 2020 with Harvey Weinstein's criminal trial hogging the headlines. The office didn't feel good either; everyone was talking about working from home in plans to guard against some upcoming epidemic, but I loved sparking off my colleagues in person. Stress made me wake up instantly at 5.00 a.m., the light from the March full moon in Virgo shining straight into my eyes. It asked me the very Virgoan question; how was I going to keep that zodiac's central focus of structure and organisation in my life cooped up alone?

The spiritual community had been predicting for years that 2020 was going to be a transformative year. In numerology, repetition of numbers is very powerful and creates what's called a master angel number. One such number is 1111 and is the one people around the world know. Spiritual or not, they tend to make a wish. Another number is 2020, which is also what we'd call a master angel number. And no one could predict how this master number year was going to go; even the best psychics could just feel the energy changing.

An awakening resource like *Soul & Spirit* magazine thrived in lockdown. However, single people across the country, myself included, did not. You have my express permission, if the shit hits the fan, to put any self-love-only vow on hold and bubble up with whatever person you can with the nicest manners, best banana bread recipe and widest-open arms. After three weeks, having nothing living to touch other than a (semi-dying) plant or myself, I had to move home. No man is an island – and neither is any woman, however let down by love she feels.

Special times call for special boundaries

For the sake of us all, I needed some special boundaries when moving back with my mother during an international crisis. Putting my maturity and growth to the test, I sent her a lightly toned message which was very serious in content. 'As long as we don't talk about three things – my weight, my sex life or my love life – I think we'll be just fine.' I shoved a few crying laughing emojis in for good measure. If we simply discussed the weather, my work and Boris Johnson, I'd be fine with that. That's the thing about boundaries; they're like clear, communicative pointers that say, 'this is how to love me best'. They worked wonders. I could love my body in peace, treat it with chocolate when I wanted and stretch it with my regular running and yoga practice.

And there was still Tinder. Come the apocalypse, there will be supermarket trolleys, fridges and Tinder left. Bored with video calls with friends, all of whom were playing fun lockdown games with their partners, I needed to see if I was missing out on all the Tinder matches. Fortunately, I got fewer matches than the last time. It seemed people in my area weren't even bothering swiping, probably because there was no sex in it. That, or I was already the reverse of the fuckboy magnet I was a few months earlier, and thank the Universe for that. Tinder is a great mirror for checking your spiritual energy levels, because you get instant feedback.

It's time for shadow work

Life coach Teal Swan calls this Parts Work, with the theory that our inferiority complexes make up many different fragments of our selves. We can have hundreds if not thousands of these many 'parts' that make us, us. When we look externally and don't like what we see, when we judge, blame and criticise, we need to pause and consider what shadow energies we are avoiding looking at internally. Change internally, see the difference externally. It's so simple, so empowering and so accessible, I'm almost mad this basic principle of manifestation isn't taught in schools!

Imagine jealousy at a friend's engagement. What belief lies beneath this feeling? Envy? What's under that? Perhaps resentment. What's that telling you? They're better than me. But is that true? No. It all comes down to the old chestnut: 'I'm not good enough.'

Go again with disappointment, loneliness, horniness. Does it also boil down to the tune of 'I'm not good enough'?

Where did that come from? Explore your childhood, your relationship to your parents, to your siblings. Think back to your formative friendships, relationships and break-ups. What was the messaging you kept getting?

Now how do you feel towards those external things? Remind yourself that those people are coming from where they are, so not to take anything personally. Your beliefs are your problem. How are you going to release the emotions so they can come to the surface?

Where are they stored? Put your hand there and feel the emotion. Feel angry, disappointed, heartbroken. It's safe. Even say out loud, 'I don't feel good enough' and repeat it, over and over. This can be intense because you are intentionally triggering your core wounds. Breathe deeply, exhaling for twice as long as your inhale. Go to the next emotion and place on your body, using your hands to hold yourself there.

Now journal everything that's been weaponised against you, or that you've weaponised against yourself. Embrace them. In your journal, write: I embrace my (shadow part) because without it, I wouldn't be able to (list one of your strengths).

Drink water and rest as this shadow energy ebbs its way out of you.

Remember how each chakra has a back that looks out into the world? Shadow work also works on an international scale. We must use our throat chakra to speak up and speak out on matters close to our heart, rather than watching from the sidelines. While healing ourselves heals the world too, we have to actively call out discrimination when we see it. It's not all love and light out there, but the Divine Feminine knows this.

Needing our needs

If this man break feels like a year-long retreat, we're doing it right. Well done. The next workshop is on, drum roll please: needing our needs.

It turns out, our need for familiar experiences, those we had before awakening to radical self-love, is what blocks us from happiness. It would be funny if it wasn't so damn annoying. See it this way: we go for fuckboys because we know exactly how they work, so we know how to work around them. When they send the Doom Text, we know when to put our emotional armour on, throw our hands up and go 'I knew this would happen'. We know they'd never come through, and we depend on it. We know we'll always be the black sheep single one of the family because we know how to play that role. Until someone gives us the playbook on how to break out of that role … ta-da!

That was my problem right there – I was attracting people who would disappoint me because my ego needed to be right. We feel comfy being the fuckgirl to our fuckboys. My beliefs were blocking a brilliant, trustworthy and loving man from stepping into my life. We need to work on the relationship we have with our needs.

Break up with your needs

When we are attached to outcomes, we cling. To detach ourselves and get us back into flow, so we can be surprised for once, Louise Hay tells us to admit that we ourselves have created the condition. The first step to empowerment is to take responsibility, after all. Add the affirmation 'I am now willing to release the pattern in my consciousness that is responsible for this condition' to your nightly roster and repeat it 12 times each night.

Then break up with more needs. Say the affirmation 'I am breaking up with the need to feel … about (your preferred gender).' Mine is: 'I am breaking up with the need to feel disappointed in men.' As these words permeated my consciousness, I started to see that, though flawed like us all, I didn't find my dad, brother and male friends disappointing. They were there when I needed them, loving me how they could best. So why do we group all men into the disappointment doghouse? The statement 'all men are shitbags' will only be true if you believe it.

So we flip the switch on our deeper-rooted beliefs. Add to your affirmation roster each night, 'My relationships always encourage my freedom and exploration.' As I said it for the first time, a smile came to my face, and I immediately started feeling energetic handcuffs tying me to old boyfriends dissolve just a tiny bit. I felt stronger, sturdier and excited to explore new things with someone new. It's all about the feeling.

If you want to go one step further (and you can never go too far) write these affirmations across your mirrors, on sticky notes, anywhere you'll see them multiple times a day. Friends may think you've gone crazy, but it reinforces your positive outlook each time. And when friends can't read your handwriting, it turns to Chinese whispers. 'Every time I take my pants off I give up the need to be disappointed?' one friend asked, piecing together my scribbles.

'Every chance I take pays off, I give up the need to be disappointed in men,' I corrected her. Well, at least you know your displayed affirmations will stay private.

Remember to be kind to yourself

Remember that having some deep realisations of what you've been subconsciously hanging onto will zap your energy. You may resist admitting to using some beliefs for keeping you safe or using other people for your own validation. That's okay – shadow work like this is difficult, but we won't dwell in our darkness because we live in our light. You're not an awful person for doing what you've done in the quest for love, because we've all done it. Shake off guilt – it will only block your manifestations from moving.

Take a deep breath and sense what's happening to your body as you release the habits. You may have some 'aha' moments, but also do welcome any tears that need to come. If you start to begrudge yourself, take yourself back a few steps and acknowledge it from a distance, resisting the need to let it attack your self-worth. Soothe yourself with sympathy and self-love affirmations such as, 'I am enough, I am worthy, I am loved'. You are practically writing a Bye Bye Bye List to what's keeping you playing small, so that you can grow into the person you were always meant to be. Be patient with yourself, practise lots of self-care and come back to this need-releasing practice when you think of more that might need blasting.

Three meditations for an instant boost

When you next have at least 15 minutes to yourself, set up your bathroom like a spa retreat. Put some low-volume, high-frequency healing music on (if in doubt, Enya), light some candles, leave your phone out of reach and don't let anyone in, even if the cat paws at the door. Run a bath with Himalayan or Epsom salts to draw out any toxins and relax your muscles.

1   **A body-scanning meditation for instant peace**
    This is also ideal when negative narratives in your mind start
    spiralling and you need to wind them in. Close your eyes and
    send your focus straight to your feet, asking yourself about the
    sensations you feel there with this concentrated awareness. Put
    your full attention on one body part at a time; how do your toes
    feel as you wiggle them? How does the hard surface of the bath
    feel against the balls of your feet? Take a deep breath and send
    the fresh oxygen down to the cells there, relishing the feeling of
    connecting with a part of your body we normally treat badly or take
    advantage of. Slowly do the same as you move your attention up
    your body, finishing at the crown of the head. Breathe in a deep
    sense of presence, knowing you deserve to take up your rightful
    place in the world.
2   **A Gratitude Gaze to feel loved**
    This is one of my favourite self-love techniques that allows me to
    compliment myself for being the divine, gorgeous goddess I am. You

can also do this naked, clothed or in lingerie in front of a mirror, depending on how comfortable you feel. With your eyes open, soften your gaze, as if you're looking at a beloved partner. Raise one part of your body at a time out of the bath, mentally putting on rose-tinted glasses as you inspect this limb.

How beautiful it is, you tell yourself silently or, if you're feeling confident, aloud. Really listen to each word deliberately, and programme your mind to believe what you hear. I know it might feel unnatural, but your subconscious really needs to hear it, so do it for the inner you. Notice how shapely this part of your body is, how unique it is. We're not talking about classic beauty by society's standards here, we're not talking about comparison at all, just you as a stand-alone human. How you love the adorable freckles on your arms, how you actually enjoy the round suppleness of your own breasts or chest. Wow, you've never actually realised how naturally elegant your fingers are, or given yourself grace for how cute your kneecaps are.

This is even more worth doing with areas on your body you don't love as much. Feel the resistance and carry on anyway. Describe these body parts in your mind with even more compliments and love, not being afraid to go overboard. For example, if it's your tummy you're not keen on post-baby, pay it huge gratitude for having grown the best human in the world, having given them a safe home for nine months. Thank each part of your body for being exactly as it is; it's beautiful because it's all yours. This could lead to ad-lib affirmations (from your bedtime manifestation ritual, page 178), because the point is to channel and improvise loving words without much mental thought. Incorporate a light touch from your fingertips as you stare at your body, treating it like a lover would, marvelling at how soft your skin is, because in this moment, you are wooing yourself as if you were your own lover. Incorporate tantric touch as a tool too. Tantra is not just about sex from the 1970s but more an ancient connection technique from the sixth century. Just warm up your hands before rubbing them where you're feeling tension to generate good energy.

3 Scan your chakras

Follow the body-scanning meditation above but instead of limb by limb, go from bottom chakra to top chakra, following the illustration of the chakras (see below). From the root chakra, take three deep breaths, and as you exhale each time visualise your outbreath causing this red chakra to spin faster and brighter, as if it's a plastic pinwheel at the beach. Move up to your sacral chakra, imagining this as even more orange, and then your solar plexus chakra, willing this to glow with a brighter yellow colour, and so on.

You could even incorporate touch too, massaging your body space where each chakra sits, generating warmth there as if

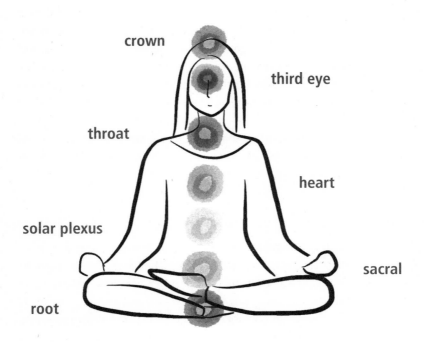

to encourage their energetic vigour. As you learn more about chakras, and yourself, you might even feel one slightly out of linear alignment with the others, so imagine popping it back into place like an energetic chiropractor. In your mind's eye, you'll finish with seven glowing rainbow lights all in line up your spine, and you'll feel energised, buzzy and electric. My shortcut is placing my hands straight on my heart when I'm feeling a little anxious or down to start healing where it's needed most.

After doing these rituals a few times, notice how you start to react differently towards your body when you get dressed or catch it in a mirror. You might start eating more mindfully or taking more gentle, mindful exercise, too. That's because you'll start *caring* about yourself, and isn't that the basis to any strong long-term relationship? With enough regularity, you might also be able to keep calmer in stressful situations and focus better on tasks. Remember, all of these should be done as an act of loving kindness to yourself, not in a hurry, or as a chore, or with any self-criticism. Any time you feel like you want to criticise yourself or a part of your body, pause, take a deep breath, and remember that voice comes from somewhere external. Each of us is incomparably unique. But remember, if a friend was saying hurtful things to themselves, you'd probably be the first to leap in to help them see themselves with more love. Can you be that friend to yourself?

If you'd rather seek company instead, be my guest. But this book has hopefully already shown you how using mindless sex as a self-care strategy gets frustrating.

Self-love in sacred movement

As we step into our Divine Feminine, we hold so much sexual energy in our bodies that we have to move it through. Get down to your local studio for some yoga, if only to watch the hot guy but pretend not to, or do this sacred movement ritual.

Friday is the day of love in Norse mythology, after Freya, the goddess of love, lust, abundance and fertility. The Cure had it right with the song 'Friday, I'm in Love'. Though we might want to spend our weekends having sex, if we're single or the world is locked down, put down your phone and dance. If you feel stuck in a rut, then this ritual will help you move like your life depends on it, even while you're sober!

THROAT CHAKRA: THE MAN BREAK

Animals use their bodies to release stress, but as humans, we're up in our heads all the time, overthinking and ruminating endlessly. Meditation and stillness work too, but this is a different discipline in that there is none. Let your body evaporate your negativity by getting the good energy pumping again and know that this physical self-expression through somatic movement (with the intention being more conscious of how good it feels rather than how good it looks) is also working wonders for your throat chakra.

Incorporate the tantric touch from the Gratitude Gaze into this mindful movement flow below and get somatic dancing! It's great for your soul, mind and body.

1   Put on some music that always gets you dancing, whether it's techno rave, funky 1970s disco beats or classic spiritual music like drumming, chanting or crystal sound bowl music.

2   Light an incense, sage or palo santo (holy wood) stick with a match and blow out the flame. Breathe in the musky scent, close your eyes and invite any negativity to slide off you. In any way that feels good, start slowly moving from side to side.

3   As though the smoke is a ribbon from a circus workshop, wave your smoking stick round your body with an extended arm and dramatic movement, spinning or moving side to side or forward and back as you do. Wave it round your chakras where you need it most, or your groin to exorcise any leftover fuckboy energy from your sacred sex area. Wave it round your crown and just above to cleanse the seven disembodied chakras above your head too. Remember to keep breathing deeply and release your throat chakra even more by singing along to the music, humming or making any sound that feels natural.

4   Pick up the pace of the music, moving your body more quickly now. This is called ecstatic dance, when all your inhibitions have dropped, and you are moving intuitively without thought. When you feel called to, or when the healing smoke has all gone, come to sit down, smiling, palms up to surrender to the Universe.

5   Sit down and recover your breath and journal in answer to these

prompts: I feel ....; I desire ....; I release ....;
I celebrate ....; I trust ....

We become easier to love

Now you're not always fretting about what that guy's thinking, or why that other one unmatched you, you can do all the fun, valuable things you never had energy to before. Learn Reiki, go on a crystal course, get massages with the money you'd have spent on dates with losers anyway, or channel more love into your relationship with your kids, friends, creative ideas or home ... your transformation possibilities are endless. One friend I shared the man break magic with has grown her Reiki side-business into a successful corporate service, simply from cutting loose the guys she'd small-talk texted with for months. Those people will lead you nowhere, but your potential can take you everywhere.

I would recommend not using your new-found spare time and creative energy to take on more work, as I did.

Now, I put being able to work so well down to the self-care routines, plus my new ability to let myself off the hook and be more self-compassionate. I was totally clear and creative again. My inner child was loving it, but I hadn't felt this free even at school, because even back then I always fancied someone. Then I landed a freelance writing gig with a different magazine, rebuilding my savings but burning me out almost as much as dating did.

How do you know you're awakening?

A lot of people report the following symptoms, but if in doubt, consult a spiritual professional or healer.

- You do all the intuitive exercises on page 111 without even realising.
- You feel pulled to haunted places, or spaces a spirit has imprinted on. Your emerging psychic connection can help the spirit be

acknowledged and move on. Don't be scared by this — a lot of psychic mediums swear that some humans are scarier than spirits.

- You are aware of a stuck energy inside you without knowing its root cause but use holistic rather than materialistic means to clear it.
- You see a mirror in everything and everyone; everything is a sign of your vibration. It's a *lot*.
- Technology seems to fail more often and for no reason.
- You have more vivid dreams but you lean in for any messages, and you try lucid dreaming, astral travel and dream journaling for waking life wellness.
- You start to be grateful for colds because you see them as opportunities to detox and purge negative energy from your body.
- When you feel a sore throat coming on, you wonder if you're withholding a truth that needs telling.
- Nature, peace and solitude are the only ways to still your monkey mind, which you can now separate from yourself and know you are not your thoughts.
- You feel an aversion to former non-serving habits such as certain drugs or alcohol, or at least much less interest in them than before. You subconsciously prefer to keep your mind and body, and thus your spirit, clearer and purer. The opposite to addiction is not sobriety, it's connection.
- You consult Louise Hay's research for psychosomatic symptoms while you're waiting for a doctor's appointment.

Enjoy main character energy

The by-product of a more distilled intuition is main character energy. You may pick up on things you don't want to know, as in this guy is just in it for sex, or she actually wants your contacts, not your friendship. As you awaken, it can be hard to keep centred in your own experience when you are so distracted by the loud outer world. If you get attuned to Reiki energy by a Reiki master, this will be even truer. Stay in that rose-gold egg (page 34) as much as you can in this growth phase.

But all in all, it will give you a positive, buzzy energy that will make others flock to you. Do not waste this precious energy on Tinder; instead, channel it back into your healing like a self-saucing pudding. Do not think you are magically psychic, too, because sometimes we over identify with the path we think we are on, get attached to an outcome and fall into disappointment. Spirituality is being *sure* of yourself and *open* to the future.

Have a heart chakra glow-up

This meditation is a lovely one to open your heart like a lotus flower and become more confident, attractive and successful.

1 Go somewhere you can't be disturbed. Sit down against a wall or bed headboard, back straight, hands resting on your knees, your legs either out in front of you or cross legged. Take a deep inhale, and on the exhale through the nose, smile. Repeat five more times, smiling wider each time. Place your hands on your heart chakra space and imagine your heart like a closed lotus flower.

2 On the next deep inhale, in your mind's eye, take all the fresh breath there. Get into the rhythm of inhaling goodness straight into your heart and exhaling any tension and negative talk out. Feel your heart expand, and now, the petals of the lotus flower are starting to open. The stronger you feel your own love, the more they will flutter open with the breeze of each inhale. They may flutter back closed with the exhale, but each movement is progress.

3 Visualise the lotus flower opening up more and more. Don't rush this; instead, delight in how much lighter you're feeling now. You may even be sitting up straighter, chest prouder. Be happy for you, as if the future you is in front of you, telling you have someone to look forward to.

4 Slowly open your eyes, blinking softly. Follow it up with a cuppa, some cacao or something sweet. Remember, your whole soul, all

the trillions of cells in your body, love you deeply. It's time you did too.

Awakening trust in men again

One surprising perk of the man break is it's quite rewarding to know you are off bounds to men. They can't have you, even if they want you. And even if you secretly fancy them, it's good to stop and remind yourself of your 'why', before you get carried away in expectations. I can't, and refuse to, stop you having harmless interactions that may or not be flirting, because we're spiritual, we're not *nuns*. But this time, you will know that you can always choose yourself instead of them. If they're nice, and when you are free to date, choosing them will also mean choosing you and your best interests.

Even if you meet that person, it will have to be slow burn, and their waiting will only prove to you that they're serious (actions show someone's true intention far clearer than words). But Ros, what if I meet the love of my life? I hear you cry. Well, they will have to wait until you're ready. That's right, men, it's ladies' choice.

But if no such miraculous love has knocked on your door, you'll know the man break is working when you're greeted with much nicer mirrors. Though lockdown was accidentally the perfect time to retreat from dating, I did have consistent social interaction. Luckily I had a Friend for that.

You know the Friend. They're so nice and totally your type – your *new* type, that is. They are the Wise Man, if you say so yourself. They're not a Spiritual Fuckboy or Spiritual Narcissist; those are in the past. You met them at one of the new groups you joined; you know, the one where you went to meet like minds to make friends but caught a crush too? The friend you watch reality TV with, albeit remotely because it's still lockdown. The friend you speak to every day. The friend you learn about and teach them about you. The friend you cloud scry together, that is, scribbling shapes on pictures of clouds, then disagreeing because it didn't look like a face, it looked like a jellyfish.

'I think he likes you, you know.' Mum wiggled her eyebrows as she walked in on a video chat one night.

Not helping, Mother.

Make your own mystic pizza

In his book *The Mastery of Love*, don Miguel Ruiz talks about a magical kitchen within our home. 'In that magical kitchen,' he writes, 'you can have any food you want from any place in the world in any quantity … You are very generous with your food; you give your food unconditionally to others, not because you want something in return from them.

'Then one day someone knocks at your door, and it's a person with a pizza. You open the door and the person looks at you and says, "Hey, do you see this pizza? I'll give you this pizza if you let me control your life, if you just do whatever I want you to do. You are never going to starve because I can bring pizza every day. You just have to be good to me."'

Sound familiar? This is a classic fuckboy with an agenda – to use you for the Girlfriend Experience but never ask you to be his girlfriend. Our pre-man break selves go, 'Oooh, for little old me? You shouldn't have!' We forget we can make our own better, cheesier pizza, with zero control for toppings. As we become dependent on their pizza, we become cursed by the deal. 'You can become a slave because of food,' Miguel writes.

'Your heart is like that magical kitchen,' Miguel points out. 'If you open your heart, you already have all the love you need. There's no need to go around the world begging for love.' Post-man break, we couldn't agree more. We find we can feed ourselves and anyone who wants with our love, with no conditions. We may open the door when it knocks, but smile sweetly and say, 'Oh, hi! Sorry, we're busy tonight. You can come in and join the open-hearted crew if you like. If not, have a great night.' If they turn down our generous invitation, we'll see it as their loss rather than any low worth on our part.

So, when the next fuckboy knocks on your door and says, 'You can only have my body, on the nights that I say, and I'm in an open relationship too, okay?' we can close the door in their face.

Codependency is emotional caretaking

If you take one thing away from this book, let it be this:

Our worth is so unattached to other people, and what they do.
Our worth is decided by us. And us alone.

That's why our man break time is so precious – it gives us time to decide what we, individually, are made of.

We look out for any way to serve someone we hold in higher esteem to ourselves, just for a hit of validation, be that a partner, a parent or boss. But when we go on a man ban, we look around us and see no partner to validate us. Really – no one we can measure our daily worth against? Nope. Does that mean we have to learn to do it for ourselves? Yes, it does.

When we've people-pleased all our lives, especially pleasing narcissistic people, we can feel scared to gaze down our own lane for the first time, and lonely too. We can second-guess ourselves that we're even in the right lane. It means believing our own pizza will feed us just fine, rather than assuming other people's pizzas are always better than ours.

Communication gets quicker

I had to learn fast when my older brother moved into my flat with me that summer. I had to lower my expectations and improve my communication in a flash, which I was able to thanks to a better-balanced throat chakra from all those affirmations. When he triggered my self-worth button by opting to spend time with friends over with me, I had to remind myself that my lane, my kitchen, my plans, my life, even my day was good enough without anyone who didn't want to be in it.

It doesn't matter what he does. It doesn't matter what anyone else does. Look down your own lane.

As one of my close work friends had said to me six months before, 'You just have to be okay with being on your own.' We might not want to be okay on our own, but we must be. It won't be forever, but it's where we start this new chapter of our love lives.

So, if people like Friend decide not to ask us out, that's okay, because we know we're good without their invitation. If they don't want to explore it further, that's nothing on us. It's just a non-alignment. We can acknowledge that someone's rejection or uncertainty of us stings, but not take it on ourselves to wonder why or scapegoat ourselves just to make it make sense. We will drive ourselves crazy if we wonder 'Did I come on too strong? Did he realise he liked me and then freaked out?' We should really trust them to communicate their truth anyway. Unless we feel comfortable or investigative enough to do the vibe-checker text, we just turn our attention back on our new default: ourselves. We were just over here looking pretty, and don't want anything that doesn't have our cosmic name tag on it.

It all comes down to trust; to trust our self-love foundations are strong when the dating game tries to rock us. To trust our partner will be along when we're both operating at our highest good. When you understand that the Universe wants the best for you, you can finally stop making the self-destruct choices and work with it. And post-man ban, these new trust tactics would be the secret ingredients to allowing the right things to flow into my life.

Slide back into swiping

So how do we keep that optimism but guard ourselves against the wrong people, I wondered? Over-seriousness can be more than a mood-kill, it can be a trauma response too, wanting to control the situation rather than see where it takes itself. I only wanted to step in on a situation, and on the Universe's toes, if I had to. But if I met the wrong people, and I inevitably would, I knew these self-love rituals would be my safety net. Life wouldn't just become a Disney film or Barbie Land, but I would be able to navigate the experiences I had far better. Just as when I came home from my travels, the world wasn't different, but I was. And girl, a year-long man ban is a journey into the self.

In both life and dating, keeping an open heart and mind is crucial, but so are boundaries. One thing I struggled with as I neared the end of my man break was knowing the sweet spot between being curious and cautious, two parts of me that had to now dance in tandem like yin and yang. I still wanted my person, more than ever, so much that it hurt sometimes, but now I finally understood that it wouldn't just happen overnight; I was working on the Universe's time, as we all are, and I was fuelled by the spirit of Louise Hay, and my two grandmother Bettys, and my spirit squad. As my love would make his way to me, I'd look up, smell the flowers and focus on me. I was still a romantic, but I was more hopeful than hopeless.

But there's a difference between healing and just the absence of dating drama. True proof of your development can only be drawn when you make different dating choices to before, and finally find fuckboy energy completely and utterly unattractive.

I had managed to reconnect with my own spark. Now I needed to reintegrate and put the three spiritual single girl commandments to the real test.

Three spiritual single girl commandments

These three commandments are designed to be easily memorable and always empowering. Imagine them like the slogans of your spiritual tag team, what they recite to you when you're down. They are the laws of thriving as a spiritual single girl, so have them in mind when in doubt.

- The First Commandment crowns self-love as the pinnacle objective, because the better you feel internally, the better you'll naturally attract externally.
- The Second Commandment reminds you, even when you don't believe it, *especially* when you don't feel it, that it's more than okay to be single.
- The Third Commandment is the holy grail, reminding you that if we swipe on dating apps with soul in mind, instead of ego, we can never lose. In other words, putting aside what we think we want and consciously choosing what we need.

The First Commandment

Dating is a mirror, so any self-love progress is instant to see.

Most people have heard of the concept of relationships as mirrors, where our partner shares and reflects our own insecurities and fears. We may vehemently deny it in some cases, denying that his mixed signals are identical to ours, or his lack of self-esteem has anything to do with ours, but it always does. We attract what we are. If we date half-hearted, we'll match with half-hearted. We also attract what we're willing to put up with. Fortunately, though, what this means is we can gain a close look at ourselves through our lover. We can be the change we want to see.

Every step you take towards a self-loving life, however subtle and however minuscule you think it is in the long run, can be shown with incrementally better matches. Becoming more conscious of your patterns? Meet a guy learning the same about himself. Started therapy? Here's someone who has too. Beginning to love your body more? Let me introduce you to a less vain, more lovely person than your ex. We talk about having things in common with new matches ... this means having more in common than just a favourite genre of music and a mutual friend or two.

The whole reason spirituality helps us grow, heal and understand is because it changes our day-to-day perspectives, which in turn influences our day-to-day lives. It works the same with love; with the right self-love practices, we can change our perspectives on ourselves, and see that progress radiating out into our love lives. Small changes in the sky, even by the tiniest degree of a zodiac sign (each zodiac has 30 degrees in an astrological chart), lead to big changes down here on Earth, in our lives. Small changes in our minds and hearts lead to big changes in our actions. That is why consistent rituals and positive self-talk every day mount up to big change to our subconscious.

I do believe some fate comes into it, but we are the catalyst, our own masters of change. How empowering to think that manifestation really bloody works: we do create our own world, and we see the return on investment straightaway!

Fuckboys: just say no

These boys won't change their patterns because of you and they won't choose to because they're dating you, and, sorry to say it, but you can't attract better than them either. Neither of you knows what's good for you. I know, this is easier said than done; sometimes they are too tempting to say no to and you are too beautiful to not try it on with. But we've got to get to the heart (or lack of) of *why* they're so tempting to us. Fuckboys have things to heal too, and these things usually centre around fear of commitment or rejection – just fear in general. They need their heart cracking open just as much as we might, because we are all just reflections of them. Get yourself away from their traumas and focus on your own. They're just a distraction, a smoking-hot smokescreen, from your getting what you really want in a partner. As Carl Jung said, 'where your fear is, there your task is'. I would translate that into modern-day speak as 'where your fuckboy addiction is, there your self-love work needs to be'. Know that you will find a man with a heart as gold as yours if you 'do the work', which is the rituals I've tasked you with in this book. It's the non-fuckboys who are the quietest and hardest to find, and who can help you heal as deep as spirituality can. They just don't have that flashy flirty energy of fuckboys we usually find irresistible, so don't be a magpie. Smash your paradigm and watch better things fall into place.

Trust in a higher power than Tinder

The reason the Alcoholics Anonymous (AA) programme works is the belief that there is a higher power helping to keep the recovering addict sober. It is the most integral element to the AA process. Bestselling author and survivor Stephen King prays to the god of his understanding in the morning and in the evening to say 'please' and 'thank you' for not letting him drink. It took me years to lean into self-love; I thought it was all too superficial for me, too fluffy. You'll know when you need to go sober from dating, to surrender and let spirituality catch you in its net, as is its purpose.

Just as how downward dog pose feels uncomfortable at the start of a yoga class, hardships like break-ups show us that we *can* stand discomfort, *we can* go no-contact with him, *we can* withhold boundaries and *we are not* the person they think you are. We are so much more than even we know. Spirituality helps us trust that when we're ready to go back on dating apps, or go out on the pull, we'll do it with conscious intention, wiser than we were with our former match.

When we 'do the work', we can pull ourselves back into our own life instead of getting lost in theirs as a distraction. Because to live in their life, where we can forget our problems, is unsustainable. We can never be our full self or live up to our potential there. We can't heal our inner child while we're camped out within other people.

Self-love and chill

Say no to people who want to 'Netflix and chill' with us. This is slang for having sex with background TV on to make a point of how casual and non-romantic your connection is. These people are typically after what we call situationships, mock relationships that don't require the commitment or exclusivity. It's fun, until they leave when the show ends and we wonder why we feel so unfulfilled. I'd prefer to watch TV alone, but when I got a cat, my little familiar called Tabitha, named after a character in a programme I loved called *The Worst Witch*, I'd accidentally ensured that I'd never be alone again. Even when going to the toilet, or eating dinner, or when masturbating. My little furry bedfellow would pounce on the spot where the duvet subtly moved between the tent of my bent knees. Crouching tiger, hidden rabbit.

Self-love – the psychological kind, not physical – has taught me to let feelings sit, speak to them, feel them and thank them, even feel compassion for them. Don't bypass yourself by letting you or your friends talk you into just getting over it and moving on to the next guy. You won't find any spiritual bypassing between these book covers, either. That's a term coined by psychologist John Welwood in 1984, defined as the use of spiritual means to 'distract from painful feelings, wounds and developmental needs', which is the opposite of what we're doing here, honey – real self-love asks us to face our internal fears. They're never as bad as we think they are, and sharing them with others is a natural painkiller. That's partly why I wanted to write this book. Because shame dies when stories are told in safe, spiritual places.

Now, after all my self-soothing inner work, even just the spark of a high-vibe thought, a fleeting moment of gratitude or the sight of a feather on my path can give me a hit of dopamine similar if not greater than a Tinder push notification that says 'You have a new match!' I crave time alone, in the retreat of my own home, because I can only hear the Universe's voice, unexplainable in words as it is, in my own company. Even I, a chatty extroverted Gemini, am claiming how vital alone time is when healing and heading in a new direction for love. Before, I couldn't even sit alone with myself, and I needed to swipe myself into a haze.

Make time for you time

As a single girl, you are divinely meant to put yourself first and foremost. I also firmly believe that when you need time out for self-care, the Universe will cancel unnecessary plans for you. We *have* to care for ourselves better because we don't have a partner to do it, and it's not something to feel pathetic about, as I used to. Whoever is meant for you will still be there when you're ready to receive them. That means you can be really honest with yourself about whether or not you want to go on that date with that Tinder boy, because your soul might be nudging you to do some meditations in the bath instead.

Self-love can be equally as gratifying even when in a relationship, and that goes for both partners, especially after a conflict. If I'm in an uncertain place on a dating journey with someone, I need a warming treat for my heart chakra, so I turn to a mug of cacao and meditation. If I'm feeling triggered, I can feel the place in my body that's tense and breathe light into it – the trick is realising you are triggered in the first place, so that you can revisit the situation calmly and not as your unhealed inner child. Yoga also serves as a great self-love practice; with every hip-opening pose, such as those on page 59, I feel repressed emotions ebbing out of my joints that bit more, being evicted from my body. Self-love keeps our hearts soft when we've been hurt, when we often want to be in our heads, rationalising and intellectualising our situations as a common coping mechanism. But, hard as it is, embracing our feelings in the soft compassion of self-love is the only way to heal our hurts.

No one said self-love was going to be pretty. If you're secretly thinking 'but I'm a parent, or carer, or work addict, I don't have time for self-love!' then I've provided you with some ways to incorporate it seamlessly into your life. If you think you're already at the right stage, or if you're not even single, add self-love rituals for good measure. There's nothing like proving you're in the exact right place than upping your self-love reserves and seeing everyone around you be happier for it. It may even allow your relationship or marriage to take on a whole other level. And like staying at a steady weight, staying at a healthy self-love level – a spirit level, if you will – takes maintenance. I know, sorry to be a bore and everything, but I guess consistency is just what adulthood is.

My core lesson is that spirituality and love are linked – they are in fact the same thing. Spirituality is a love of the Universe. When I realised that I was already in love with the Universe, I began to feel inner peace in a world full of chaos, trust in a world of uncertainty, and self-love in a world of couples.

The Second Commandment

You are not a black sheep, you are a golden sheep.

Shake off the feeling that you are the *only* single person left on the planet, because I know how much it can feel like that. I have been where you have been, kissed the same frogs, nicked the same tee shirts from our situationships. There is no shame in being single; being in a couple is a society construct. We came into this world alone and will exit it alone. Remember, everything happens for a reason: if you were meant to be in a relationship right now, you would be. The Universe keeps showing us time after time that if you keep looking in the wrong places, outside of yourself, then that is the root of the problem. It can be solved with Commandment 1. Feel free to go and read that Commandment again before revisiting this one.

Rectifying your own single status in the wrong way can start a downward negative spiral, too. 'Just one more one-night stand, maybe he'll fall in love with me! Then I'll have someone to bring home to meet my mum!' we goad ourselves. No, he won't, babes, I'm sorry. If a man is in it for sex, he always will be. And your mum probably wouldn't like him anyway.

I know what it's like to go out to dinner with girlfriends and realise you're the only single one and feel shit about it. Even at work, I found myself thinking everyone round the meeting table would be going home to other halves but me. But when you heal, when there's nothing to report to friends – it's not that you're not dating anyone right now necessarily, there's just no drama to it because you are in such flow with it – it feels damn good. You've set your boundaries wisely. You're a drama-free zone because you finally let the Universe do all the heavy lifting and you're just here enjoying the ride, greeting what comes, shrugging off what leaves. With all that work in the First Commandment, you deserve to clap yourself on the back.

But if you feel so left on the shelf that even your mother remarks on how single you are, in public too, I feel you. When I threw a small soirée to celebrate this book deal, at the flat that I single-handedly own, at a party *celebrating my singledom*, my mum, tipsy on champagne, still helpfully reminded me that I was indeed single and she was still grandchildless. As entertaining as that was for my friends, I busied myself with hostessing, rolling my eyes at the irony of it all.

Down with single shaming

As society defines women as married or single, I don't blame my mum, or anyone of her boomer generation. Note that men never need their marital status pointing out. I'm seriously considering petitioning to get the word 'single' cancelled – Emma Watson had it right with 'self-partnered'. You can even marry yourself these days – author of *Reader, I Married Me* Sophie Tanner did it. 'Ms' was a step forward for women, and now there's the prefix 'Mx' (pronounced *mix*), to go along with the gender wxmn (you're on your own with how to pronounce this). Once we take the stigma away from being a single woman with its sad undertones and reframe it as a woman of mostly unlimited means who can do whatever the fuck she likes, or whomever, we can move forward towards a future of equality.

But don't get me started on how we are incentivised to couple up; the single supplement is simply an unfair charge. Hotel rooms, rents, rollercoasters, chicken breasts, everything comes designed for pairs. It is possible to get by as a middle-class single woman, but people from lower-salary tiers of society and disadvantaged backgrounds would see the disparity way more. All I really need a partner for is to use their torso as a laptop stand while we're watching sitcoms in bed, but my American soul sisters could have a real need for social security or medical insurance. Society is skewed towards couples and screws the singles, especially single women when you take into consideration the gender pay gap and especially with the cost of living crisis. I argued this point when trying to get a pay rise, just so you didn't have to, and nope, my boss did not buy it. And the years of being single, I don't really think the odd free drink or dinner being bought for me by a male date, thanks to so-called 'pretty privilege', really evens out the gender pay gap.

It's when we turn that single shame on ourselves that the real insidious trouble begins. When we're beating ourselves up over whether we're skinny enough, confident, motivated, positive, good enough is when the patriarchy has penetrated us and we become pregnant with its bullshit. At my lowest times I blamed myself for why I couldn't get a boy to text me back when it seemed like the easiest thing in the world to other people. I would come to realise that guys want emotionally available women as much as we want emotionally available men and fuckgirls exist, too! Seeking comfort and validation in other people isn't exactly sexy, so shake off the single shame and get down to the rituals, and you'll feel more fulfilled and at peace before you know it. You may tell someone you are single, or read this book in public. It might just break the ice with a gorgeous stranger or new friend.

The Third Commandment
Date the person who sparks something in *your soul*, not your ego.

Ram Dass said, 'Souls love. Egos don't.' Time after time, we go for the fuckpeople because our ego desperately wants them to choose us, meaning we must be one in a million. Oh ego, you are the spiritual version of a cockblock; you really do keep us in the comfort zone, what with your defence mechanisms, coping habits and blocked-out emotions. We repeatedly choose familiar relationships, good or bad, because of it. But our soul wants us to have an ego death, break free, to evolve and to find that person we don't normally go for, the one who's not 'our type', the person who is actually, wait for it, good for us. I know, shocker. They may only become attractive to us when we finally appreciate our own qualities, but this is where Commandment 1 comes back in yet again.

We mistake highly infatuating trauma bonds with love a lot of the time, because these types of unions can feel like the earth moving, which is what we expect when we find our soulmate or twin flame. That's what we've been indoctrinated to think. Some of the more extreme-thinking people I've come across believe *only* those with trauma are ones in relationships, because as a healed single, we're whole already and don't need the crutch of a partner. That

THROAT CHAKRA: THE MAN BREAK

sort of thinking is a slippery slope into spiritual snobbery, and not a stance I agree with. If someone helps you be your happiest, healthiest and highest vibe you can be, have at them, I say.

When we let our soul do the swiping, rather than our ego or sex drive, we can feel that spark, that divine click with someone through the screen. You can't force spark as much as you can't teach charisma or become a dog person if you're born a cat person. By all means, go on a first date with the person you fancy, but do me a favour and think about a second date – is there a real spark or a genuine enjoyment of his company? There are plenty of questions we need to ask ourselves on a potential match.

Throughout my story, I mistook the spark I had with people as real potential for something more than sex, but the secondary ingredients that are meant to grow, such as trust, common interests and shared happy memories, just didn't. Sometimes sparks flew but our fire died prematurely. Sometimes I felt all people wanted to see in me was my sparky sexual energy, but my inner self, along with my vulnerabilities, all of which were masked by a confident facade, scared them off. If anything, baring our souls to someone – when the time is right, of course – is a perfect filtering practice. The wrong people would swiftly remove themselves and the right person would stick.

How do you know you're ready to date again?

- You feel excited about who you could meet now that you know that you can't go wrong.
- You're ready to learn more about yourself in the mirror of someone new.
- You can put your flirting powers to the test with someone you like, as well as your boundaries.
- You know your deal-breakers, and what you're not willing to spend time changing their mind about.
- You now see the fun in conscious intimacy and authenticity rather than unconscious ego-scoring.
- You're excited to subtly ask for his date, location and even time of birth to judge his Sun, Moon and Rising signs accordingly. Questions like 'were you born in the same town as you live now?' or the game

of 'let's compare our silly serious faces on our driving licences' will tell you what you need to know. You're even excited to cast an astrology compatibility chart to check what's called synastry — two people's likely compatibility in a relationship.

Open up your throat chakra

This chakra is linked with healthy communication, self-expression and even a balanced diet. It doesn't just encompass the neck, but the face, jaws, ears and even base of the skull. I think of it as the energetic voicebox, because it mainly comes down to how well we are communicating our truth. Follow this short meditation below to stretch and release it.

1 Sit down in a quiet place as always, back straight against a wall, legs crossed if comfortable. Close your eyes and take some deep breaths. On each inhale, tilt your head to the side to stretch your neck, then exhale as you come back to central. Repeat on the other side, as well as forward.

2 Put your hands lightly on the front of your neck. Take a deep inhale, and exhale in a 'hahmmm' noise. Feel the voicebox vibrate as you release the sound. Repeat a few more times until you have warmed up your throat with sound.

3 Come back to a normal deep breathing pattern and picture your throat chakra as a light blue wheel in your neck. Imagine it glowing brighter and brighter and so big that it becomes bigger than your neck and starts to surround your body in protective blue light.

4 Feel yourself within the blue bubble of protective energy. Know that no words can cut you in here, or drag you down, only uplift you. You also don't feel the need to criticise, demand or shout in here, because all communication will be calm and peaceful. Words are a vehicle for love and respect only. Energy can deter people with just one look.

5   Open your eyes and journal your first thoughts. Write about your
    feelings and what you wish you could say to people but don't feel
    able to. Let yourself be surprised by outbursts and epiphanies now
    the energy is flowing between your lower and upper chakras again.
    Even just getting it down on the page helps — that's why fake
    letters and texts never intended to be sent are so helpful, because
    it releases the need inside you. How will you start to enact your
    inner truth bit by bit, each day? Voice note yourself just to exorcise
    it from your mental load.

For further assistance, carry blue crystals, for example lapis lazuli, blue lace
agate and sodalite. And even better, wear them on a long chain around your
neck or meditate with them.

6

Third Eye Chakra: Conscious Dating

Affirmation: I connect with all of those around me once again easily and seamlessly. I am happily single and a queen of my own kingdom, and I enjoy tasting the fruit of my fellow singles on offer. I manifest all the luck I need to swipe the right person at the right time and enjoy those in the meantime.

Cue the music, because you and the Universe are coming in hot. She's our wingwoman now.

Congratulations! Now you'll be in the dating pool of normal people. When I say that, I mean people walking around the planet with difficult emotional baggage, the same as us all, but still seriously looking for someone to love. By this point, you no longer allow someone stringing you along for meaningless booty calls. Once you raise your standards, you'll have graduated out of the fuckboy pool and promoted yourself to a higher league.

By October, I was back on the market feeling magnetic. When you re-emerge from your own man ban, you should be feeling totally abundant and excited to see who's ready for you. If, like me, you receive a text from an old flame then swiftly get hit on by your new neighbour, you'll already be learning not to allow everyone access to you. You'll filter boys like a subscription to Tinder Gold would. After all that time chasing, all you'll have to do is mind your own business, attract effortlessly and select intuitively.

Let's see what mirrors we find this time, I thought as I pondered dating again. If the problem before was taking things too fast, I was curious to see what sparks could really fly while slow dating (to assess compatibility over time). I was even willing to give 'dry dating' (to assess compatibility without an alcoholic drink) a go. I was a changed woman.

So with no rush, no beer-goggles and no compulsive need for a man's attention anymore, we're set. But we're going to need our secret weapon: a strong intuition in the form of our balanced third eye chakra.

Third eye, open for business

The third eye is probably the chakra in our body you've heard of most. It's called the sixth chakra or *ajna*, which means to perceive, and is a different kind of psychic sense to our gut sense, sitting around our solar plexus. Situated between and just above our two actual eyes, it 'sees' what we don't, such as a troublesome Tinder match, even if we can't explain its reasons. Tune the solar plexus and third eye chakras and psychic power can be yours.

First, check back and make sure your heart chakra is in balance as much as your third eye. Because when you blow this truth channel open and you start receiving these acutely sensitive nuances, information never at your fingertips before, you'll need a loving, self-compassionate voice to support you through a new perspective on the world. Your open heart will provide a compassionate voice to others, too, even if they and their subconscious agendas are the ones causing conflict.

While preparing to re-emerge from a year-long man ban, feeling as though I was a hermit crawling out from my meditation cave, I received this download (a notification sent directly to me from a higher power) during one of my daily meditations.

Go ahead and date, but stay in that self-love state you've been gassing about all the while. We dare you.

Self-love showed you that everything within you is worthy of love. Shadow work showed you that the darker bits of you that hide even from yourself are worthy of love too. So learn not to take things to heart, even in the cut-throat world of modern dating. Lots of people assume we can't do self-love and dating at the same time, but we can. Think of them as two separate Fool's journeys happening at once. The challenge of this chapter is to keep the self-love spark alive even when dating tries to dull it.

Quality, not quantity

We know how it feels when we have plenty of matches in the apps but zero in our bed. Creeping back on the boy bandwagon, I chose Bumble as my cupid of choice and decided to be selective not just with who I swiped right on, but who I then opened a chat with. Being much choosier than pre-man break, I only swiped right on about one in about ten people, if that, and probably only opened a conversation with two in ten matches. Now, with my improved profile tips (page 217), I get better matches and want to open a chat with most of them, saving me both time and energy in the long run.

Crystals to attract a strong, intimate match

Place these babies in your bra, baths or under your pillows and watch as you manifest more passion into your life.

- Carnelian for self-confidence.
- Red tiger's eye for loosening up the libido.
- Rose quartz for the heart chakra.
- Rhodochrosite releases fear of intimacy.
- Garnet for passion.
- Pink tourmaline for emotional support.
- An evil eye charm – not a crystal, but this amulet can help to repel the fuckboys, just in case. You just can't be too careful.

Manifest a good match in your day to day

Remember, the more you love the deepest parts of yourself first, the deeper love you'll attract. The more specific you can be about what you want, the more it will come to you.

Before we get to the swiping side of things, carry on your ad-lib affirmations and give the Universe the green light to bring him in. Your delayed gratification will have worked, with studies showing discipline being the number one trait of successful people. Re-read Chapter 5 and you will turn heads with no conscious effort; your aura will just be on fire. Set intentions for new love under every new moon and charge your heart chakra crystals under the light of each full moon. Make sure your bedroom is a loving space, with a calming feng shui. If you shave your body, be well-groomed so that the 'oh no, I haven't shaved my legs!' fear doesn't negate your chances. Remember what they say about making space for a man in your wardrobe, bed, life? It's true — you want a space the right person can slot right into.

Keep the playful energy up by daring the Universe to show you your next partner in the next profile you're shown on an app. Visualise him in your mind's eye then open your eyes to see who flashes up. If you believe 'there are no guys for me on here' that's what you'll get.

That's because our brain has a particular software called RAS (reticular activating system), which directs our attention to what we ask it. When we set intentions on finding a certain type of guy, the RAS acts as a filter that Tinder would probably charge us for and flags the resources that align with our intention. We manifest more of the matches we want because we're more aware of what to look for.

Lots of us seem to have a love-hate relationship with dating apps, downloading them in hope and deleting them in disappointment, over and over. Meeting first in real life is preferable, where people's energy is clear and upfront, but unfortunately we live in a Tinder age where that's minimal. They require two different approaches, but both involve mystery, because mystery is the prerogative of the Divine Feminine.

In real life: play the long game

If you spot someone *you* like, eye contact is your signal here. See the 'look, linger, head tilt' move below. In short, it acts as an invitation for them to approach.

1   Look – the eye contact should be a warm and bemused smile so that they see the spark in your eye.
2   Linger – hold their eye contact for a second longer than you would normally, about two or three seconds in total is fine.
3   Head tilt – this is optional, but its body language says, 'I'm considering you'.

The extra seconds he looks back at you is your green light. Intensity and patience for him to come over is the key. Don't go to him; play the long game. Once you've got their attention, feel free to put on a show, putting on lipstick or dancing – they'll be watching. If they are interested, they will come to you. If they are not, they won't. It's actually very simple when you break it down. When they come over, they'll break the ice, even if it's to check if you were looking at them. When the time is right, do a quick version of The Eyes (page 78). You'll know it's landed when he pauses mesmerised, or takes the flirting up a notch.

But what if you can't catch their eye? The trick to that is to have done the shadow work in your man break to be glowing with effortless confidence. They won't miss you. That sure was one big epiphany of mine – that men can read our energy better than we can read our own. We may occasionally tell ourselves that men are stupid, but they can sense our repressed feelings better than we can. The flipside is they can also sense when we've broken through them. When we're at war with ourselves, we only attract people at war with themselves too.

If you want to lean in more, feel free. I'm not saying don't go up to guys, I just mean you simply don't *need* to, and in my experience making the first move sets the precedent for lazy or insecure men who will always want to be chased. Dating coach Matthew Hussey calls it 'dropping the handkerchief', as women may have done in days gone by to summon attention from a man. I call it something more millennial: dropping the scrunchie. No kidding, recently a guy literally lurched for mine as soon as I had accidentally on purpose tossed it to the floor. The ball is back in your court when they hand it to you.

So, make the first move or slide in the first DM if you must. Far be it from me to stand in the way of destiny. But from my experience, if you make the first move, he's unlikely to lean in because he won't have to. Remember, in classic partner dance, the masculine leads.

On apps: be upfront

On dating apps, it can be such a roulette wheel as to who we'll click with in reality, even if the online chemistry was good. I'd love there to be a blanket rule that good on apps means bad at relationships, and vice versa, but my research shows it is not so. How are we meant to discover our divine compatibility using two-dimensional tools like pictures and words? Even though apps try to keep up with our increasingly conscious dating needs, with voice notes and even experiments into AI, we shouldn't rely on them. Shockingly, only 10 per cent of people in committed relationships met online, and according to other research the age group most likely to find that successful online reunion are aged between 43 and 58. So young people need all the help and positivity we can get when it seems the odds are stacked against us.

A profile is most magnetic if it's brief: three or four sentences and three or four pictures being upfront about what you want and what you have to offer. In one night club, however big it is, there's only a finite number of single men. On apps, you'll be shown so many different profiles you must have strict policies about what you swipe right on. 'Yes' is only powerful when it's used sparingly, and a good date to all is a good date to none.

An attractive dating app profile includes a hint of the real you with a pinch of mystery. It may sound obvious and shallow as hell, but physical attraction is paramount in men's brains, and a filter on your pictures is not the mystery I mean. First, experts recommend treating your profile like the story of you. Choose a clear headshot, not selfies, then continue storytelling by sharing pictures of activities most authentic to you, such as rock climbing, yoga or dancing at a festival. Make the story even more cohesive by only including pictures of you with your current hairstyle. Include a picture or two of you with family or friends, but avoid lots of group pictures. In retail speak, confused customers never convert, and we want buyers. If you're always the designated photographer, ask friends to catch candid pictures of you on your next cocktail night.

Leave the pictures of activities such as drinking or babysitting your niece for social media, as well as the ones of you in sunglasses, which don't show the window into your deep soul. People need to visualise themselves with you, and they can't do that if they don't know what you truly look like. Chapter Five will remind you that the real you *is* beautiful enough without filters or enhancements.

Writing your profile

You don't need to be a writer to create a magnetic profile – your energy will do that, even in the Tinderverse. Your first sentence explains who you are with maybe a little goofy joke. Mine used to say 'I'm a package deal, I have sass, class and ass', which got my personality across but ultimately invited people who didn't take me seriously. Now it says 'former magazine editor, now self-employed writer'. Ambitious men, who are the men we want, will be impressed by the career transition. They're already intrigued.

Your second sentence describes what you're after. Men need to know what role is vacant in your life, so they know their purpose to fulfil. Now they're largely redundant, even for procreation, they don't know anymore. My second line says 'Looking to fill the role of loving, affectionate person in my life. Could it be you?' Now there's a challenge they can prove themselves by rising to.

Your third sentence is what you bring to the table. 'Fab little spoon, excellent listener.' What more does a bloke need? A chat can facilitate the rest.

Don't be tempted to detail what you don't want on your profile, e.g. single dads or smokers. Experts say doing this gets you half the matches of people whose profiles say what they *do* want. As when we manifest, we must always use active 'I want' statements rather than 'I don't want', because that's a sure-fire way to call it in anyway.

Serve a beeline

On apps like Bumble, women have to message first within 24 hours of a match, and then the guy must message back to secure the match, otherwise it expires. This is so that women don't get inundated with upfront sexual invitations as on other apps – that's the theory, anyway. But how does that work with my 'lean back, stay warm' approach?

It requires from us an intriguing message to get the guy's attention with the same 'come hither' energy we'd serve him in a bar. Make them feel truly seen by asking a question or serving a compliment relating to their profile. Sometimes, people still won't get back to you, and that constant rejection mounts to what I call Bumble Burnout. It's tempting to delete the app and go back to Tinder, where men can message first, or just quit it altogether. But be honest with yourself: it will only lead to downloading it again. So take a few days pause and only swipe on people whose energy feels fantastic, even if you can't work out why.

If you're intrigued, 'I have a question for you and it's not the one people always ask you' will pique their curiosity.

If you want to be coy and flirty, say 'The answer is no' or 'The answer is yes'. They will want to know the question.

My favourite is 'Hi, (name). I like your (something on their profile that genuinely made you swipe right). What made you swipe right on me?' Gets a response 100 per cent of the time.

If you don't know what else to say, on an app or in reality, a classic is 'You look familiar, do I know you?' No, it's not a chat-up line. It's just an innocent icebreaker that serves as invitation to chat. The worst thing he can do is say 'no' and leave the conversation.

Trust you'll be shown the way

We're not playing hard to get – we *are* hard to get. But so are the Wise Men we want, because they know their value too. Fuckboys are hard to want and hard to get – no thanks! There's the Power of No again. Your prerogative – no, your job – is to be able to discern between the two types of men and exercise the Power of No both in bars and on apps, so that the path is clear for the one you'll say yes to. While it's easy to get a date with just anyone, most matches will just want to get inside you, not your life.

Apps also work on algorithms, so toggle your profile frequently to get the top of each 'pile' of profiles that the app has deemed right for each version of yours. To help, either change your bio a bit or increase or decrease age and distance limits, and the app will take you to a whole new set of profiles. Or, leave it a week and let the app sift the best ones to the top of the pile for you, ready for you when you log back in after a week of self-love. Each profile is like a different path of destiny. It's ladies' choice which one we follow. And you know you trust the Universe's cosmic interference when you shrug off accidentally swiping the opposite way you meant to, but also because you refuse to pay the fee just to backtrack.

Swipe with these rules of thumb

Remember these pointers when you next log on to a dating app.

- Photos make people look better than they look in real life, plus they have your hopes and expectations splattered all over them. You may think you're looking at someone amazing, but you are only seeing potential. The good news is, people may not be as attractive in the real world, but their energy may be better than you ever imagined.
- These apps were designed to keep you hooked. The swiping function was inspired by a psychology experiment that saw hungry pigeons appear to gamble for more feed. You are not a pigeon; you are an evolved, conscious human. Ground yourself often so as not to get sucked into a black hole. As if it's a gambling app, set a time limit and stop when you hit it. Know that happiness doesn't lie at the bottom of this match queue. Unclench that jaw, relax your shoulders and take some deep breaths through your nose down to your stomach.
- If you are manically swiping to a point of obsession, consider the meditations and affirmations in this book as more self-serving for time and energy than apps. It might be that low self-esteem is driving you to connect with someone external when your inner child needs you to connect with them first.
- Manifest consistency of messages, not speed. Find a pace of conversation that works for you both – that could be a message exchanged every five minutes or five days. Someone good for our nervous system will be consistent; by contrast, a fuckboy might have

erratic timing because he's just had a different girl cancel on him and he's suddenly free tonight.

- Don't get jaded when you get to a stage with a person where it feels like a Mexican stand-off: who's going to ask who out? Typically that's after Instagrams or numbers have been exchanged, and both know the other is lukewarm interested. Guys these days seem to want to be chased just as we do and no one wants to come across too keen anymore. If you do want them to make that move, make them feel comfortable and reassured that you won't say no when they do.

The mirror theory, in practice

A lot of people on the apps these days are trepidatious, in-between life milestones and just looking to date to pass the time or gain validation. In a recent survey, the number one reason people admitted to being on apps was for validation, the second being to seek connection (note, not commitment). Both may have been true for a guy we'll call Scorpio and also for myself. But it was a good match with plenty of green flags. Tick – we got into a consistent back-and-forth conversation. Tick – we had a love of travel in common. Tick – I was now interested in me and he was interested in me. My new 'lean back' approach was working, and my third eye was batting her eyelashes. She could sense an impending 'do you want to meet for a drink?' message.

Despite my awakened approach, we can still be guilty of playing games because we're gripped by fear of rejection. Desperate not to appear desperate, we make ourselves wait a comically long time before responding to messages. I hadn't yet learnt I could be my warm self even while leaning back, so I donned my old Cool Girl energy. I'd even make him chase me to confirm a day and a time. But it was quite amusing to watch, and we're only human, so my connection-blocking ego was still somewhat in the game. If you feel the same, go easy on yourself. You're probably still raw from ripping layers of ego off yourself in the man break.

Slow dating lacks one thing: drama

Ah, the optimistic joy of first dates. You've shared the good, carefully curated bits of yourselves, so you feel like you know each other more intimately than you do. That sweet fake familiarity is intoxicating; you're still strangers, after all, and as much as I might have been holding back my real self for fear of rejection, so was he, so are we all. Before the man break, I would have already coloured in all the grey area with imagined potential. Now, the more I date, the more I realise how little I know about someone, and let those gaps go unfilled. I focus on my own potential rather than some guy's.

After a year celibate, I'd recommend slowly reintroducing sex into your life so as not to get 'honeymoon cystitis', which is just a more romantic UTI. As much you might want it, keep doing your self-loving bedtime rituals as you did before, even if you're manifesting good sex with the guy when the time is right. It's *slow* dating, remember, so focus on positive emotional experiences to deepen bonds before consummating those bonds. Just know you're going to have to go back and heal that sacral chakra all over again, and that was back in Chapter 2.

That's why the clichéd 'third date rule' – or any rule for that matter – doesn't align with conscious daters, so that's why I made sure our third date was an outdoor activity date. It's not about earning our bodies or anything intentionally feminist. It's about us knowing enough about the person with whom we'd share our bodies, sacral energy, precious time, bodily fluids. Nowadays, I don't use any rules, and as long as I can consciously answer my questions 'why do I want to sleep with this person?' and 'what exactly am I looking to gain from it?', I go with the flow, and most of the time totally sober.

If you want to wait, communicate it. All you need to say is 'I really like you and I don't want to rush anything', and that respectful honesty is hot. But I abstained from saying anything with Scorpio, as we do when we hide from our own truth. I'm sure he

THIRD EYE CHAKRA: CONSCIOUS DATING

could sense the conflict inside me – between old me and new me – and it wasn't hot at all.

Put the ritual into spiritual

If a year of self-love had taught me anything, it was that I could deepen my connection with myself through rituals. Surely then, rituals could help deepen our connection with our partners, too.

With Scorpio, I wanted to transcend our sexual connection into an intimate one with exercises like synced breathwork and extended eye contact, but I felt too vulnerable to suggest it, thinking it was too intense and might scare him off. I let him get away with sex positions which felt mechanical and which required no eye contact at all, which just made me feel even more vulnerable. I know how nerve-wracking it might be to suggest these, even if you usually take the dominant role in bed. Men rarely feel shy in asking for what they want to try in bed, so suggest trying these. Be confident, explain honestly why you'd like to try it, and he might follow your lead and be mind-blown.

Try these together

Know that you can do most of these with clothes on, and they don't have to lead to sex if you don't want them to. The eye contact may be intense at first, but if he can't hold your eyes, he may need to hold space for himself in a mirror first.

- Start face to face with crossed knees touching, or straddle him, wrapping your legs around his hips and pushing both sacral and heart chakras together. Take deep synced breaths together, feeling his stomach press against yours as you both breathe in.
- Another time, look into each other's eyes for a whole song of your choice, suggesting a silly or sexy forfeit if one of you breaks eye contact.
- Listen to guided meditation together just before sleep.

- Increase post-sex aftercare, having intimate conversations and sharing secrets cuddled up, or cooking together. If they start playing the guitar after sex, chuck them out.
- Establish a private love language, like leaving little surprise silly notes for each other or completing some sort of private goal together which only you two can celebrate.
- Show each other a conscious effort for open communication. Download a free app like Agapé, which asks both of you a daily question but you can only see the other's answer once you've answered yourself. The more common ground you find, the closer you will feel. Some of the strongest couples schedule this in as a shared priority.
- Have a favourite song, band or date spot together that when you play it for each other, or take one another to, it always means 'I like you' without having to say it.
- Have a code word or phrase when overwhelmed to pause disagreements.
- Use massage as a bonding tool, specifically yoni massage or lingam massage. This can be a transformational tool for you both, but requires technique, so research a local practitioner who can show you how to do it properly.

Caution: none of these are to be used with fuck buddies. There is only one activity to do with them before boundaries start blurring.

Every connection is different - that's its magic

When we look around at a yoga class, if the person next to us is resting a different hand on a different leg, we assume it's us going wrong. So when everyone's new relationships are going strong and ours aren't, the easiest thing to do is assume it's because *we* are not good enough. Now that I know that not to be true, it seems so lazy of our ego to jump to this conclusion without considering other options.

We assume the ones in our friendship groups who get married are the most desirable, but desirability is so irrelevant to timing, it's almost laughable. During my courtship with Scorpio, another lockdown came and people around me started establishing social bubbles with their new boyfriends. If we weren't moving at the same pace, that meant my connection with Scorpio wasn't as strong as theirs. We were still riding the label-free limbo. When one of my closest friends told me she bubbled up with her now fiancé after their second date, that was it. Degrading sex positions I could deal with, but submitting to them and still being rejected for a label, I couldn't. I suggested bubbling up, the 2020 version of asking someone to go steady.

'To be honest, I don't think we're there yet,' he texted back. 'But shall I still come to you on Saturday?'

We must see progress where we can, and pre-man break us would probably have rather skinny-dipped in the Bermuda Triangle than ask for what we want. So, in his spirit of honesty, I told him I wasn't ready to go into intimate bed-sharing territory, asking him just to come for the day. My bed was my self-love sanctuary now – I had been very careful in consummating our status as 'seeing each other' on the sofa instead. Looking back, I wasn't ready to look him in his eyes let alone bubble up. See the mirrors at play again?

Even though he was totally fine with postponing it, in my guilt at self-serving rather than people-pleasing, I got horrendously drunk. Dr Nicole LePera, the psychologist behind the popular Instagram account @the.holistic.psychologist, excuses us there. 'We pull back to the familiar, the thoughts in our mind, the discomfort in our body, and before we know it, we're right back in our familiar,' she says. There was alcohol again, hiding me from the truth my third eye could see, plain as day. That he was just someone who'd got lost in the matrix, and who belonged on my old path.

How to have The Talk - when you see a future

Okay, so you really like this person, you've been seeing each other a few months, but you don't know where you stand with him. Are you a thing yet? Does he even want to be? Can you introduce your children yet? You're trying not to let it bother you, but your spirit squad won't let you forget it. Allow me to introduce the Vibe-Checker Chat.

Whatever happens, you'll be okay because the Universe has someone better queued up if this doesn't go to plan. This chat will only make the fuckboys run away; others will at least try to stay and chat it out. It really separates the wheat from the chaff, as it were, or the 'fuck' from the 'boy'. It also goes for anything you need to bring up, like odd behaviour you feel bad for questioning, or a hurt feeling or a crossed boundary. Remember, you can only control your words and your reaction; you're not responsible for the whole conversation, just 50 per cent of it. Visualise each of you sitting on opposing sides of a counter if you must. Just know that you can't lean over it.

First, preface the chat with something nice. You're dating the person, so I'm guessing you want to be sweet and let them know you do like them. If you don't even want to admit that, maybe someone should be having this chat with *you*.

'I'm having such a great time with you.' 'I really like you.' 'I think you're lovely – and I just wanted to check something – that we're on the same page.' This nice little preface also keeps their defences down, which is crucial to open communication. Now, here comes your question.

'I was just wondering where you were at with dating?' This is an open question, and you can trade it for others. You don't want to accuse, pass blame or project. If he says, 'well actually, I do want to keep talking to other people,' believe me when I say that honesty is more useful than a lie just to keep you happy. With enough self-validation in your self-love tank, this truth might sting like rejection but you'll recover fast. With a good enough third eye too, maybe you even knew he was going to say that and you just needed confirmation. And with enough self-respect, you'll know to take the answer you trust most, even if it's given away in his facial expression and body language rather than his words. Or, if his answer is positive, then you've made progress and been brought closer together.

Just don't do it how I did. Scorpio was forced to spend the next day making toast for a very hungover me, and with my defences down, my needs came tumbling out. 'Do you like me?' I asked him in bed, batting my lashes. Cringe. He rolled his eyes, smiled and replied sarcastically, 'What do you think?' Answering a question with a question – not quite the sincerity our manifestation boards are made of.

Have The Talk – when you aren't aligning

The true mark of emotional maturity is how well people can communicate in the testing times, not how they weather the good easy times. So when you've prefaced your chat with an anti-defence line such as 'I've really enjoyed getting to know you' or 'I think you've got so much to offer', then followed it up with 'but I don't think we're aligning as much as I'd hoped,' your honesty will be appreciated. The word 'align' is like a no-fault divorce; neither is to blame.

The deeper, harder work you do on yourself, the more you can't *not* be open and honest, especially if you've been gaslit into submission in the past. Just make sure your throat chakra doesn't blow out and share too much truth, because it's always best served with compassion. Sometimes, we don't need the whole truth. But in general, you know the reward of real vulnerability is always worth the discomfort. That's why people fear a spiritual woman – her self-acceptance can be intimidating, her intuition disconcerting, and her open and genuine nature can be disarming to people who are closed-hearted or have something to hide. She's a mirror who inadvertently forces people to look at themselves. She might not always be popular, but being her is worth the work.

Déjà doom

Break-ups feel so shameful because as women we feel we need to be good enough to be 'kept'. Could I have done it differently or better, we question ourselves. When Scorpio ended things by text days after our first official sleepover, but suggested still meeting up for sex, I questioned every little thing I'd done. Why had I been fuck-zoned (like being friend-zoned, but instead propositioned just for meaningless sex) for what felt like the millionth time? Maybe he'd been thinking with his groin the entire time. Maybe I'd been thinking with mine.

We can be so choosy, and we can still get stung by a fuckboy. Well, it can't work out with everyone. We know deep down that dating is for trying people on anyway. We're still getting to know ourselves in our twenties and strengthening that solar plexus, after all. But we do funny things when we're taking rejection personally. Sometimes we delete their contact, as if ripping a name from a number makes his texts less powerful. We delete every text straight after we send it because we still find it hard to hold our emotion. Instead, we need to love ourselves harder to trigger a real change in the outside world. We need to sage the room to clear the bad energy of his messages, and chant affirmations 'I am worthy as I am' and 'I complete myself' as soon as we get off the phone to our girlfriends.

In retrospect – it's always in retrospect – we realise some people were our perfect mirrors. Scorpio wasn't ready for a relationship and neither was I. Maybe he was an accidental fuckboy – someone who waits as long as needed to get sex, like the good guy he thought he was, but it's still what he was in it for. Maybe I was still a fuckgirl, still only dating for my own validation. But we still need to see progress on our healing journey where we can. Where he is less of a fuckboy than our last, we are less of a fuckgirl than we were. And luckily, we're nowhere near narcissists anymore.

Magnetising better than a man

The beauty of the man break is that it shifts you in ways other than romantic. Just by taking a year off men, I had become more at one with the Universe in other, unexpected ways. Christmas week was hell with the magazine, and we had half the time we normally did to get it to press. I did it as always, but I couldn't help thinking I deserved a bigger, better salary for the job I was doing. In that moment, I caught myself in a lack of gratitude for what I already had, and automatically, as Gabby Bernstein said it, 'chose again'.

'I am grateful for what I have and it will only get better', I decided to affirm instead. The next morning, I won a cash prize in a work Christmas raffle. Merry Christmas to you too, Universe!

It also lets us know when it's time to cut off connections that don't serve you. I don't mean from men (they were doing that for me, if anything) but from a girlfriend I felt only got in touch when she needed something. Protection techniques wouldn't work here. When misunderstandings kept popping up, and she got ever sharper and more ungrateful, I took one look at the energy of that 'exchange', put my vow of self-love first and dumped her. We don't need low-vibration people to like us. In fact, it's actually a compliment.

What if I was making the wrong decision? I panicked. What if I'm too sensitive?

Do you think you're the problem here, seriously?

I found it more nerve-wracking than breaking things off with a date, but it's as important. Not that we can go around calling everyone a toxic narcissist or an energy vampire, but I'll say this: if your mental health has got better since you called for space with them, you made the right choice. And the Universe may gift you with validation by bumping into a mutual friend who had the same experience with them, even years later.

After communicating with them, I find it good to do some cord-cutting, writing a letter then burning it or expressing anger or passive aggression by deep breathing and pushing against a wall or hitting pillows. Chant 'I release them with love' to keep your energy high and if you feel overwhelmed, journal on how you feel – it may be useful to read back later.

Each connection raises your vibe

Forget Black Friday or Blue Monday – it's all about Super Sunday, the first Sunday of January. Record numbers of dating app sign-ups, matches and conversations happen on this day across the world, and some apps see an increase of as much as 70 per cent.

It doesn't take a genius to figure out why – it's slap bang in the middle of cuffing season, most singletons have had to watch happy couples ring in the New Year together, and it's the time of New Year's resolutions and good intentions and gym sign-ups. So while it suggests more impulsive dating decisions than conscious, it gets people's year off to a flirty start. It's exactly when I matched with the Wise Man.

Wise Men are the transcended version of a Spiritual Fuckboy. Think Spiritual Fuckboy if he'd gone through rounds and rounds of therapy, deep dark shadow work and maybe a heartbreak to really bring him into his emotions. My Wise Man was no boy – he was a mature man who knew himself, knew his astrology and really leant into the technical side of spirituality. Where Supernova waxed on like an uneducated hippy, Wise Man spoke like he was delivering a Ted Talk. He was up front with how busy he was, and where he was at with dating – no love-bombing to be seen. It was clear he had had his own Spiritual Fuckgirl episode in the past, and we clicked immediately. Our distance was long, but it was okay, as I had grown accustomed to no boyfriend, holding my own hand as I fell asleep, and using a draught extractor cushion as a boyfriend pillow. I was in the NATO crew, the cross-section of modern daters who are officially 'Not Attached To Outcomes'.

But the one thing I didn't expect from dating with self-love was how you start finding the green flags not in the men, but in *yourself*. They might only be glimmers, like catching how lovely you look in the mirror on your way to a date, or clapping yourself on the back at how you approached an awkward question. But they're there, and you *see* them now. Sometimes, you fancy yourself more than you fancy them. When that happens, applaud yourself. And though we want opportunities for love, my video call date with the Wise Man did inspire an even bigger opportunity, one that made me feel like I was the one doing a Ted Talk.

Power to the people, not one person

If people say they're spiritual, mediumship is usually high on their list of interests. With the right psychic, it can be so awe-inspiring watching them connect to the next realm that I've seen it even convert the spiritual non-believers. So while I wasn't getting asked for a second video date with the Wise Man – he'd said the lukewarm response of 'let's do it again sometime' after our first – I'd send our text thread to the 'graveyard', which I call my WhatsApp archive, and seek connection elsewhere. (FYI, it's better tech feng shui to store any pics in a cloud then delete old message threads. But if you must keep old chat threads, when you sweep them into your archive, make sure you uncheck the 'Keep chats archived' button in Settings. That way, the archive will appear at the bottom of the list, out of daily sight.)

I decided to go on a live video date with my Instagram community instead and show them an example of a medium at work. If it was good enough entertainment for the Victorians, it was good enough for us. The people needed connection too; it was lockdown again, and I knew psychic mediumship to be a comfort, a positive tool to bring divine guidance to a struggling human realm. The same gang of ladies would join me each Friday night like a virtual beauty salon. We needed girl time, and apparently I needed cosmic guidance.

'They're telling me that now is not the time for boys. Now is the time for creative projects,' the medium said during my on-air reading one Friday. She seemed to have immediately connected with Betty, and my grandfather Stanley, both of whom I had spontaneously mourned that time in George's living room in Brisbane.

But that's no fun! I thought. Here I was exploring my charming self outside the dating framework already, but they wanted to smack me on the back of the hand, the medium said. 'Stop bothering with people who only want to waste your time,' she channelled. 'The time isn't right yet. You're too deep for them, and they back off, wanting something just surface level. Someone's coming, but not yet.'

It was true, I had to admit. While it meant I had plenty of anecdotes from Bumble to share, such as all the divorcées who seemed like they were the only ones into me, and how I'd attracted an odd spate of Nigels, I did feel like I was about to be sucked back into old ways.

It's funny that spirit doesn't just predict our future love life but can give us validation on relationships in our past too. It proves it's never too late to heal a hurt. 'Your nan is pointing to the heart chakra,' she said. 'Five years ago, you pushed someone away from you who wasn't serving you well at all. You said it was now or never, and she wants to say congrats.' Oh, god. That would be Supernova. 'You really changed the chapter there,' she nodded.

I don't expect everyone to turn to a psychic medium every time they need guidance, let alone live broadcast it. Most people I know don't believe in it, and just nod to humour me or make fun of it, even if they are secretly very intrigued about who in spirit would want to connect with them to give them a few tips. Their first question is always 'but do *you* believe in it?' Our own intuition needs to be our first port of call of course, as most reputable psychic mediums will only read for someone every six months anyway. But that feeling when life confirms predictions is like nothing else, and I was going to feel it. The Wise Man might have been light years ahead of most in spiritual maturity, and had somehow become a good friend, but he still couldn't offer me meaningful sex, let alone romance. Now I had to work out if the Ten of Cups, the 'happy ever after' card I'd pulled from a tarot deck, predicted a change of heart in him. And how far I was willing to ignore my dead grandmother's warnings.

Switch up into higher self mode

Who said just because your third eye is clear now that you have to listen to it? Despite all the work you've done to heal your fuckboy wounds, I wouldn't judge you if you fell back into your pre-man break self, because fuckboys offer the cheapest love and the best-looking bargains.

So, when faced with a choice whether to sleep with someone or not, ask yourself questions a therapist would. 'How will I feel after?' and 'Which version of me will I have to answer to?' are good places to start. Your decision, such as to hook up with a friend or fuckboy, might feel liberating at the time, and hell, women have fought for a long time to be sexually liberated. But you may deal with any residual feelings of vulnerability, shame or anxiety embedded in you for a lot longer than the moment itself lasts. Only you know yourself well enough to know what you're doing. That's why 'sleeping on it' works so well: according to online education body The School of Life, at night time and first thing in the morning we can access our neocortex. This is where all the juicy visualisation and empathy occurs, and with it, our ego falls, allowing our consciousness to heighten. That's why it works even better to do affirmations, journaling and meditation during these times.

Try this instead: switch to what your higher self would see. She's up there in your mind's eye, knowing what's best and wisest. What would she be telling herself to do with the benefits of all her wisdom? That's right; you can choose your reality, and can choose again at any point. You can have free will *as* your higher self, and never feel like you're missing out on the fun you didn't choose.

Eclipse energy is pretty extra

When you go through any kind of life transition, however small, look at what phase and zodiac the moon is in. I promise you, it will help guide your way out of it. When the moon has waxed up to full, think of it like a mirror telling you you're full too, and you need to release whatever negativity you've been holding on to.

I broke it off with my Wise Man a few weeks later on the

supermoon solar eclipse in Sagittarius, a free-spirited air sign. It reminded me to let go and find freedom, and boy did letting go of my expectations for that man feel good. The clincher? Learning that even with a boyfriend, or boyfriend figure, it still doesn't mean they can get you off. Sex with Wise Man, which I expected to be the most intimate of my life, was an awkward bumping of not just mismatched uglies, but souls.

I was slowly mastering slow and conscious dating, which is realising you feel bothered by something and being brave enough to make changes accordingly. I was learning that the word 'no' was a one-word spell, one big, fat empowering incantation that pushes away anything not on our highest path in the space of one syllable and two letters. 'Fuck that' is another spell that does the same thing, but faster.

Always use protection – and boundaries

'Real sex and casual sex are *so* different, aren't they?' I mused one day to a girlfriend over lunch, almost buoyant I was so giddily grateful not to be lusting after someone and was back in Chapter Five energy. 'It's so easy to get attached, they should have different, I don't know … holes!'

'There are other holes, you know,' she teased.

'Ha,' I responded. 'Yes, thank you for that. Ooh, maybe I could start to visualise condoms as a metaphorical barrier, like a boundary, so I don't fall in love with the guy. Like, a level of emotional protection as well as physical.'

'Not sure if that's how it works. Do you want to share a dessert?'

It goes without saying to always use protection against STIs and unwanted pregnancies with anyone, not just casual partners. Consciously think about the consequences and what you would do (really, conscious thinking is just being brave enough to face up to the truth). In fact, even if you're not trying to date them, think twice about whether to sleep with them at all if they try to get out

234

of wearing a condom by conveniently 'not having any'. Casual sex, as long as you're conscious that it will never lead to a relationship, can be a great growth opportunity in which to practise open communication, as well as keeping expectations low and boundaries strong.

It feels counter-intuitive to say no to the things that feel good in case you get lured into 'catching feels', which means dates, gifts, and even mutual friends are a big no-no as they grey the line. My advice would be to keep your energy cleansed more often by carrying a selenite crystal to cleanse your aura as soon as you leave theirs (do not meet up in your own sacred space) and journal more often to keep abreast of your thoughts and emotions about it. If you catch the dreaded feels, don't panic – communicate, and take them as a sign you're ready for something more with someone else.

Still just the bridesmaid

If we're serious about finding a person, our person, we can't give the Universe mixed messages by fucking around with the wrong one. I finally understood that, and I never wanted to be in the grey area again. I was approaching my 28th birthday and I felt so powerfully single. Now I was finally grateful to be single, blissed out to be unattached completely. I vowed never to abandon myself again. Only conscious choices for my highest good ahead. I could see clearly now the fuckboy fog had gone, and I hadn't felt like this since the man ban!

And then that person comes along to show us where we still need healing. It's a good thing, if only we look out for the lesson. When a message came in from a friend – who, coincidentally, I was a bridesmaid for – asking if she could set me up on a blind date, it (a) felt somewhat nineties, and (b) reduced me to being just the token single friend. Though friends try their best to set me up with friends, strangers, even co-workers, it can sometimes have more the effect of a pity party.

After a period of guys talking about themselves, it is so refreshing to have a guy lean in and be so engaged in you. At the party where I met the man in question, anyway, I was in a bubble of his undivided attention, and it felt nice, if a bit intense. It felt like finally my turn to be seen by someone other than myself. In person, he was charismatic, charming and drop-dead dreamy. His energy was gentle, not intimidating or dominant. His shimmering eyes and plump pink lips gave me a smile that said to me 'you are the most beautiful thing I've ever seen'.

This feels familiar.

Yes, doesn't it? I've missed it, I replied to my inner voice.

As you comfortably lean back, you can observe that a guy likes you when he leans in. But this guy was intense, and leaning all the way over the metaphorical counter. As we lay down to stargaze the summer sky on our first date – one he'd planned and picked me up for – drinking cocktails from a tin, I felt invited to nestle up into the warmth of his neck. The spark was well and truly there.

This felt so different to the Wise Man, because meeting in person first, not on an app, I could feel our sexual spark practically pulsing. I just knew nothing we did was ever going to be casual. And maybe that's the trick – it shows how much you need that fiery spark which then keeps the fire burning in a sustainable union.

Oh. My. God. Are we going to be able to finish our book actually loved up?

Pace yourself with the expectation timeline

Sometimes our imagination still runs triathlons ahead of real life. Use this timeline to stop you getting attached to your 'happy ever after' outcome. It'll slowly guide you through the first three months while you scope someone new out. Plus, it reduces the risk of falling for love-bombing because with this timeline, you're unable to look into the glorified far future with them.

Use this for both app dating and meeting someone in real life. Our intuition can scope out the very first impression of someone, but this framework works after a good connection has been made. Remember, it is your responsibility only to show that you are all those things too, and you'll need multiple examples of each stage. Think of it more of an art than a science.

1 Start practical: 'I hope they are single and available to chat.' Some people these days aren't, sadly, and could already be in a relationship (or if you're non-monogamous, disregard this). So, to start us off, let's just expect the bare minimum: that they are on the dating app to find a date, just like you, and they're up for chatting at least.

2 If you're satisfied that they are indeed single, expect that they are a down-to-earth and kind person. Any creeps or weirdos will hopefully drop away now. You can also add in lifestyle choices here, such as sober, spiritual, has kids or not. Compromise or don't but establish this before going any further.

3 Then, if they're single, available, nice and normal, and you're interested, pin your hopes only on the fact that they are interested in you in return. Imagine absolutely no further.

4 If you feel they're interested also (even better if they tell you), pin your hopes on them being funny, and not just as a coping mechanism. If this chat is going to carry on anywhere, you want to be having fun at least!

5 Then, if they are single, available, nice, normal, interested in you as well, *and funny* … they're too good to be true, run (I'm kidding). You'll probably be getting your hopes up now, so take your self-love up a notch. The thing you want to see now is that they're honest. Whether that's to tell you about the baggage they have, or give a valid reason why they might need to cancel a date, you want to see that this is a safe place for truth telling.

6 The next expectation to keep you from racing forward is that they're consistent. For example, that this person is maintaining a good back and forth with you and that there's follow through – they actually do what they say they're going to. Crank up your self-love affirmations to keep yourself steady and more in love with yourself than their potential.

7 Now for the intimate connection. Hold up, because I've been stung here when a guy I swore was 'it' practically blamed his impotence on me. If they're single, available, nice and normal, interested, funny, can handle both your truth and theirs, and they consistently

show up, then congrats! You have met a rare breed of Wise Man. If you've already had sex, do you feel comfortable to tell them how you want it? Can you build intimacy without sex? Can you be totally yourself with them, and let some mystery now drop away?

We welcome in the worship

When we love ourselves, but we haven't been loved by another for so long, we're hardly going to turn it away when it turns up. This is exactly the worship and attention we deserve, we think. It arrived just at the time half my six senses were about to disappear: taste, smell and intuition. I'd finally got Covid.

Though I wouldn't recommend it, I was grateful for my two-week quarantine to slow McDreamy and me down. What I would recommend is booking a solo trip for straight after your first or second date to keep grounded in your own love. As soon as I recovered, McDreamy didn't leave my flat for a whole weekend. My ovaries had taken over any sense of intuition, but I was about to have my stomach-sinker moment with McDreamy. On what was our extended second date, he told me he never wanted kids.

When you both want different things in life

Some people still believe that with wrong timing, they're still the right person, but really, that still makes them the wrong person. If, say, they want to move away next year, or one wants children by a certain age, it puts a deadline on your dating. But if you really do believe in the abundance of the Universe, then riddle me this: why don't you deserve the right person at the right time? Why do you think you're only worthy of being dated recreationally to pass the time before their deadline?

Kind and calm communication can help when putting your needs on the table and only then can a compromise be found, even if the compromise is ultimately letting each other go and exploring your own paths alone. With enough self-love practice, you'll know in your gut if this person belongs in your future or not.

Of course, you can pay for tarot readings on the matter, ask your pendulum or do your own reading, but they'll only reveal the answer you know already deep down. And though it's so painful to let them go, you'll look back and be glad the Universe shimmied you in that direction.

By all means, be curious about people you have a spark with, and follow it, if that's what feels right to you. But if you feel your lives are not aligning, know that the wrongness you feel about it all is *not because of you and your worth.*

Trauma can repeat itself

The phrase history repeats itself is true, and even truer is that boyfriends repeat themselves too. That's why it's so easy to trauma bond with the next, and so hard to break the pattern. It's disappointing when you think the man break will fix everything, but it doesn't. Though my man break had shifted me a few gears internally, my traumas were still brooding under the surface, too far for solo shadow work to penetrate.

Just as with Supernova, I had a stress dream about being kidnapped, as if I was a child helpless before an adult. Like Supernova, McDreamy loved to impress my friends. As with Supernova, McDreamy love-bombed me with notes and cards, calling me 'perfect', and that would probably kick off the hypervigilance in me to stay that way in his eyes. And as with Supernova, I was his biggest cheerleader, hyping him up on his own potential far past the realms of a realistic partner. If this was meant to be slow dating, this trauma bond had tripped me up and I'd fallen down the rabbit hole, falling at a pace so fast I couldn't control. How did I fall so fast with such a strong self-love foundation?

His charm, my girl. And charisma.

My nervous system was stressed out for some reason; I was waking up at 5.00 a.m., and my appetite was a lot smaller, which I now know to be a sure sign of anxiety. I was losing weight subconsciously, physically shrinking because of his preferences, instead of growing happier. I was calm only when I was around him and anxious if not. When it was just the two of us, he sent me into a frenzy.

Venus vibes

So often when we're stuck in a sex spell and tangled up in our infatuation, we can't see straight. In sex with McDreamy, I finally felt safe to be in my Divine Feminine in bed, in my submissive and caring state. My Venus in Taurus was exalted, for it was hedonistic, passionate ecstasy, and he got me high with almost as much as a glance. Look at your Venus; where is it and what does that zodiac say? Most of all, I loved to be worshipped by someone who couldn't help but do the Gratitude Gaze on me, clothed or otherwise. Was this what they meant by sexual healing? Maybe I *could* heal from sexual love as well as self-love.

This is the love I wanted, no? So why couldn't I fully let go and trust that this was it?

MAYBE BECAUSE IT'S NOT RIGHT?

They want Barbie girl, but you're Barbie goth

There's a difference between being positive by default and being positive authentically. Once we've braved deep heart-opening spiritual work, we can re-emerge into reality with a high, radiating vibe, but deep and rich, and *only* so powerful because of the expansive depths you have explored. Bright *only* because you have gone in and peeked around in its shadow, as if the blacker the yang half is, the whiter the yin appears. Calm *only* because you know what chaos feels like. This deep self-acceptance shines out from within us, ridding the need for heaps of make-up or Botox that would only hide the true authenticity we now want to take pride in. Maybe that's not a lot of men's type; maybe men like McDreamy still do prefer the type of woman who just agrees and submits, as I was when I met Supernova. Maybe we all do, because who is taught how to manage conflict these days?

Maybe that's the type of 'positivity' McDreamy thought he was getting in me, and what he was used to – someone who never bothered to dive into her depths. I worried more that I wasn't Mrs McDreamy material, rather than if he was Mr Moody material. I was half blonde, but I was multi-faceted, like a shiny amethyst crystal cluster. And you know one thing about crystals? The more facets a crystal has, the more faces they have to reflect light.

And some men love to manipulate their Barbie

Be wary when the first 'I love you' comes to resolve an argument, especially if it's a rushed conversation. This is usually a manipulation tactic when they're scared to lose you, like when they sense you getting your coat. Just ask yourself, is that the cute, considered way you'd want your beloved person to declare love to you? We'd had our first argument the night before, when he had totally ignored me at his best friend's wedding. I'd felt lost, punished and empty because of it. Mere hours later, I existed back in the world because someone *loved* me again. So of course, I said it back. We were now boyfriend and girlfriend, and that morning seems to be when the problems started.

After a few hours of being apart, a distant inner voice returned. *See it through, see it through, you must see it through.*

Have a chat with the Universe however you feel most comfortable, be that inside your mind, on a journal page or out loud, just the two of you. Ask it to show or tell you the things you need to know, then make your decision, trusting that the Universe will hold up its end of the deal. Always make the most empowering choice, and you'll feel instantly more resolved. I felt so confused, the opposite of empowered. Was I going to go all in on this wonderful loving feeling I wanted to explore, or deny myself it due to our differing futures? I didn't even want children yet. But I wanted regrets even less.

I chose to go full in and see where this love could take me. I let his sex spell power up into a love spell, and for a few weeks, I was blissfully happy with my decision. But by the end of summer, and the end of our three-month honeymoon period, my inner voice was nagging at me again. Can't I ever turn this thing off, I scolded it. I needed to seek help in a spiritual guru I had met through the magazine.

'I want rid of any old stagnant energy and to get to the heart of why I feel disconnected from my partner in sex. When it's over, I feel vulnerable, low and needy, rather than empowered and loved,' I'd told the healer in a consultation.

Maybe because he's pumping his trauma into you, not love. And I needed you to see it.

'The themes you mention are so common,' Alexandra, the remote self-love healer, emailed back. 'We all carry such deep imprints of feminine abuse.'

Alexandra went on to tell me that we often feel at ease in the early stages of a relationship because we can put on that mask of being the sexual goddess – which we are. But we are now realising that sex and intimacy have been coming from a murky and masculine-controlled space. 'It is not uncommon for women to completely lose their sex driving during their advancing stages of awakening, either. Therefore, sickness, such as your UTI, manifests as a way of pushing partners away.' Sex with him did feel masculine-controlled for sure – it was all his kinks, as I still didn't know mine – and my UTI had come screaming back.

Then she got into past lives, which overwhelmed even me. 'You also carry a lot of prostitution energy from your female ancestors as a form of survival,' she said. 'There's only so long a woman can operate from the external part of her being seen as a sexual being before the emotional vulnerabilities, childhood trauma and emotional neglect begin to surface,' she warned. 'This is when we decide if we are emotionally safe with a partner. Spirit shows your primary wound is the Father, hence why you feel that you need validation and to be kept close by your partner.'

Hang on, my *father*? I never considered that.

Alexandra finished by bringing through, in her words, beautiful healing codes from my spirit team to activate a deeper healing within my cells, something they'd been trying to do the whole time. 'You don't need to be anyone but yourself to be loveable,' she finished, which brought me a wave of emotion. I felt a sense of relief, validated in how I was feeling. I had been feeling disempowered, needy and co-dependent again, as I was with Supernova, rather than the hippy, happy powerful woman I was just months before.

Three months in, the power struggle begins

'You can be very emotional, can't you, princess, like, very sensitive?' he pointed out one day. Though it made me want to punch him in the face for being so patronising, I wouldn't let it land. I hadn't done all that shadow work to then deny what made me me.

'I am,' I nodded proudly. 'I wouldn't have my job if I wasn't. Can you imagine how hard editing a spiritual magazine would be if I didn't have all my feeling skills?'

It would snowball. 'All women are just far too emotional, don't you think, baby?' he'd tell me another day. Maybe his red flag of secret resentment of women had been there all along. Maybe I'd seen it and tried to paint it green, but it ended up a murky shade of shit. I'd found a committed man, but he wasn't as conscious as I wanted. I wanted him to be an ally to my feminist values, to be open-minded. I felt like Goldilocks trying to find a man who was just right.

Visualisation for releasing control

When a relationship feels heavy, do this meditation to feel lighter of heart.

1   Picture yourself packing your relationship troubles into a heavy, masculine leather weekender bag, full of your arguments and fraught texts and tense energy. Where once your connection felt as easy as carrying feathers, now sense what could be in the bag – bricks? A whole house?
2   Acknowledge how weighed down you feel and put it down on the floor to see what happens. In your mind's eye, did it just sit there and sag a bit? Realise it's not your responsibility; neither is it his. You don't need to control, mother or cling.
3   Acknowledge how you feel now. Do you feel a physical weight has been taken off you? What's in the bag now?

Trust that if you are meant to be together, you can find common ground and work this out. Because the Universe doesn't want you to try harder, it wants you to feel more at ease.

When disdain arrives, it's time to go

Before long, our initial fiery spark had got out of control like wildfire in a forest, sweeping through our relationship, burning anything salvageable.

'Can you make space for me?' he said one day as we sat down to eat dinner on the sofa. We were rarely at his because he lived with his mum, a slight red flag I never cared to see. Besides, McDreamy wasn't my ideal man manifested, I was becoming sure of that now. 'You always take up the whole thing.'

Instantly, after so long being a powerless girl, his princess – the Queen in me was awakened. I flinched as though I'd been stung.

'Don't you dare talk to me like that.'

'What?' His eyes were wide with surprise.

'This is my flat. Don't you *dare* talk to me so disrespectfully,' I bit back. I was unsmiling, hard, serious. He sat down beside me submissively; he was the told-off child this time.

I had thought because we were so good together physically, we were meant to be together. Without the rose-tinted glasses, I found it almost amusing how bad our match was; a closeted Brexiteer who, albeit politely, asked if I could wear a dress next time we went out, and a liberal leftie daydreamer who would only do what she was told in the bedroom and nowhere else. Maybe McDreamy came into my life to show me exactly why a relationship wasn't the emotional container I idealised. Instead, it was more of a prison for my insecurities to breed. I hadn't realised it, but I kept my captor close for immediate reassurance, just as Alexandra had said.

In this process of dating in my twenties, I learnt, more by a process of elimination than anything else, what love is not. It is not sex. It is not even romance. It is shared goals, morals, lifestyles, and most of all, a shared perspective on this one tiny life we are given on this curious, chaotic planet. An ability to accept each other without trying to persuade the other out of their free will or highest good. Love is friendship, but also holding each other to account. It's swapping who's dominant and who's submissive without pride or ego. It's chasing each other. It's being flexible and being reliable, and it is shared trust and shared truth.

The biggest revelation of the man break was that it helped me in each break-up more than in each relationship. Falling in love, I had slipped back into old, anxious ways. Come the break-up, I felt lucid and calm again, but self-aware enough to know this was the euphoric relief stage and pain might come on strong soon. But I felt proud knowing my break-ups weren't the end of the world anymore, and to me, that victory was a very surprising by-product of a very sad experience. So give yourself kudos for progress, just as I did for getting myself out of this dead-end relationship in double the speed of my last, with Supernova. Maybe if I'd made more time for self-love rituals, rather than relying on him for love, it could have been double the time again.

The day after we finally broke up, I crumbled, and knew deep down I had to go no-contact otherwise we'd never leave each other alone. That night, all the social media apps crashed around the world, as if the Universe was keeping me from peeking at his Instagram. It was the kindest intervention it could have made.

Activate your third eye

This is an easy one now you're so used to meditating and your five lower chakras are all open. Find your quiet place and sit against a wall with your back straight and hands resting on crossed legs.

1   Focus on the middle of your eyebrows, breathing deeply and sending all your oxygen there. The third eye chakra is said to be a doorway to the spiritual realm, so as thoughts come and go, visualise them as if floating past a window like clouds.
2   As you get deeper, see a purple orb form itself in the middle of your eyebrows and spread outwards until your body is holding this purple light in every cell.
3   To finish, bow your head, put your hands together as if praying and touch your third eye with the tips of your middle fingers. Touch the heart with the tips of the thumbs. Try to repeat this meditation daily or try third eye-boosting yoga or even just mindfulness. Welcome in the wave of intuitive thoughts, keeping the heart chakra also balanced and open with regular positive affirmations.

7

Crown Chakra: Purple Flags

Affirmation: I connect with all of those around me once again easily and seamlessly. I am actively healing and choosing a different pathway than before. I am ready for the next step in my spiritual journey and see my life full of divine love. I know that I am love.

You are just one step away from having healed all seven chakras and your perspective on being single is hopefully radically different from when we started. How do you feel? Are you breathing deeper? Are you more aware of your thoughts? Are you feeling more positive about your romantic future?

We've reached the top chakra: the crown. Not just because you're a queen of your own energy but because that's the name of our seventh, and most important, chakra. The *sahasrara*, meaning 'thousand petalled', is associated with both white and purple light glowing right at the crown of the skull of the energy body. It's such a big deal it's said to be the giver and receiver of spiritual consciousness – *oo-er*. It's most concerned with a connection with the whole of the Universe, helping us blast through self-perceived limits and living (and dating) free from ego. With a balanced crown, we finally feel free to date with our soul bared and guard down. We're ready for someone on a similar vibration to perfectly align with *us*, rather than us changing to align with *them*.

So often when we feel a low vibe, or even feel isolated or

247

dissociated, it's this chakra that's blocked. The best way to describe it is feeling as though Mercury is in eternal Retrograde, because you feel constantly prone to mental breakdown. I'm not saying that every ailment the same as this can be automatically healed with only spiritual means. We honour mind and body alongside the spirit, after all; that's why the industry is called mind-body-spirit (MBS). However, we can use our spiritual insights to become aware of where we are out of balance, and that is always the first step in healing. The crown chakra may also be askew if we are excessively egotistic, or fixed and inflexible in who we are. When that happens, the ego takes on a superior identity as if higher evolved than others. Sound familiar? This kind of hyper-spiritualisation is the exact vibe of a spiritual narcissist or, worse yet, cult leader, whose arrogance puts them on a pedestal to preside over others. When you work on your own chakras in depth, making sure you're connected both with the Universe but also are grounded in your own earthly human experience, you'll spot those people a mile off. My advice would be to give them a wide berth.

Imagine the chakra system you've learnt throughout these chapters. Right at the bottom is the red root, and right at the top is the white or violet crown. Usually, one partner (in a heterosexual relationship, it's usually the man) is in a Divine Masculine space. This person is grounded and *grounding*, level-headed but passionate, and provides the safe space of the relationship. We're talking energy here, so this applies even if he's not physically masculine-looking or masculine enough by his society's standards.

Picture the Divine Masculine sitting at the root, giving the relationship a firm foundation. Then, the partner taking on a Divine Feminine would represent the opposite, up at the crown. She brings the magic, mystery and wild spirit into the relationship, seeing as women are said to be naturally intuitive and in tune with nature. When the two come together in love, they meet in the middle at the heart space, and when they communicate, they meet at the throat chakra. She's the yin, he's the yang, and together they make a divine balance. In fact, so crucial is your root to your crown that some healers say your crown won't open unless your root is, so revisit the meditation on page 56 first before doing the one at the end of this chapter.

You know that saying 'root down to rise up'? A relationship is like an energy see-saw. The stronger our root, enjoyed by both, the more magic in our crown, enjoyed by both. It's a useful way to visualise and manifest a healthy, divine and balanced relationship. With this reciprocal energy, a relationship becomes a divine ecosystem keeping itself strong and steady. Have you ever been around a couple that are almost glowing with love and mutual respect, even if it's not their wedding day? Root and crown, tied up with a big bow.

Start spotting purple flags

You might have heard of metaphorical flags of the red or green kind in dating. Like in a traffic light system, red flags suggest poor or unattractive qualities, but green flags are a sign of potential. Of course, most come down to common sense; for instance, we would all see red flags in dating a murderer, or at least I hope so. Some are much more nuanced and subjective; for example, I now find red flags in a man who overpromises or love-bombs, but others might not dislike it nor even see it. There's also a 'beige' flag in the dating dictionary, which is a sign that a person is dull or 'vanilla'. Again, that's subjective. Someone single might well be looking for a seemingly 'boring' partner after years of being with unsteady or unpredictable ones.

Purple, to me, is the spiritual colour of the rainbow. It's the colour of amethyst, the most intuition-boosting crystal, and violet is the colour associated with the crown chakra. It's the cliché shade of curtains on psychic stalls in centuries gone by, yet it still hints at spirituality in a lot of modern marketing campaigns. Therefore, a purple flag is a sign of wild coincidence, suggesting that the Universe has played cupid. Maybe you and a potential partner have an unexpected friend in common, or you went to the same uni at the same time but never met. Perhaps you share the weirdest favourite films, or you share the same irrational dislikes, or you hit it off after matching on a second dating app after letting the match expire on the first. Regard the other flags as pointers on your dating journey, of course. But when a purple flag pops up, take note. It may be a nudge from the cosmos telling you there's something more to explore here.

Rebound into healthier territory

Don't underestimate the power of a change of scenery. Travel is a lot of spiritual single people's best rebound, especially when they're conscious not to use a human as a rebound. Falling in love with a new city can help us fall back in love with ourselves because we see ourselves happier, expanded, just like a healthy partner can help us fall in love with ourselves more. At some point though, your body, where the feelings are stored, will demand you process whatever you are holding on to.

As I was on a boozy backpacker week in Portugal with Tina, I welcomed distractions from my painful feelings in the form of custard tarts and clubbing. Believe it or not, the Portuguese guy I pulled in a nightclub didn't help to heal me either – shocker! Underneath my chirpy day-to-day self, even underneath the relief not to be carrying the metaphorical weekender bag that was mine and McDreamy's relationship anymore, I was not feeling hot at all. The fastest, most fail-safe solution was Will. He was a nice boy from back home who I'd matched with in the dating drainpipe of Tinder before flying to Lisbon.

You can tell you're in emotional pain or have internalised anger when such feelings manifest themselves faster than it takes to say 'narcissist!' Before you know it, you've sent short sharp messages back to your ex because his out-of-the-blue contact triggered you, shattering your pretence as a level-headed, healing person. But maybe this hurts more because it reminds you of a previous relationship you were re-enacting. You might be in denial as to what you must grieve all over again. But to call it out is to clear it.

In a vibrational state that low, we have no idea how to be with someone emotionally available and good for our nervous system. Even if they don't give us anxiety, the brand new territory can. So when I sprang straight into dating Will before I'd even unpacked, I proved the ping-pong effect was alive and well. Will was the exact opposite of McDreamy. He was younger than me, athletic rather than alternative, and was fine with me taking the lead. With reins I wasn't used to having, and didn't even want, I caved and directed us towards a wine bar, even though I had planned on having a dry first date. *Always drive on the first date, Rosie, always drive!* I kicked myself. We had a few purple flags, and he had plenty of green ones. I should have been ecstatic to go on a date with him.

Surprise potential

But we know that deep down, when we are ready for one, a happy relationship is built on more substance than an initial spark. Maybe I was turning against the idea of a spark, scoffing at it even. Maybe with Will, he could provide exactly what I needed, even if I didn't fully want it yet. Even if he wasn't my typical type, it was so refreshing to be with someone whose calmness rubbed off on me even in my most anxious moments, and who said I made him feel the same. Even my friends and parents loved the sound of him, which was new. Still, my intuition wasn't so sure. I needed the Universe to come and guide me forward on this new pathway, which I felt I was walking hopefully, but blindly.

And like clockwork, the Universe is always there to match us up with our next move. That week at work, I interviewed a psychic who worked in tandem with tarot and astrology to channel spirit in her readings. My angle to the feature was the question she gets most from clients. 'Well of course, it's to do with love. It's usually "when will he ask me to marry him?" It's hard to break the truth sometimes, that some of them might be being led on, kept on a string. Some have such little self-value and self-esteem. My readings allow them to see how capable they really are.'

Her answer was totally relatable to me. Sometimes I'd feel being single was like being in an endless waiting room of a train station. I'm picturing one of those old-school art deco ones, with white orb lighting, rows of seating and shiny brown wood floors and fittings. We might chat to those around us to pass the time, but we're there to board a real relationship train. Well, a good psychic can tell us that a train is or isn't coming, and an excellent psychic can even tell us the time and platform. Even though I had a great Christmas and Valentine's Day (yes, I admit it, a cuffing season) with Will, I didn't feel like I knew him all that deeply. Though I was sick of constant 'conveyor belt' dating from the apps, I wasn't sure I wanted to get on a train with Will either. Confused again rather than empowered, I booked my appointment with the psychic.

Wait for your mic-drop moment

If our mind is open enough in psychic readings, the truth may be hard to swallow but it leads to breakthroughs.

'There's a loner in you that likes being single,' the psychic told me a week later.

Loner? Me, the biggest people person I knew? How was that possible?

'Well, you've had to get used to your own company, it seems,' she replied.

Maybe it's something to do with being spiritual that makes us want to tread our own path, alone, back to the self, uncovering layers of conditioning, back to source so we can start again afresh. Embracing selfdom was literally the point of the man break, but now it felt like it was working against me. Yes, I did prefer being single than in a relationship that felt more forced than fateful. It wasn't that I viewed single as safety anymore. It was that single now equalled self-love and optimism for finding the right connection eventually. It felt like trust. Freedom.

'Though McDreamy had a magnetic charm, he was also commitment-phobic,' the psychic continued. 'You two were mirrors,' she said. It was true; I had felt like we energetically kept each other at arm's length because we knew it wasn't meant to be. Both of us with one foot in, one foot out, similar to a three-legged race on sports day.

'This new man – Will? He does not want to settle where he currently is,' she went on as she pulled a Knight of Pentacles card. She then pulled a Temperance card. 'Ah, though he does bring balance to you. Ah, yes, the Hermit card. He's gone into himself. He's not your soul energy, but not your rebound either. Be glad you met this guy. He helped you get out there, he's like fresh air for you. But within four or so weeks, you'll be done with this story.' Again, my free will kicked in its defences. I'd break off with Will when I wanted, thanks very much, spirit.

Always the headstrong one … but that makes us us.

Then, my world as I knew it changed. Just like in Bali, I'd been caught off guard with a prediction that was going to lead me on. I teach not getting attached to outcomes, and now there was one trying to attach itself to me.

'This summer, you're going to meet someone who's going to change the way you see yourself.' Oh god, just when I get to a good place about being single, my Saturn decides to return and make everything dramatic.

'We move into phases just before or in our birthday month, so maybe it'll be around June or July time for you. He'll be sporty like Will … but also artistic. He's talking to someone you're in contact with right now.' I had a purple flag with someone I hadn't even met yet? Was that even possible?

Sure is, honey.

'Hmm … Two of Pentacles … yep, you'll meet at a work-related event,' she said. 'He's half-English … and he's well-travelled. He has family overseas … but you're unsure for some reason. He's quite a complicated Pisces, but he thinks he's gone to heaven when he meets you, as you'll give him a super-hot "come to me" vibe.'

Well, hot damn, I was almost proud of my future self for nailing the exact vibe I'd been working on. But I was already wary; the Bali healer had told me I was going to meet my someone from abroad too, and that hadn't happened yet. Did they see the same person? I was sick of getting my hopes up on empty predictions, even if they were made with the best intentions. How did any psychic see him for sure? And as always, how could I help it come to fruition, like the control freak I was?

'There are many options in astrology,' this psychic explained down the phone. 'But when we are ready, there can be different transitions – planetary movements into new zodiacs – that cause the same thing,' she said. 'You couldn't possibly *not* meet someone,' she confirmed, sensing my hesitation, my reluctance to believe in case I was let down. I had become used to trusting my own intuition more than other people now.

'Just keep your vibe high, keep calm and keep inviting things in as I can see you already do. When you meet him, get him to talk, but don't probe him. He's not as open and self-aware as you; he's two years behind you in terms of emotional development.'

Me, probe someone? Surely not!

If you're told by a psychic that you're going to meet a mysterious stranger, and you don't tell your girlfriends straightaway, I don't believe you. It becomes the talk of the night. 'What else did the psychic say about him?' 'When do *you* think it'll happen?' they clamour. But it's hard to know what to do with a reading; share it out loud as if you're holding the Universe accountable, or never tell a soul, tuck it into a drawer and try to forget about it?

The correct answer is both. Feel into the sensations it would bring about when it happens, then once you've absorbed those glorious feelings, taught your subconscious what to look for, let it go. After all, a cake won't bake unless you walk away from the oven. I knew myself well by now, and though I'd make my life count in the meantime. I knew by summer I'd be looking for him at every work event I went to.

CROWN CHAKRA: PURPLE FLAGS

Smash your self-fulfilling prophecy

But I was still seeing Will, while simultaneously dealing with the trauma bond left behind by McDreamy. I wasn't ready for my person yet, Universe!

According to studies, about a third of women in the UK have reported they experienced post-coital dysphoria. It's when, rather than dancing in the street after the deed is done, your mood plummets and a sense of sadness or emptiness comes about. Despite trusting Will and consenting completely, I was experiencing it frequently, not that I knew it at the time. He saw it and sat with me as it passed over my sad little head. Though I started setting some boundaries around sex, for example asking him not to seduce me while I was still waking up, even if he was messing around, I began to get an unfortunate case of the 'ick'.

The Ick: a spiritual argument

Getting 'icked out' means we become disgusted by something our partner does that seems irrational to everyone else. While it is not such a severe sign as a red flag, we instantly find our partner less attractive than five seconds before. It happens frequently in modern dating, which is probably a sign we've all become such immature morons so fearful of commitment that we ghost someone over something so trivial as their mismatched socks. I know I've icked out people by as much as gasping too loudly at a film. Sometimes even coming across too interested on a dating app can ick someone out and get you unmatched. You literally can't win.

We get the ick because we fear we'll be judged by the same harsh standards too. It's the homogenisation of behaviour, the end of quirkiness. If we judge another person as stringently as that, we need to turn the mirror on ourselves. The more we let ourselves off the hook, the more we'll allow others their quirks, even find them endearing or more original for showing them to us. Even the most attractive man on our manifestation board might have the weirdest taste in stoner movies, for example, or have a less traditional way to use a knife and fork. The way I see icks is they're the gap between expectation and reality. Newsflash: we live in reality. If something really bothers you, communicate. If it changes how you felt about them before, communicate with yourself. Is it your ego getting scared off?

If someone gets the ick with you, tell them, in the sweetest way possible, to fuck off. Then see if they do.

Acting on my ick-cident

It turns out, as I learnt, taking your own advice *does* work sometimes. I calmly journaled about where I felt Will and I were and weren't aligning, then did the Vibe-Checker Chat over the phone when I concluded I didn't want to continue seeing him romantically. At least my throat chakra seemed balanced, even if my crown chakra was so off-kilter that I felt dissociated and depressed most days, struggling to get out of bed. It was disappointing to have to push him away, and I felt bad, like I'd led him on. But it was a relationship I had to try on, and it was no one's fault it didn't fit. I guessed I had missed the spark all along. I figured I really did need it to get past that elusive three-month relationship mark.

Aching for our exes

Out of my cuffing season romance, March was going to be a reset month. Without a man as an emotional plaster, I had no choice but to step into shadow work again, and sort through what made me trauma bond so much to McDreamy. I was proactive in my pain, so I saw it as self-care to get myself on a waiting list for counselling. But any self-love rituals I tried to do felt vacuous now because I somehow resented myself for making the healthy choice and breaking up with McDreamy. 'Imagine if we had an emotionally strong man to root us down, how far we could fly,' a fellow spiritual single friend mused at the time. Even though I felt untethered to the ground like a lone balloon, I believed that like a cosmic wind, the Universe would float me onto the right path eventually. I finally fully trusted that I'd get the cosmic relationship I wanted one day, delegating the 'how' to the cosmos.

Despite being optimistic for the future, missing someone who made us feel so special and seen can be so debilitating to everyday life. You're allowed to miss them, and there's a difference between that and ruminating. Missing allows you to feel all you need to feel without bypassing; dwelling only sucks energy out of you when you're stuck in a feeling loop and can't quite move on to trying new things. I even resented McDreamy for not wanting the same things as me, unable to see that it was the Universe stopping me from settling. Our minds are in the present, but our hearts are in the past.

Heart healing

Place your hand on your heart chakra, close your eyes and ask yourself if it's really them you're missing, or could it be you're longing to feel about yourself and the world how they made you feel? Go back to your Bye Bye Bye List and question if how you feel right now dissolves any of your feelings towards the items on the list. If it does, you might want to explore what you would say if you saw or contacted them. I don't usually recommend it, but if our intuition is screaming at us to get in touch, who are we to question it? Otherwise, keep reading this.

Take note of something you feel you particularly miss right now about relationships; could it be someone to cook for, or someone to text good morning and good night to? Someone with whom you shared a secret language? Those were all things I ached for, but we can find those experiences in friends and family and, well, our animals, if they're clever enough. Find comfort in self-care, self-compassion and solitude, and seek things to look forward to, even if a psychic is the one telling you what those things are. The best way to empower ourselves is by being shown how capable we are, after all.

Move deeper into the core

As we heal our lives, we might find life's tests getting closer to the bone. This is good – it means the outer layers of hurt have come off, and we're closer to healing those more deeply embedded within us. As an onion, those deeper rings are more bitter to the taste. Just as I felt more comfortable with conflict and expressing my boundaries within relationships, I had passed through to my next test. A deep trigger from your childhood may be your relationship with food, or your body, or with siblings. One that was nestled deep in my consciousness from growing up was conflict at home.

Note to self, take first impressions with a pinch of salt not just with dates, but housemates too. I had been so cautious of toxic males, I forgot to look out for female ones. I'm sure you've been there too, living or working with an energy vampire, someone who rants and trauma dumps and never catches you in return. That unfair exchange of energy is draining, and we allow it because, on surface level, we can handle it. Add to that situation two single girls living together, and it can be tricky to tiptoe around the sensitive subject of sleepovers with boyfriend, even if they were quiet and respectful encounters. If you're feeling unsure about a situation, a reading can never *hurt*. I grabbed the tarot cards always on my coffee table and immediately pulled the King of Swords in reverse, alongside the Tower card, which I interpreted to mean someone blunt or calculating was about to cause some sort of upheaval. I didn't know it was her until the next day, when she texted me with her notice and moved out swiftly after.

Girl, you're ready for your King of Cups

We've met the Knights, the mascot for transformation, but let me introduce to you the most exciting court cards to look out for in your reading. The Kings are the power cards of the Minor Arcana. Whereas Queens symbolise a nurturer or mother figure, Kings bring the master energy. Yes, I agree, it's got a bit of stale patriarchal energy to it. But they can also relate to a matriarch at the head of a group, such as a family or company. They're a positive card because they represent the climax in whatever story is being told.

The Kings, right way up, represent power and mastery in different ways.

- Kings of Cups, the water/emotion suit: success in relationships and community connections.
- Kings of Pentacles, the earth/wealth suit: wild material success.
- Kings of Swords, the air/ideas: expert in practical decision-making.
- Kings of Wands, the fire/power suit: the ultimate lead in creativity and power.

What happens when this 'happy ever after' energy gets flipped and you pull a King card upside down (reversed)? Think about what an unruly King would do. He'd become dictatorial, evil and barbaric. Where you see a King upside down, it could point to an abuse of power somewhere. As with any suspicious character, in the tarot or in reality, you should be cautious.

Surrender, don't search

Try as you might to look out for the love coming your way, it really leads you down some dead ends. Glastonbury Festival, my favourite time of year, had come around. I was reporting on the festival for the magazine, so that counted as a work event in my eyes. Knowing there were 200,000 people or more there, my odds of finding an unknown person weren't exactly great. Despite that, I held onto hope.

In a sea of hot, happy couples, I got on to Tinder to find him, acting on impulse and forgetting all slow and conscious dating insights. Within the hour, I had hit it off with a good-looking guy from London who was an animator, a perfect artistic match for me indeed. But when he showed up outside our designated dance tent as agreed at midnight, it wasn't the glorious meet-cute of my imagination. In my nerves, I had put on too much make-up, and this guy clearly preferred the natural look and laid-back vibe of my friend. Unluckily for him, she had a boyfriend. It was like a very shit Cinderella story.

I choose myself, I choose myself, I choose myself, I chanted under my breath. *Even if no one else does, I will always choose myself.*

We are the mirror, after all. If we don't choose ourselves, who will? If we don't believe we're worthy of someone's love, how can we ever attract it? Next time I was somewhere that amazing, I swore I wouldn't be so in my head or in any app. Instead, I'd look up and surrender to the magic in my here and now. Lesson learnt, I guessed. I let my hopes drop along with my shoulders, exhaling with relief.

Manifest the man ... with a beer mat

Manifestation implies that we have some control, but really we only have a request slip we turn to the Universe, and she does the rest. But that request slip is our tool. Some people write fake cheques to manifest themselves a fortune, and others decorate an elaborate manifestation board. I'd visualised him, I'd tried masturbating him into being and I'd written to Juliet and posted it in her house in Verona when I was holidaying there that May. I even have a WhatsApp chain with a girlfriend where our texts are messages to the Universe. A few women I know swear by the sketching method, drawing a stick man, denoting him with qualities they wish for in a man, then pinning it up in the bathroom so that they can see him every day. Others think that if you give the sketched man any face at all, you'll just get attached to one look or outcome. I have one more trick, and it's a quick ritual you can do on a girls' night out.

At the pub or bar with your girlfriends, find a beer mat. Take out a pen and write the qualities all over the beer mat you wish for in a man, even if it's black ink on a darkly coloured mat. To activate the man on the beer mat, clink your glasses together, tap your drink down on the beer mat and then take a sip. Take the beer mat home and forget about it, then let a man walk into your life. He may even wander over to see why you're writing on a beer mat, or you could even ask him for a pen as a beeline. It's witchy, subtle and quick, harking back to witches' beer-making history.

That is the trick, being so certain about what you want that you can choose which words will take up such little space. It's easier said than done in a Tinder world with what *feels* like so many options but likely very few actual real connections. If you don't know even five specific qualities you'd write on your beer mat, just be wary that you'll only narrow them down by going through the motions and dating people you don't want, like a process of elimination but with sex.

And just like that, you easily manifest magic

As I signed off the festival review, without mention of my disaster date, and sent the issue to press, I was struck with gratitude to have had my exact experience. It had led me to my latest favourite affirmation: I choose myself. There I was, in my summer chalet room in the Alps, on another magazine review, with no need for dating apps. I was just going to hike, eat, write, repeat, and it was going to be bliss. No more hopes and expectations, I vowed. I was in my own Paradise Valley, the alpine wonderland I'd imagined during meditation in lockdown. If I could manifest this place by accident, I could manifest a man exactly when I wanted to. After my luscious post-deadline victory bath, with jets and all, I emerged into the lounge feeling like a new person.

It's when our guard is finally down that the Universe strikes, as it always had for me. As I sat down for dinner, I glimpsed the man that the psychic had seen in my future months before. It was July, I was there for a work event – it hadn't been Glastonbury. Every little detail had been correct, his zodiac, his nationality, and I'd totally forgotten to look out for it.

In one instant moment of eye contact between me and this man, this stranger who felt familiar to me but couldn't be, my Saturn Returned, and everything changed.

Find that divine spark – it's in you

As a parting gift, I'll let you in on a secret.

All that spark-chasing and it was in you all along, waiting to be found and embraced not by a partner but by you. The Universe, your spirit team, your higher self, they're all inside you already too. You were always your higher self; you no longer have to pretend to step into her shoes. So get out there and be her.

Open up your crown chakra

Though you're a chakra-healing pro by now, this is the simplest one of them all. Simply sit in lotus pose or with crossed legs, back straight, chest proud, or lie down in savasana as though it's the end of a yoga class. Close your eyes and breathe deeply, sending purple light up to the very top of your head with each breath. You might feel lightheaded doing this, but take a moment to actively feel the ground below you, gravity holding you steady. With each beam of light streaming to the crown, trust that you are an extension of the Universe. Know that you are exactly where you are meant to be, and smile as you feel the Universe pour its love directly into you through the portal of your open crown.

Om Shanti

More Ways to Use This Book

- To spark answers as an oracle: hold the book closed in the palms of your hands, then simply ask a question, either in your head or out loud, open the book at a random page and focus in on a random paragraph or line. The ritual, lesson or story in my text could reveal an answer to your query.
- To spark discussion: find questions for book clubs on my website, rosalindmoody.com, where I suggest wine and crystal pairings for the book club evening too.
- To spark journaling: grab a notebook and use the panels and text as inspiration for your own love-life journaling. What has my story helped you realise about your own?
- To spark healing: flick to the index on page 267 to see how I suggest using various rituals together.

Acknowledgements

Thank you to all my friends for the endless love and support: you are my heroes. You've heard me drone on about this book for years and I couldn't have pushed through the late nights and triggering moments without your hype. In particular, thank you to the friends who beta read the manuscript for me. There were an awful lot of drafts.

Thank you to my agents, Jane and Maddy, for seeing such potential in the proposal, and to Theresa for making the connection. Thank you to my editor, Hannah, for getting this book to the finish line with such sensitivity. For Charlotte, Amie, Sarah and Beth at September too. Thank you to my publicists, Katie and Gabrielle, for helping to push my story out into the world.

Thank you to everyone at *Soul & Spirit* magazine, colleagues, readers, designers, columnists, everyone, for your love and light. It formed my spiritual education and it was the best job in the universe.

Thank you to Louise Hay and the team at Hay House for allowing me to share quotes from her book *You Can Heal Your Life* (1984, Hay House), so that I could show you how this book helped me and mine.

Thank you also to don Miguel Ruiz and the team at Amber-Allen Publishing for allowing me to use quotes from *The Mastery of Love* (1999, Amber-Allen Publishing) to share the Magical Kitchen analogy with you.

Thank you to Elisabeth, my astrology teacher, who proofread this book for me.

I acknowledge that the land I call Australia in this book is in fact sacred Gadigal land. Thank you to every person I met there; I'll come back soon.

Thank you to the real-life characters in this book for teaching me more about you, me, friendship and vulnerability. Even the 'villains' of this piece – thank you for showing me which paths not to follow.

Thank you to my counsellor for holding space for me to truly validate my own feelings and experiences for the first time.

Thank you to my family, who have never quite understood me but supported me anyway, even when I didn't understand myself.

Thank you to Tabitha for finally making me a crazy cat mum. You are a fabulous, though bossy, familiar.

Thank you to me, for having the guts to finish and release this book. A lot of people talk about writing a book; trust me when I say it's no mean feat finishing one. Especially one that forces you to look at each of your fuck-ups in excruciating detail. I doubted myself but I wrote the book I always knew I could write.

Thank you to my two grandmothers, Betty Mobbs and Bet Lyons, for always encouraging my creative side and reading my stories. I didn't realise when I was little that your maternal and paternal grandmothers weren't meant to share the same first name. Maybe that was what inspired purple flags.

Thank you to you for reading my first book. I hope it helps you to heal from your spiritual narcissists, fuckboys, ghosts and grim situationships. Most of all, I hope it helps you to find the spark inside you, so that when you discover (or rediscover) it with someone else, you can seize it with both hands.

And so it is.

Index of Self-Help Rituals

For super quick self-help, here are the rituals and activities in this book grouped together according to need. There's space to write your favourites down too.

INDEX OF SELF-HELP RITUALS

INDEX OF SELF-HELP RITUALS

My favourite rituals

....

....

....

....

....

About the Author

Rosalind Moody is a writer and former editor of the UK's leading spiritual magazine, *Soul & Spirit*. She has been told off in every job she's ever had for talking too much, and believes she finally has found a vocation for it. She has interviewed many successful people including Caggie Dunlop, Angela Scanlon and Daisy May Cooper and has been a guest on multiple leading podcasts such as *Witch* on BBC Sounds and *White Shores with Theresa Cheung*. She's been featured on radio stations such as Psychic Today, Wellbeing Radio and Hay House Radio, which amassed 2 million listeners in one show. She is a writing coach and also programmes Mind Body Spirit festivals across the UK. She has hosted events for Teal Swan and expert panels for LA-based show Conscious Life Expo. She is a fierce campaigner for getting spirituality into the mainstream so that more people who feel lost can find themselves. She believes in connection, creativity and always having a cup of tea in hand. She lives with her cat in Herne Hill, London.